THREE
MINUS
ONE

Lovingly provided by

Now I Lay Me Down to Sleep
Remembrance
Care Packages
Our Journey Together

www.nilmdtsremembrance.org

THREE MINUS ONE

Parents' Stories
of Love & Loss

edited by Sean Hanish
and Brooke Warner

SHE WRITES PRESS

Published 2014
Printed in the United States of America
ISBN: 978-1-938314-80-3
Library of Congress Control Number: 2014932684

For information, address:
She Writes Press
1563 Solano Ave #546
Berkeley, CA 94707

For Norbert Krekorian Hanish
b. July 12, 2005

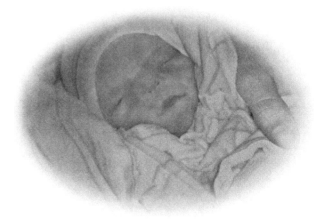

Contents

Introduction

Sean Hanish

My wife and I were expecting our first child in the summer of 2005, less than a year after we were married. We bought our first home in an area of Los Angeles with wonderful schools, narrowed down our favorite names to a shortlist, and my in-laws held the requisite baby shower which filled an otherwise empty room to the brim with toys, clothes and a crib which would soon hold a mewling, nursing, beautiful bouncing baby boy.

We went to the hospital, but we never brought him home.

His heart stopped beating on a Sunday. My wife discovered it without me by her side on a Monday. We met him on a Tuesday. Beautiful but breathless. Stillborn.

I thought that stillbirth was something that only happened when carriages we were crossing the continental divide, pre-hospital horror stories that had gone the way of the Hansom cab in our fuel-injected, Internet-saturated world.

My wife and I hid, as if on an island of grief, sorrow and disbelief. This all-too-typical reaction is due to the lack of discussion and knowledge surrounding this type of loss which, when the pall lifted, turns out to be far more common than can be believed.

Stillbirth is a taboo word and is not used in the medical nomenclature in the United States. Instead, it is known as "fetal demise" or "fetal death". No matter the term, it is defined as a death after the 20th week of pregnancy and before the child's birth. Definitions vary slightly by country but not by much and, sadly, neither do the dismal statistics, or the guilt, shame and isolation which surrounds this unique and devastating type of loss.

In the United States alone, over 26,000 couples a year deliver a stillborn child—that is 1 in every 160 births and more than 6 times the number of children who die of SIDS every year.

If one includes neonatal death, which is the death of the child within the first 28 days after their birth, the numbers nearly double to 1 in every 85 births or over 50,000 per year. This is greater than the amount of people who die in traffic accidents across this country each year.

If one goes a step further and includes miscarriages, then 1 in every 4 women and couples have been touched by a loss which still remains silent, misunderstood and ignored by society.

From personal experience, I can tell you that the impact that one stillbirth has on the mother, the father, their family and friends is devastating—a shock-wave of pain and guilt, and then, too often, silence. The majority of those affected, especially the mothers, suffer in this silence often believing that their grief and trauma is theirs to bear alone.

It is made worse because family and friends do not know how to talk about this subject. They simply don't know what to say or how to say it. They don't want to make things worse but by trying to protect the parent, they often ignore the child they loved and carried to term or, even worse, suggest everything will be better when they have another healthy baby. These all-too-common responses only deepen the pain and isolate the grief-stricken further.

This book has within its pages nearly 100 testimonials to the love and loss, pain and heartbreak, anger and denial, joy and wonder of what it means to be a mother, father, aunt, grandparent and friend of those who have lost children in this shocking way.

The film "Return to Zero" which I wrote, produced and directed is based on the experiences my wife and I had when our son was stillborn which is why the majority of the stories included in this book are about stillbirth. I sincerely hope that these stories, along with their companion pieces about neonatal loss and miscarriage, will resonate with you no matter what loss you have experienced.

My hope is that this book and the film will help to open up discussion around these taboo topics and in doing so give family, friends, and, if possible, our society a way in to discussing this loss, or at least a toe-hold to begin the discussion.

My thanks goes to all of the courageous people who, despite the natural human instinct to shelter their pain and push aside grief to look forward to a brighter day, have relived their worst days through stories, poetry, photography and artwork in this book, a book which has one simple purpose: to help break the silence.

For those of you who are afraid to turn the page—terrified of the horrors that you might find—I hope you will understand that at its very essence this is a book about love.

Love for our children who we lost but for whom that love endures.

Love in our hearts for the beautiful lives which were here with us for only a brief time but which left an indelible impression and a lifetime of memories.

Love for those beautiful ones who are, and will forever be, our precious children.

Introduction

Brooke Warner

When I met Sean in 2007, he was working on another screenplay—one that I hope he'll someday produce. It was a tragicomedy loosely based on his own family-of-origin dynamics. It was some months before he told me about losing his son, Norbert, the inspiration for his film, *Return to Zero,* and now this collection of stories you hold in your hands.

Everything about these two projects has been a labor of love. I've seen writers I've worked with over the years want things badly. I've seen them manifest their dreams and land agents and publishing deals. But never have I worked with someone whose singular focus created a movement—which is what Sean has done with *Return to Zero*, online on Facebook and more broadly with his community leaders and so many others who've rallied around his film.

The depth of emotion and sorrow a person experiences due to early pregnancy loss, or infant loss, is not only hard to measure, it's very hard to articulate, to express. It's hard to be a listener, too, and to put yourself in the shoes of someone who's had this experience if you have not. I knew Sean years before I had my son. I met others during that time who'd experienced similar losses, too, and I felt their pain and listened with a compassionate heart. But I could not fathom the loss until my son was born. Only then did I fully realize how meaningful Sean's work was to a larger community—to give voice to losses many people don't want to talk about, or don't know how to talk about.

She Writes Press is honored to be publishing *Three Minus One* as a Passion Project (read more about what this is on our website), and I am humbled to have had the opportunity to partner with Sean to collect the voices, experiences, and range of emotions of our contributors into this anthology.

My hope is that *Three Minus One* brings its readers comfort, if they've also experienced a loss, and a new understanding and deeper compassion, if they have not experienced such loss. Books on this topic are difficult to find because many publishers are worried they will be hard to sell. Readers don't want to buy books on grief. Sean and I hope the opposite will be true for this book. We already know that voicing our grief is healing. The next step is sharing. Share the stories in this book far and wide, and keep in your hearts the parents and their little ones who have passed. Through the sadness and tragedy of these losses, there is such great hope and resiliency, too. I'm proud to have been witness to these stories and to have been invited to be a participant in Sean's healing journey.

"You're Going to Be a Daddy"
Sean Hanish

"**N**ext time I see you, you're going to be a daddy."

Those were the last words I heard before my phone rang late on a sun-filled morning in Malibu on July 11, 2005.

For some reason those words on that day, "you're going to be a daddy", landed in a way they never had before. Perhaps it is because I had space in my brain to take it in having just finished the biggest project of my commercial directing career minutes earlier. Perhaps it is because those words were said to me by Cindy Crawford in the driveway of her picturesque Malibu estate. When she said those words I realized that we had crossed the threshold from colleagues to friends.

Most likely though, it was because my wife had gone to the doctor that morning and, late in the third trimester of our first pregnancy, I could very well become a daddy at any moment. I would come to find out days and years later that when I heard those words for the first time that Cindy was wrong, I was already a daddy.

We've all had those moments when we've received a call, the call. And even before a syllable reaches your ear the silence, the stillness, the fear reaches you first. The feeling starts deep inside—you know something has already gone terribly wrong.

Filled with a serene sense of accomplishment, I pulled onto the

Pacific Coast Highway. The phone rang. I answered. A wall of silence hit me and nearly knocked me off the road. Then, through gasps and tears, my wife struggled to tell me: "He's gone."

The next few minutes are a mosaic of memories. Images and emotions I have tried to piece into a coherent narrative but it's gone. You can't glue the broken glass back together as it's breaking.

I hope that I stayed calm long enough to let my wife know I would be there right away. I know that before I hung up a flood of tears had begun. I know that after we hung up through the disorientation of disbelief and white hot anger I screamed, alone, thrashing at the wheel, trying to put the broken glass back together piece by piece.

It felt like traffic conspired against me, a full two hours of torture on the LA freeways until I walked into the kitchen and saw my wife seated next to her mother and our doula. Another realization hit like a jab… our son was still inside her.

To be asked how you want to deliver your dead son… to be asked if you have thought about having a burial or cremation for your son who is still in utero, these are questions so macabre as to make Edgar Allen Poe blush, but they are so very real. The shock helps. A simple but effective protection mechanism, tens of thousands of years of development, leaves you detached, dizzy but able to go through the motions of breathing, walking, surviving. Shock is your friend at first. And that's what it is in those minutes, hours, days, weeks afterward—shock. The goal is simple: survival.

There is nothing you can do, nothing you can say to make it better. It is torture. I wanted to fix things… to do something, anything. And yet there I was at the kitchen table helpless, at the delivery of our son hopeless, then holding him in my arms lifeless.

As a husband, a partner, a man you are a passenger on the pregnancy express. You can look out the window and watch the scenery go by, her belly grow, her skin glow, and if you're lucky, catch your baby's elbow as it presses against her belly like the dorsal fin of some alien sea creature making it more real for you. But you're not the engineer.

When the crash comes you are struggling with your own emotions, grief and loss, desolation and depression, and watching as your wife, your partner, your life jumps the tracks. Twisting metal tumbling out of control in slow motion. Prepare for impact.

The crash came, our son born into silence. Beautiful. Heartbreaking. Holy. And then gone, forever.

The two of us entered our home, prepared for a family of three now stripped bare in a few hours of all infant accoutrement by my wife's family who swept in like a SEAL team. Our stark baby's room remained a visual metaphor for the gaping hole in our hearts.

The need to do something, anything became overwhelming. We were gifted a rose bush. I decided to build a patio for that plant, a memorial to our son. The only thing I've built in my life up to this point was with Legos. To call me a novice in the construction arts is to insult novices.

I enlisted the help of my handy father-in-law who helped lay the foundation and steer me clear of disaster. After that it was me, a ton of bricks, buckets of cement and a case of beer. It was like some kind of zen trance. Brick after brick. Line after line. I kept at it.

The days were punctuated by visits to my wife's bedside to check on her dutifully though looking at her brought back everything that hurt… everything that I wanted so desperately to change and forget. Not only have you lost a child, but you've lost your wife. For some it's temporary, others permanent, and most of us somewhere in between. Your relationship never recovers from this, it can only grow together or apart. Neither is wrong.

Brick after brick. Sweat. Wipe. Following a steady rhythm of sadness. I finished the patio—by far my greatest (and only) construction achievement of all time—the day before the memorial service. Goal reached, yet no reward.

The balloons disappear into the sky--my wife and I strain through tears to see them. Surrounded by family and friends, nearly everyone invited made the trip from miles and states away. All of that love helped. The support was incredible. But eventually, their sorrow fades as it must. The neighbors stop the parade of dinners from the oddest pot luck ever. And there we are, left with each other—I never thought that looking into my loved one's eyes would be like staring into the void.

We all grieve differently, especially in this instance. The engineer blames herself for not seeing the signals. The passenger who survives the wreckage blames everyone, everything and nothing. What does it matter when everything you thought up to that instant, everything you believed in is lost?

The change lasts forever. You're never the same. Your relationship is never the same. Yet, here we are, my wife and I nearly eight years later still together. Three children in our heart, two in our home. We love each other, but so very differently than before. I'm not sure there is a tomorrow but each day builds on the next like bricks in that patio, but this memorial will never be finished. It is work now, this marriage, like all marriages but unique in its difference.

Three years ago I quit my commercial life and dedicated myself to building a different kind of memorial—this one with images, shots and scenes—one which I'm (hopefully) better at building. It's a miracle that this film was made—a testament to leading with your heart. We built it and they came, the actors, the crew, and the parents of lost children like wind at our back when we needed it the most.

I'm just one dad. This is one story. One life. And no matter what is gained with this film it will never fill the void that was created the day I lost my son.

What I have learned is that I was a daddy on that day in July 2005. And I am a daddy now--a daddy who never met his first son until after he was gone. Yet, that son has left me a precious gift--I lost one life and found a new one, one which I cherish with all of my heart and will for the rest of my life.

Keeping Kian Close
Gabe Johns

The Tiny Voice That Saved Me

Alexis Marie Chute

*M*y milk has just come in.

I am highly aware of my body as I greet each person in the over-whelming receiving line before me, its long tail whipping out the double doors of the hall and around the corner of the church. My breasts are hard. Full. I shrink into myself and cower my shoulders; this is not fair, the timing is so very unkind.

Greeting the next person in turn, I put on my most grateful yet half-hearted smile. "Thank you for coming," is all I know to say. Our family had not expected this many to attend the memorial service; we had only printed sixty programs bearing two tiny footprints on their covers. I scan the room in search of my husband Aaron, mask-ing any visible annoyance on my face while I growl in my head, "I cannot believe he has left me to do this alone."

Just moments before, Aaron and I stood in front of this gather-ing and spoke carefully planned words, each deliberately selected despite the inadequacy of all words. The faces of the audience shone silver with tears in the flare of stage lights. Women, openly raw, sat beside somber, uncomfortable men. Once the memorial concluded, Aaron and I were led to this simple hall to be greeted — so formal, so dignified.

The words from my mouth were simple and in the same breath, monumental in their lack of simplicity: "Good-bye." I said good-bye to my life, or I should say, the vision of what I thought my life would become. Good-bye to my dream of the perfect family. Good-bye to a predictable marriage. Good-bye to innocence, naivety, normality. Good-bye to my son.

Good-bye to Zachary.

When I became pregnant for the first time, I received the godlike capabilities that all mothers innately possess. It is the ability to tell when a child is lying to your face, or where a tiny set of hands may have hidden a cup of milk just before it turns the electronics drawer into a hot box of putrid fermentation. It is the unexplainable capacity for wild crazy love for a small human that only ever needs and takes — and yet somehow you cannot give enough. It is that same love that makes the endless giving strangely pleasurable.

In the time before Zachary's diagnosis, I often took my daughter Hannah, a buoyant and single-minded one-year-old, for walks along a small birch-lined trail not far from our home. When a wolf warning was announced this past summer, I imagined coming across a scraggly yet sleek ash-gray creature. Famished, its low gaze would pause on Hannah who stood several paces ahead of me, before it ran at her, teeth exposed. In that moment, this wild mother-god love within me would pounce forth with animalistic ferocity all its own and tear the beast to pieces until it was nothing more than a mass of muscle, bone, and fur.

Nevertheless, I did not have enough divinity to see this coming.

As we arrive home after the memorial I am a whistling kettle, the why questions piercing darts into my bedraggled brain. Later, with Hannah asleep in her crib and lullabies dancing in the hall, I stand in front of the bathroom mirror. Naked. The heat from my warming shower casts a dreamlike swirl of steam around me. I wish this were a dream. Am I living someone else's life I ask the person looking back at me; it is an idea which I nearly convince myself is the only logical answer.

This cannot be me in the reflection, I am not this woman with breasts dripping colostrum onto her toes. It makes no sense. My arms ache for my son. As I think of him, of a baby's cry, my milk grows to a trickle—but Zachary did not cry. I will never know the sound of his voice.

I'm crippled by the lack of an outlet for my anger; it is as if my hands have been severed from their wrists. Control is a taunting illusion dangling before me, and I cannot grab hold. Who is to blame for this? No answer. I am bitter at Aaron, who left me while I greeted the long line of fellow mourners. I abhor the doctors that pressed me to terminate Zachary's life before it even began. I loathe the funeral home that demanded a strict collection time for my son's body and then arrived two hours and fifteen minutes late. I said good-bye every minute for 135 minutes, the sorrow of injustice mounting until the funeral-home worker finally arrived. I could have killed the man.

I had planned to file a complaint when we went to collect Zachary's ashes a few days later but was too startled by the tiny silver urn, a heart with shallow etchings of painted white birds hovering on blue wind. Holding the heart in my hands, its weight likely no more than two pounds, I listened to the audible swoosh of my son's ashes as I rocked him back and forth. Too few ashes it would seem, but a newborn's bones are small, only a tiny collection of dust and hope. I was too distracted to yell, and instead whispered, "Just get me out of this place," in Aaron's ear.

Zachary's heart failed. An intimate evil — a tumor so large and dense that echocardiograms appeared white and sound waves could not penetrate the mass—had wrapped itself around the married chambers of my son's heart. Like a tailored coat, it fit so perfectly they almost became one and the same. Operating was not an option. Zachary's heart would be minced along with the tumor.

Despite the doctors' dour predictions, Zachary survived labor and was born alive. He did not cry; he did not open his swollen eyes.

He lay upon my breasts making small movements amongst my kisses. That was all. A silent film—no words but breathed "I love you's" from trembling lips.

My mother-god within could not save him. I had no answers, no power to attack this tumor as I would a hungry wolf. I was helpless and thus cheated. The indifference of nature's force raped a lifetime from my cradling arms. This incomprehensible 'act of God' split my chest, exposing my still-beating heart and the fear I was unaware resided within. As a child, I was scolded for wishing to die before my mother, my love for her so great I thought it would be the better way. I did not understand it then.

I do now. It is as if I have died along with my son. In the natural order I should precede him, surrendering my last breath long before would he gave up his own. Yet I am here, living, while he is ash in a cold silver heart in my hands. I am somehow transfixed in a purgatory of life and death, trapped in a no-man's-land of the soul, neither places of substance, both ghostly and unwelcoming. This is a time and space outside of time and space. There are no walls, no doors, just the muddled openness of abstraction. To stay in one place serves no illusion of rescue yet to run with no end is a madness all its own.

Then I hear it, the voice of my savior, calling me out of this darkness, forcing me to live, breathe, be present in each new day, to make plans, dream a new future; calling me to hope and love and forgiveness. The voice is small yet demanding, knowing though not comprehending.

"Mommy!" Hannah's first morning call from her crib. "Eat!"

Seamus

Aoife Goldie

*I*f you drive west from our apartment, it takes less than half an hour before you hit that quintessentially English countryside—woodland, rolling hills, and fields divided into patchwork quilts by hedgerows.

I've watched that landscape change through the seasons. Listlessly, I've gazed out the car window at frosty skeletal trees in winter, the burnt yellow grass in the peak of the summer, the turning of the leaves in autumn, or the snowdrops, daffodils, and crocuses tentatively peeking above ground in early spring.

We've made that journey often since May 2011.

His final resting place. The place where John and I will also be laid to rest one day. A place of both immeasurable pain and perfect peace.

When I had imagined the end of my pregnancy, it was all sweat and grunts, exhaustion and pain, and John urging me on, willing me to dig deep for one last push—then a rush of joy as his first little cries filled the room.

In reality, my labour was largely silent. Whispers and knowing looks. Solemn faces and broken hearts.

Shock had dragged me underwater, distorting sounds and slowing everything down. Placed a Vaseline-smeared pane between me and everyone else. Left my mouth agape, mute and ineffectual. Scrambled my brain, making every decision difficult and foggy.

Inside my head I tried to trace the way back…

John and I fell in love in a little-known ski town in New England; all cedar-clad gingerbread houses, decked with winter-long fairy lights, sparkling in the crisp air. A small town inhabited by larger-than-life, bearded and burly, gruff Vermont-sters, frequenting the bars, glugging back frothy gallons of Bud Light to a soundtrack of nineties rock.

John was in his second ski season when I took a break from law school to fly out for a visit. His pseudo-celebrity status as a ski instructor had me all googly-eyed and weak at the knees. His command of the terrain, weathered complexion, and strong legs all conspired against me and I was a goner…

It was the happiest place in the world for us, and the place where John proposed to me in 2008.

For weeks after we were married we joked about how grown-up it felt to be calling each other "Husband" and "Wife." And as my belly grew and swelled with the promise of the best chapter of our lives just around the corner, we giggled again like school kids as we talked to my bump, referring to each other as "Mummy" and "Daddy." I remember it felt glorious, trying it on like that.

When our midwife returned, she raised the bedsheets and gently explained, "It's time. Your baby is coming."

A second midwife came in to assist, and I held John's hand. In the moments that followed my boy was with me. I felt it like the sun on my skin. However gone he already was, he was there. It was just the two of us, together. He looked after me, helping me all the way. Such a good little boy. I pushed, twice, and it was done.

Seamus slipped silently into this world at 7:06 p.m. on Friday,

May 20, 2011. Bottom first—if only we'd had the chance to tease him about that over the years—with his little clenched fist held against his face, and his umbilical cord wound tightly around his neck eight times.

The midwives whispered as they disentangled my boy, working away at cleaning up his little limp, lifeless body before handing him over to me.

The most precious gift.

The best thing we ever did together.

And in that instant I felt like I'd forgotten to breathe, like my heart would burst with love…pure, new love like no other.

"*Look.* Look what we did. Look who we made." It was in that moment that John felt like a Daddy. Wide-eyed and mouth ajar, his voice was a half whisper and higher-pitched than usual, choked in utter wonderment. His large hands tentatively took their first touch of his son, clutching his little fingers, stroking the side of his soft, soft face. His face lit up with such pride as he took his precious son carefully into his arms and cradled him close. It was the image I'd longed for…but the colors were all wrong.

I think both of us expected him to open his eyes, screw up his little face, and start to cry—but all the wanting in the world couldn't breathe life into our blindingly beautiful little boy.

And he was. He truly was. I wish the world could have seen how beautiful he was.

In the early days, it just about broke me to say the words…"*My baby died.*" Hearing those naked, blunt words out loud always clubbed me over the head. The pain was so raw. It pierced and seared, and we raged and wailed.

For weeks, months maybe, as I closed my eyes and tried to sleep, a clamminess crawled through my skin, and my heart began upping its tempo as I drowned in the memories, pulled under by images I didn't dare face and thoughts that fed the rabid anxiety that gnawed at me endlessly. Flashbacks caught me as I folded laundry or made the bed. The ghosts of times gone by bound my hands behind my back and grabbed me by the jaw, twisting my face towards that room…forcing me to feel it all again.

I thought that I might die;—that my poor little heart would break and that my life would end. In fact, each morning that I woke in those first few days without him were savagely disappointing - —that I *hadn't* passed in my sleep, that people would *not* solemnly whisper of me, "*'Twas death by a broken heart.*" That this bloody heart kept on beating when Seamus's gave up on him.

How had we ended up here? From choosing his nappy bag to the words on his grave marker? From picking a buggy to the outfit he would be buried in?

I wanted to watch him grow up in his own beautiful boyish way— stamping his Wellie-booted feet through muddy puddles, building sand castles, snowmen, and Lego towers, poking at frogs with sticks, digging for worms, building tree huts, roly-polying down hills, flying kites and balloons, dunking soft-boiled eggs with toasty soldiers…

But our lives were irrevocably changed. We didn't live them anymore, just glided through, afraid to touch anything in case it broke.

Life is different now.

Now I live with it. The bottom-line pain. That pure throb and tenderness that never lessens. Just as I rise in the morning, brush my teeth, and dress, I grieve. It has woven itself into my day. The pain feels routine. As familiar as the feeling of water hitting my skin every morning in the shower, so I grieve. Sadness and longing for him are as natural and mundane as pulling on my socks. It is in every moment, in every breath, in every beat of my pulse.

And yet, I consider myself one of the lucky unlucky ones. For somewhere in among those desperate early weeks, we stepped out onto weak and spindly newborn foal legs. The lure of two pink lines gently nudging us forward. And after thirty-seven long weeks and a second labor that almost ended in a second lightening strike, Hugo gave an almighty scream and began to cry. That sound encapsulating so much: unquantifiable relief, overwhelming joy, and unspeakable pain.

He was alive. Our little bringer of happiness. Our so-so-special second son.

It's only on rare occasions that Seamus is mentioned nowadays. Life is fantastically hectic with a toddler in tow and a belly swelling with another new sibling that we daren't dream of taking home.

I marvel at my new plastic persona. So adept at conversational pleasantries…frothy words, silicone smiles.

But maybe that's okay. Maybe I just want to hold Seamus a little closer. Tuck him safely under my wing and tend to him a little more privately. He's not a story to be told, a terrific tragedy…gossip fodder.

He's my baby.

But there are still those moments that I wish…that someone might just intuitively know…that, actually, I am not okay. Yes, still.

That someone might cup my weary heart in tender hands and soothe it a little.

That even after all this time, even after mastering the art of not crying in public, even after having had another baby, and conceiving a third, I'm still feeling the sharper edges of this life.

Just hiding it better.

We are so lucky and unlucky. We are so blessed. We are still so cheated. We are so happy. We are still so sad.

And we simply love—all three.

Executioner
Heather Bell

And the baby is dead but
we need lettuce in the house, maybe some bread
for morning toast so

I am at the store touching the potatoes at the spine,
the slim wrist of carrot. And the baby is dead so

this entitles humans to talk about their dog's death,
or gerbil's. This means I am expected to sympathize at

their loss. Because all death becomes, somehow, equal

when a childless person hears of a baby's slow start and
quick giving up.

So here is a poem I have written while curled up behind
the cartons of juice at the supermarket. Because the

crushed apples on the floor in the produce section were
her ears and eyes. The skin was so raw from sadness

that I knelt there to watch for too long.

And your dog might be dead too but you did not have to
watch him fall from inside your body like pieces of bird.

Teeth to knees, I spread her deadness in the bathroom
like it is the ocean and she is a gift.

The Turn

Susan Blanco

I leaned back on the uncomfortable exam table until I was flat on my back, exactly the position the doctors advise against when one is seven months pregnant. The technician squirted the warm, viscous gel on my belly and began to move the sonogram wand around.

"She's still breech," she announced.

I had been going to yoga class, practically living my life upside down, trying to get this baby girl to turn head down. My husband and I had been trying to get pregnant for three years, ever since Izabelle. After more losses than I care to recall, we finally had a healthy pregnancy that seemed to be sticking. But she was breech. And I *really* didn't want a C-section. So I tried everything from inverted moves to playing music for her to shining a light at my belly.

"I know this is going to sound a little crazy," said Sandy, my doula, "but let me suggest something. You haven't done anything to prepare for her. Maybe this baby knows you're not ready yet."

She was right. We hadn't decorated her room or washed her clothes or unpacked the new stroller we bought, even though our son begged for us to try it out. Some voice in my head told me that if I didn't acknowledge this baby, I'd be less anguished, less disappointed if something horrible happened.

So I invested. That weekend, I bought a crib and asked my husband to put it together. We got a changing table, and I decorated the walls with butterfly and flower decals. I washed her newborn clothes and put them in her closet. As I folded those impossibly tiny pieces of clothing, I began to talk to her.

"Baby girl, I have a story to tell you. You had a sister, Izabelle Rhea, who once lived where you are now. I was twenty-four weeks pregnant when I learned that her heart had stopped beating. That was the most tragic day of my life, and no one can explain why it happened. I miss her so much, but I'm so happy you have come to me. You are not a replacement for your sister, but you do complete our family. With my age and all of the babies we have lost, doctors told me I'd never have another baby. And yet, here you are." My face was wet with tears as I slowly and methodically ran my hands over my bulging belly.

"So I've decided to name you Milagros Ziva, my brilliant miracle. I love you so much already. I'm looking forward to the moment when I can see your face and hold you close in my arms."

Something changed that weekend. I suddenly felt lighter, like I could walk better, more comfortably. I could also feel her hiccups lower in my abdomen.

"That sounds about right," my OB told me at our next appointment. "Let's see where she is."

And, there, on the sonogram, was my beautiful miracle, head down and ready to go.

The Emptying Out

Lisa Roth-Gulvin

I howl like a wild animal—nature's groan of lost life—as a nine-week-old fetus slips from my body. Sitting on the toilet, I rock back and forth. My arms are wrapped around a cramped, throbbing, womb, my heart is curled into a fetal position to mimic what might have been. I hear my husband calling to me from behind the door that separates our loss. I know he wants to break down this door and rescue me from my anguish, but that will be impossible. He is paralyzed by the sound of despair echoing from every wall. I know that in order for him to survive, he will lock this sound away forever—and I will not. I will never forget this emptying out of life.

When I was young, I bled with relief. Now my blood reminds me of my loss. It is death. I can stand still while death comes from inside me. And I can do this without the decay or withering of my DNA. But I am dying anyway, so I cry without weakness or shame—I weep and weep and weep. I have never been this lonely in my life. But I am not alone. We are everywhere. We ride the bus, we push a stroller, we go to work. We women of dead babies do not exist and yet there are so many. Our bodies mock us; they are destroyers of dreams, nature's murderesses.

Look at them, I think, as I sit curled in a ball by the window. *How do they continue to exist in this terrifying shuffle between joy and despair? How can it be that no other person feels this gigantic hurt and anger? Why is this loss, more than any other, immune to distraction, consolation, and recovery?*

In the other room, my husband puts on his tie. *How long*, he thinks, *how long before my wife is finished mourning?* And I, still curled in a ball, watch people who are unaware of my grief and think, *How can he go to work everyday, moving effortlessly away from the pain?* I do not understand that he buries his hurt in the comfort of daily habits. When he closes the front door behind him, I dress my heart up like a clown and pretend I am happy. I drink imaginary tea with my two-year-old daughter on bright, blue cups made of plastic. Between sips, my eyes wander back toward the window—the one full of people without loss.

There will be no burial. No beautiful, lifeless, body for a preacher to pray over. No one will hold my shaking hands. Nothing will fill my empty, aching arms. There will be no memorial service, no hymn sung. No "closure" for my enormous loss, as I stand alone on a cracked precipice overlooking my fragile sanity.

Some people, out of ignorance, will try and still a grief that cannot be stilled. So they will offer words where words do not belong, and without thinking they will remind me of my beautiful, healthy, little girl whom I am grateful for—I really am. But this cannot silence the quiet, constant, begging of a mother's prayer for solace. And when someone remarks, "It's God's will. You can always try again." My anger swells into a rage that I cannot keep inside. At night I stand in the shower, covered in water and tears, sobbing, "I hate your God. Your God is a hypocrite," over and over again, as my rage moves into an unfurnished heart where my baby once lived.

Time tumbles forward, awkward and without meaning—as time often does without hope. And I forgive, but I do not let go, and I do not forget. I walk like a ghost, and mourn in silence until quietly, little pieces of light—my child's ballet recital, a writing course where I put sorrow on paper, a trip to honor a grandmother's memory—break through my shadow of loss, and l begin to reclaim my spirit.

Then one day, a small piece of paper tucked in a forgotten journal finds its way back to me. Reluctantly, I pull back the folds—first right, then left. Names. It is covered in names: some in pen, some in pencil, some crossed off, some written by me, some by my husband. The words drift off the page like forgotten music. I read them out loud, returning to the gorgeous memory of life that was. And know it is time to release my baby—whose heartbeat is seared in my memory. The name, like a feather, floats on the breeze of my breath, as together we soar away from my prison of sadness forever.

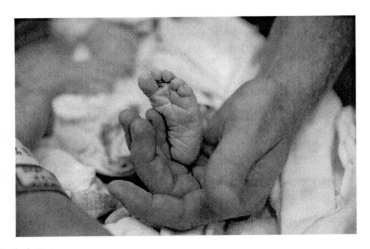

Bentley's Feet
Stephanie Nalley

The Almost-Fives

Abbie L. Smith

*T*here are two kids who always remind me how big my boy should be. I see them so rarely—only a few times a year. So what are the odds that within one painful week, they both accosted my eyes, attention, and heart?

The first encounter was at my best friend Cristen's house on a Sunday afternoon in April. I'm still in the foyer holding the hand of my twenty-one-month-old daughter as she greets the birthday girl, when I turn around to see a familiar woman walk up the sunlit path and through the open door behind me. Suddenly, I am nauseated, well aware that the young girl holding the woman's hand is the one I never want to see.

She was due to enter the world just weeks before my boy. Her mother is Cristen's other "best friend." The three of us were so excited to have these two babies due at the same time. Cristen already had a son who would be just over a year old when the new ones arrived. We lived with this idealistic notion that two new babies would be the perfect additions to friendly visits; and that they would, in time, make the perfect playmates. How naive were we to live with so much hope and certainty?

The tall blond girl with bouncy curls distracts me, hurts me, and pulls at my curiosity in ways I would much rather ignore. I see her mother and her only at birthday parties like this one or other functions occasionally hosted by our mutual friend. The possibility of us three women enjoying one another's company together has long been shattered.

Inside Cristen's house, the mother feels awkward, as do I. She acts as if she doesn't see me standing right in front of her as she walks in and chats with the little children gathering around us. In the first few years it only seemed to be *awkward*, but now it seems to be something else. Is it disdain? Disrespect? Misunderstanding? In her mind, should I be different? Do I come across as a bitch? I'm sure I will never know exactly. She doesn't look me in the eye as I muster a pathetic "hi" in their direction with what must certainly be a blank look on my face. *Don't look at the girl*, I tell myself in that frozen moment. *Look at the mom. Be friendly. Smile. Act NORMAL. Breathe.*

I doubt she knows what her presence and the presence of her daughter do to my inner being as the day goes on. How it rattles my core. My eyes try to dodge that child when the cake is being cut, but then I seek her out with sick, painful curiosity during present opening. How tall would he be? At least her height. The mom and her husband are not as tall as my husband and me, and my subsequent children are tall for their age. He would be, at least, her height. Would he be her friend? Would he be laughing? Would he be running with her? Would he be blond?

He would be—though maybe brown-eyed to her blue. He *would* be joy and laughter. He would unite us in a common motherhood where we are now driven apart by drastically different experiences. We would have a bond. In reality I don't often care about that bond, but I am keenly aware of its absence when I'm in the presence of that child and her mother. I can't touch the child. Hug her. Say hi to her. Acknowledge her much. It hurts. It rips at my heart in ways that make it hard to speak. Those two friends don't know that. They don't know what that child does to me…and let's not forget the effect of her mother, who has, for nearly five years, gone on to enjoy what I have lost. No, not lost. He is not lost. My little boy did not wander off. He died.

The second encounter happened the following Wednesday. It was a beautiful spring evening. My husband made it home early, so we rushed our two little girls out of the house in the double stroller to wander over and watch the end of a baseball game at the nearby high school. An hour later, we happily make our way back down our street with a grinning infant in the stroller and our "big girl" walking on her own. It is one of those rare times when our family life seems perfect, and it is a perfect night for a walk—that is, until I see the neighbor and her child.

Nearly five years ago, my unfortunate new neighbor was out for a stroll when she spotted me outside my house. She eagerly came up our driveway to introduce herself and her brand-new baby. It was the first afternoon that I left my house alone after Isaiah died. I had just returned from approving the final drawings for his headstone. I was shattered. I was a wreck, and there was Jill with her brand-new baby.

"Do you have kids?" she asked.

"I was just pregnant, but my baby died."

How's that for a conversation killer? It was the first time I was ever asked that awful question. I hadn't practiced my responses. I didn't have the arsenal of statements I now choose from when asked. She couldn't possibly know how to respond, so she rushed off with an awkward good-bye, mumbling something about her contented, grinning child seeming hungry.

Since then, I've chatted with Jill at another neighbor's jewelry party and tried to explain my story of Isaiah to some extent, until she used the word "miscarriage" in her misunderstanding of what I was saying. Sadly, I don't think it is possible to break into her mental construct of what my dead child meant to me when she ran into me that first sunny summer day. Like most people, she has no reference for the word "stillbirth."

On this sunny Wednesday evening, Jill and her children are out playing. I don't see them often and the times I have, I've tried not to look at that girl. Of course, I fail in my attempt to avert my gaze. I don't want to catch Jill's attention because I don't want to be forced to smile in such close proximity to that little girl—the "should be Isaiah's age" little girl. Instead, I walk down the opposite sidewalk quickly with a cursory sideways smile to dodge her mother while staring at that girl from across the street. She's Asian and, I assume, is smaller than my little boy would be, but she seems SO BIG! Is that what almost-five looks like? She rides a big girl bike down the road and looks after her little brother.

Isaiah should be watching after Paige and Quinn. Isaiah is invisible on our family walk as we pass the people I try to avoid. He's with us, but invisible. On our perfect family walk, I see him on his bike laughing with his toddling sister, Paige, who is looking oh-so-sassy in her shades, bright-colored clothes, and curly pigtails; just as I saw him at the birthday party last Saturday excitedly hovering over the gifts right next to that tall blond girl with bouncy curls.

He's not lost; he's just invisible. Since they—Jill and Cristen's friend—can't see him, I don't feel like talking to them and their children. As I duck into the garage away from an always friendly, but somewhat confused, Jill, I think that she will never see him walking with me.

Dragonflies

Shannan Fleet

Could I ever determine which is harder? Cradling your slack body still wet with birth or being leached of warmth by this pink granite as I press my face against your flat grave marker. Your indelible name, written out in rhythmic gouges pounded across stone, cutting into my cheek. My shirt soaks up the water from last night's rain as I settle in six feet above you. My fingers constrict, closing on fistfuls of grass. I'm too numb to startle as a dragonfly alights on the back of my hand, tickling me with an iridescent flutter of wings.

It was an unusually hot spring, and the heat made your big sister fussy as I struggled to situate her in her canopied raft. But soon we relaxed into the cool water, delighting in the relief. She giggled with glee as I bobbed in and out of the water playing peek-a-boo over the side of the raft. I dove under her and rolled over so that I could tickle her pudgy, pruned toes. I felt you roll too, as if you were trying to snatch at those same toes! Were you trying to play? I surfaced behind your sister, laughing and clutching my swelling belly, thrilled by the flutter of first kicks.

On the road near the cemetery, engines drone ceaselessly, a steady stream of cars pass by mere feet from our visit. The ever-changing but constant presence of strangers increases my loneliness. I should be holding your tiny hand instead of blades of grass. My eyes dart about as I catch flashes of metallic blues and greens in the periphery. I feel susurrous movements in my hair, a gentle tug here and there, tangles forming; I am somehow sure the dragonflies are beginning to ravel up in there. I look and see that the first dragonfly never left me, still brushing my hand with opalescent kisses.

Your sister, your Da, and I all went to see you. The ultrasound technician entered the room all warm smiles and cool jelly, and there you were! Emerging from mists of visual static, my beautiful daughter. But we had no chance to celebrate you; two doctors came in all whispers and pointing. I perched on the edge of the bed, every muscle taut with anticipation. Did my mounting dread frighten you as my cortisol coursed through our binding cord? As the doctors spoke of abnormalities, perinatologists, trisomy 18, and "options," you devolved from my "baby girl" to "the fetus."

I drove us home as the bright-white light of the sun drained the color from the world around me and my mind buzzed with the beating of a million insect wings.

I hear the keening before I realize the sound is coming from me. I want to scream the earth open, tearing back turf and soil, rending a hole—a way to you—and letting the dirt collapse in behind me. Let it swallow me deeper and deeper into the comforting abyss next to you. But instead I lie here as an ever-growing number of insect feet send tingles across my skin.

You and I held on for fourteen more weeks, and during that time, I got up and made sure that your sister was bathed and fed and had a little fun every day while I tried to keep her from cutting the soles of her feet on the sharp shards of our grief. She and Da cast my belly all slippery fingers and scrunched noses as the plaster set. But there were times when she needed to be kept away. Your Da helped me find an outlet for my rage at the unfairness of your short life: we bought a cheap stack of dishes, and with a black marker, I covered the white surfaces with my anguish. Then I smashed them all to porcelain dust.

Did you hear me plead for forgiveness after I begged you to stop kicking? Every kick was a reminder of what we were to miss. Did I confuse you when I would then gulp glassfuls of orange juice to get you to move if you had been still for too long? I prayed that you would never stop kicking because I would never be ready to say good-bye.

I planned a funeral for you while you still grew in me.

A tickle on my cheek causes my eyes to twitch open. Dragonfly wings obscure my vision, and it's as if I'm seeing the horizon through an oil-slicked puddle. More continue to descend upon me. Their tiny feet prickle my skin, causing gooseflesh despite the heat, as they vie for purchase. I can't hear the cars or the wind or anything over the vibrant thrum of wings.

The funeral home called to tell me your casket had arrived and that it was the most beautiful casket they had ever seen. The esteem in which they held the casket gave me a twisted sense of comfort. I needed to see it for myself, to be sure that it was right for you. My fingers glided along the handcrafted red oak and silk linings. Somehow, I knew it was right, but it was so small, so impossibly small. My throat constricted as tears filled my mouth with salty bitterness, and I could not swallow. The air went out of me in a rush, and I collapsed to my knees, clutching my stomach, and choking back the acrid taste of bile.

I felt you roll then, like that day in the pool so long ago, for the last time.

I cling to the grass as the dragonflies envelop me and begin to beat their wings in unison. I will my body to go limp, to resist the upward pull, anything to stop them from forcing my leave. My grip begins to slip; the wet grass too difficult to hold. Why can't I stay? Why can't I scrape out a hollow for myself here, over you? I could let time cover me in layers of leaf litter and grime until I become an indistinguishable part of the landscape.

At the hospital, Da and I were led into triage by a string of questions and chased by an ultrasound machine on a cart with a squeaky wheel. You appeared on the monitor and the only sound was the crinkle of plastic sheets as I leaned in toward the screen, scouring for the slightest flicker of movement. Your arms lay across your chest, a tiny fist resting on each shoulder, and your head was bowed. You were utterly still. My breath hissed through clenched teeth as I released the air I unwittingly held.

The hospital staff hung a paper dove on our door, a peaceful portent belying the agony lurking within our room. The doctor broke my water, and I rode waves of pain, ebbing and flowing but relentless. I resisted, but I had to push. The nurses tensed. Breech. Breathe.

Push. I couldn't do it. Push. I panicked and pleaded. Push. It was too soon. Push. I wept. Push.

The inexorable pull of the dragonflies stirs me to motion, and I try to shake them free. Instead, I lose my stay on the grass. The glittering cloud lifts me to my knees when I hear a familiar tread. The dragonflies disperse in a frenzied roar of shimmering wings. I blink my eyes clear and see little feet. I raise my head, and immediately, I'm transfixed by your sister's gray eyes. She giggles as a dragonfly dances from my hand to her cheek, sweeping delicate kisses across her freckled nose and finally flying away.

And then you were on my chest. Your silence ripped my heart asunder and I wondered if there existed enough sutures to mend those tears. Your sister came in to the room, and I dammed the bulk of my sorrow. She climbed into the bed, and I read her a story about water bugs and dragonflies as I cradled you between us. It was a story meant to instill a hope of seeing you again, and now I cannot see a dragonfly without thinking of you.

Your sister smiles, wipes the tears from my dirt-streaked face, smooths my hair, and dusts the grass from my knees. "I miss her too," she says and kneels over to kiss your grass. Rising, she slips her hand in mine and we walk back to the car together. I turn around before we leave to smile at you, thankful for my beautiful daughters, and tug the door shut.

Skin

Chiyuma Elliott

I believe in the *clish* as the beer can opens.
In the deep cut of river through strata,
in coarse sand, in skin. In the new ink
on that spot on my back I can barely reach
with the sunblock. *I want their names*, I told him,
the years they died. In black.
Sometimes I believe in needles.

I believe in the skin's eruptions. Quiet totems
of flux. In the young man named Omar
who sees pimples, asks for my digits.
I could be your mother, I say. This is a lie.
My babies die. Their leaving's a red blur
that makes my face welter and blossom.

The toddler splashing in the shallows—
I believe in her green hat. In her mother,
who looks up and her eyes say
when did you lose her? In the way my hand
automatically reaches for my abdomen.
Which means *six weeks ago.*
The way she barely nods.

I believe in the almost-quiet. A cove
where the river slurps like a first breath.
We've come here because the ranch
is separating cows and calves, for miles
the air is raw with their screams.
Each cow hears her own baby's cry
across the paddock. She moans all night,
even when sleeping. Then the trucks come.
Then everything just goes dark. I envy that.

The Second of July

Lainie Blum Cogan

July 2, 2013

Hannah was born eighteen years ago today.

Two weeks before my due date, my husband and I were riveted by *Braveheart* in the multiplex on Route 22; sometime between Murron's execution and the defeat of York my water broke all over the upholstered theater seat. We rushed out as abruptly as the amniotic fluid, and I only felt mildly guilty about the mess I left behind.

We drove home, packed our bags, and sped to the hospital. Like children, we excitedly called our parents and told them to plan to arrive the next morning, as the nurses said delivery was not imminent. When nothing was happening in the morning, they injected some Pitocin to get things going, and I was slightly disappointed that my natural childbirth plans were going out the window. Well into active labor, the baby wasn't progressing down the birth canal. Fearing she might have to perform an emergency C-section, the doctor ordered a heavy hit of anesthetics, while she was busy trying to extricate the baby.

When my child was finally suctioned out, the doctor asked, "Are you sure your dates are right?" The umbilical cord disintegrated in her hands.

That the not-crying baby was sick was obvious. What exactly was wrong would take weeks to discover. I was whisked away to the recovery room, as my brand-new baby girl was intubated and hurried to the NICU. Seth broke the news to our parents and conferred with the doctors. In a state of utter confusion reserved for innocents faced with unimaginable trauma, I refused to see anyone. After initial tests, it was confirmed that our daughter had a herniated diaphragm, which meant among other things that the organs that were supposed to be situated in the lower abdomen had floated up through the perforated diaphragm and were crowding the lungs, which had not developed properly as a result. Her ears were set low and she was missing a rib. We learned that doctors do not like to see a constellation of abnormalities, as this generally indicates a serious genetic syndrome, but they were reticent and revealed the story only page by page, reluctant to speculate about the plot that could only be determined with genetic testing.

Over the next forty-eight hours, droplets of information would condense and slide down the foggy window of confusion, painting an ever-clearer picture of Hannah's impossible situation. Although the doctor suspected that Hannah's condition rendered her "incompatible with life," they would have to wait until she grew strong enough to endure the tests that would confirm his suspicions that she would never grow strong enough to survive.

The doctor quietly told us that it was hospital policy to resuscitate this child, no matter how many times she started to fail. He had done so, he informed us, the previous night when Hannah's frail body had gone septic. When he predicted it would continue to happen, we soberly prepared ourselves to accept her fate and fight for our child's right to die if it came to that.

Meanwhile, we desperately wanted to bear witness to the existence of this precious child who was teaching us the most important lesson we would ever learn about being parents. We spent our days with our daughter and slept in a makeshift bedroom in a hospital lounge. We invited everyone we knew to come meet our Hannah.

At 2 a.m. on July 7 a nurse urged us to come to the NICU immediately. We quickly washed with the foamy antiseptic soap that smelled like hospital and candy and slipped into blue sterile gowns before rushing to Hannah's bedside.

"She's septic," the doctor quietly told us, and we exchanged knowing glances. We sat down, as the merciful doctor unhooked the ventilator and put Hannah into my arms. It was the first and only time we saw her without the breathing tube obscuring her tiny face. We allowed nature to take its merciful course as she died in our embrace.

In the ensuing months, genetic testing confirmed Hannah's "incompatibility with life."

"They lied to us," I told my best friend from grade school, who now lived across the country. "We did our homework and ate our vegetables. We were supposed to be rewarded for doing everything right." It simply never occurred to me that something like this could happen to someone like me, and it took some time to assimilate personal tragedy into my arrogant, entitled worldview. The best I could do was to accept that I—at age twenty-seven—had now received my cosmic quota of heartbreak. It would be smooth sailing from here.

Over the next three years, we gathered our courage and were blessed with two healthy and beautiful children, the first of whom is named Samuel, the name of the child for whom the Biblical Hannah prayed so fervently. He's nearly seventeen now. But I was wrong about the tragedy quota. Life has since thrown us a series of calamities and trials. Rather than rage against them, I have learned to be thankful for the serene moments of grace in between. And there are so many.

I still think of Hannah every day. Together with her little sister, Mimi, I still light a candle for her every Sabbath eve and holiday. I still cringe, unsure how to answer when people innocently ask me how many children I have.

More than anything, though, I am deeply grateful Hannah was here. She drew us deeper into the humble human community that suffers. In her five short days on earth, she taught me that the most important role of being a parent—a lesson I try to implement every single day—is to be a steady and stable advocate for my children and to lovingly do what's best for them regardless of the personal price for me. Through her, I have glimpsed the vast perspective of the universe, which gains new poignancy as I reach middle age and my parents' generation begins to recede: In the context of eternity, there really is no difference between a life that spans ninety years and one that lasts five days. The distinction is in the impact that life has on others.

Bearing Max

Wendy Staley Colbert

During the last trimester of my pregnancy, both the prospect of my baby's disability and the prospect of his death frightened me. From the time I was seven months pregnant, I knew he wasn't expected to live long. I wasn't sure I was up to being his mother. I wasn't sure I could handle the pain. I wasn't sure I could love him enough and then let him go.

The ultrasound technician picked up anomalies during the second trimester in a routine exam, pressing the wand against my slippery, swollen belly over and over to get a detailed look at his abnormal kidneys. Additional abnormalities showed up as my pregnancy progressed. Subsequent scans showed six toes on each foot and an extra flap of a digit on each hand. An amniocentesis early in my seventh month provided the damning diagnosis.

"Your son has trisomy 13," the genetic counselor said. "Trisomy 13 babies don't live long. Each of the cells in his body carries an extra thirteenth chromosome. He will be severely developmentally disabled. He will never walk, talk, or feed himself."

Shocked, I sat beside my husband Mark, beginning to realize the hopelessness of our son's condition even as we felt his kicks through my cotton, floral maternity dress.

I went to my baby shower the next day, and made the hard decision to keep the news to myself a little longer. I wasn't yet ready to reveal this shift in our world. I choked back tears and smiled wanly as I opened pale-blue terry-cloth onesies and the stackable blocks I knew my son would never use.

We met with the genetic counselor the following week, and she reiterated that trisomy 13 is a random genetic mutation that occurs only once in five thousand newborns. Many trisomy 13 fetuses are miscarried. Most infants born with the syndrome die within the first three months of life.

I was seven and a half months along now and completely lost my appetite. I bitterly thought, *So much for skipping coffee during my pregnancy. A lot of good that did.* The impact of caffeine on my baby's deformed body seemed absurd, but I kept up my nutritional discipline anyhow.

If we wanted to investigate ending the pregnancy, we could take our case to the hospital ethics board. My husband and I were glad this option was available, but decided we would prefer to let nature take its course. We didn't want the potential burden of guilt from the choice of such a late-term abortion in addition to our already palpable grief and my growing fear. I worried that the baby would die inside me, and was reassured each time I felt him kick. Even worse, I worried that I wouldn't know how to care for a disabled baby, that I wouldn't be able to love a disabled baby enough.

A woman with whom I'd worked had carried a severely disabled baby to term only to see him stillborn. She told me, "Be prepared that your baby may not look like a normal baby."

The mother of a trisomy 13 child whose son was kept alive by a feeding tube offered to stop by for a visit in the coming weeks so I could meet her son. Now eight months pregnant, I declined—I thought I would break down crying upon seeing the severity of his disability and felt ashamed that I might not be able to welcome her son as she so joyfully had.

A few days passed, and then my water suddenly broke as I stood up to leave work one afternoon, three and a half weeks before my due date. On the drive to the hospital, I felt relieved that my son had beat the odds so far.

I labored for hours, and as my baby's head was crowning, my ob-gyn said, "I'm sorry—it doesn't look good—I don't think he made it." I sobbed as I continued to push.

My son was born. I heard his strong cry, and I began to cry for joy myself. Our son's scalp wasn't fully closed and had an open wound on it, and our doctor had assumed as his head was crowning that he was dead.

We named him Max James. His eyes never opened. He had extra digits on his feet and hands, and numerous other physical and mental defects we couldn't see. But I was relieved to find him beautiful and felt a rush of love for him, smoothing the wisps of fine hair behind his ears as I held him. He was tough, all right—he squirmed and stuck his chin out, his legs kicking, his fingers clenched into fists. He was unable to breastfeed, so a nurse showed my husband how to finger-feed him, dropping little drips of pumped breast milk from a tube attached to his finger into Max's mouth.

When we got ready to take him home, a nurse leaned into the backseat of the car where I was strapping five-and-a-half-pound Max into the car seat and said, "Now, you enjoy every minute with him, won't you?"

My original fear of not being able to love Max turned almost immediately into a fear of him dying. I was conflicted: I didn't want him to die, but I also didn't want him to live a life of such limited quality.

At home, we held Max constantly. He even slept between Mark and me in our king-size bed. As we were drifting off to sleep our first night home, Max's breathing became congested and raspy. We could hear fluid in his lungs. Mark rushed Max into the bathroom and clapped him on the back until gobs of green mucus landed in the white basin.

Over the next couple of days, we had a routine follow-up visit with a nurse, who was alarmed that Max had dropped nearly a pound of weight. She instructed us to force-feed Max formula and recommended a bili light blanket to help treat the jaundice. Max aspirated formula while the nurse was in our home, and before we knew it, she had resuscitated him and called 911.

Back in the hospital, the ER doctors told us they couldn't get all the fluid out of his lungs and that Max's time was limited. We took him home. Mark put *Kind of Blue*, his favorite Miles Davis album, on the stereo, wanting Max to hear beautiful music. While it was still warm out, Mark carried Max outside so he could feel a soft summer breeze on his cheeks. Mark held Max, resting our infant's bare chest against his. Max seemed to calm at the feel of skin against skin.

As the evening darkened, Max's breathing grew more labored. I changed him into our favorite outfit, sat with him in my arms on the couch, and sang "Silent Night" to him. I felt scared to see him die and even more scared to feel him die. I didn't want to be the one holding him when he died. I didn't want to feel his body stop moving, feel his warmth cool, hear the silence when he stopped breathing, see his stillness. I handed Max to Mark, and he to held him next to me.

A few minutes later, Max lifted his arms to us in what we would later learn was a physical reflex, but felt to us like a desire for one last hug. He drew his last breath and died. Mark and I both cried as we wrapped Max in his fleecy pastel baby blanket and laid him for the first time in his crib in his bedroom. It was the only night he would spend in his room.

I went to bed and cried all night, imagining terrible scenes, like flies landing on my baby's corpse in the next room. When the funeral home came to pick up my baby the next day, I snipped a lock of his hair to keep before I let them take him.

When I finally returned to work after my maternity leave with only pictures to show my coworkers, I placed a framed photo of Max on my desk. It was a close-up of his serene face, his eyes eternally closed, a baby cap covering the open wound on his head. You could see the fuzz of downy hair on his rounded cheek.

I found that I drew strength when I looked at his picture. I aspired each day to be more like Max—to be bolder in my embrace of life, to be more fearless, to be more accepting of the harsh realities of life. If my four-and-a-half-day-old infant could meet his demise and go so fearlessly into the night, surely I could do the same someday.

I wasn't as brave yet as I aspired to be. I hadn't been brave enough to hold my baby while he died, and I felt ashamed of that. But I was braver than I thought. I'd been brave enough to love him. I'd been brave enough to let him go.

Masters of Disguise

Gabriela Ibarra Kotara

In memory of my son, Kain Cohen Kotara, 12/25/12.
Stillborn due to a cord accident at forty-one weeks.

*T*here's no greater actress than a grieving mother. A "bereaved" mother.

I had never even heard that word before my son died, and here it is, the word I identify with daily. I am—*we are*—"deprived of a loved one through a profound absence," according to Google's definition.

Yet, you would never know it when you look at me.

Physically, I wear the scars of a mother. I have stretch marks etched upon my once-tight skin, but even if a passerby noticed that, the truth of what has happened is still not visible.

To everyone, I am just another woman. Somebody's wife, somebody's daughter, somebody's sister. But I am so much more than that, even if I don't show it.

I am a bereaved mother.

I am a woman who holds her baby silently in her heart instead of noticeably in her arms.

I am the lady grocery shopping, who avoids the baby aisle at all costs and has to fight back tears when she places her purse in the cart seat where the baby is supposed to go.

I am the woman who listens with a breaking heart to every cute anecdote her friend tells about her new baby.

I am the wife who buys a pregnancy test every month, hoping and praying that it'll be positive.

I am the woman who no longer has her innocence. The woman who fears the "impossible" and is a living part of the statistic—one of that 2 percent chance.

I am that cautionary tale. No one wants what happened to us to happen to them.

I am also the woman who gets told how strong she is, how amazing her will to keep going is, when in reality, I'm a basket case. Up one minute, down the other.

I am all of those and more. But when you see me, you have no idea.

Not one person notices. I am a master of disguise, feigning the old me. The *before* me. We, as bereaved mothers, wear the cloak of normalcy, but truthfully, we are anything but normal.

It is not normal to hold your cold, dead baby's body in your arms. And it is not normal to lower a tiny casket into the dark, cold earth. But I did it. And you probably did it too.

And although you may keep your grief hidden in an attempt to control something or to have some semblance of normalcy, it still is in your heart forever and always. You are not alone, and you have more sisters in this "bereaved mama society" than you will ever know.

We wear the masks together, and only the lucky ones get to see who we really are. Who our babies really are. Not one of us is the same person *after*. But you'll learn to take that mask off a little more each day, until the world and all those around you can know your story, and the camouflage is wiped clean off your face.

Until that day comes, wear your disguise proudly, strong sister.

Untitled

Katie Sluiter

I didn't know what to do with my hands. I kept running my thumbs over my fingers and adjusting my rings.

The room felt so full. An exam room is not made for four people.

I could feel that my eyes were wide with apprehension. I stared silently at Cort hoping he could provide me with some sort of reassurance, but when our eyes met, I could feel his worry match mine. The deep line in the center of his brow mirrored my own dread.

I turned my focus on the professionals in the room. I searched the face of my nurse for the look of routine. I scrutinized the doctor's demeanor for the assurance that all this was normal.

But instead I was asked to lie down. To try to relax.

While the nurse busied herself, I found my words. "Is this going to hurt?"

She paused suddenly, stopping in the middle of her prescribed procedure. Her face softened. She looked at my husband and told him to come stand by my head and hold my hand. And that no, it would not hurt. But it would probably be a bit uncomfortable.

It was. Uncomfortable.

But more uncomfortable was the silence of the doctor as he searched. And searched. And didn't speak.

I could feel the burn of the fiery tears in the corners of my eyes. But I wasn't going to let them come. There was business at hand. I had to know the facts and not let my emotions take hold of me.

Both my husband and I stared at the black-and-white screen, attempting to see whatever the doctor was looking for.

Finally my husband asked the doctor if everything was okay.

"Well…" And he didn't continue.

He didn't have to. I knew. I asked if we could take a break so I could use the bathroom.

I can't remember if I really had to go or if I just needed to leave the room.

When I came back there was no need to lie back down.

There was nothing to see.

Onion Bread

Corrine Heyeck

About a year after our daughter Brenna was stillborn at almost thirty-eight weeks, I was talking with someone about what it is like to live after your baby dies. How compliments about strength given by well-intentioned observers have little meaning, because we're all just getting through it because we have to.

There really isn't another choice. So each of us learns to fold the pain into our lives, which are ever changed but moving forward nonetheless. There is no going back to the person we were before, because there is no way to undo the past.

It occurred to me that we're a lot like onion bread.

Although basic bread involves the simplest of ingredients—flour, yeast, sugar, salt, and water—baking bread is a complex process. There is proofing the yeast, mixing together the ingredients, kneading the dough, letting it rise, punching it, forming the loaf, letting it rise a second time, and then baking it.

Once an ingredient—like onion—is added, there is no going back. Dough is sticky, especially at the beginning of kneading. If you've ever made papier-mâché, you know the binding power of simple flour and water. It is like glue. The dough picks up and holds onto whatever it touches.

Once the onion is added, it is there to stay. Even if you managed to pick out each and every one of the tiny pieces, the flavor of the onion would still be present in the finished loaf—even if it isn't as pungent.

Baby loss is like an onion dropped into our life's dough. We may have started out ready for a nice, comforting bakery loaf slathered in buttery goodness. But then came the onions, and the recipe changed.

First they made us cry, stinging our eyes and making our noses run. But even through the blurred vision, we started the time-consuming and arduous task of folding the onion into the dough. Somehow the rest of the dough eventually mellowed the burn of the onion so we could again see what we were doing.

We glanced up and everything around us still looked mostly the same. While tears poured from our eyes and our throats choked against the burn, life marched on.

And so we continue to knead. Every day. The onion is still there. It is no longer a separate ingredient in our lives; it now is part of our definition. We're all still bread, just like we are all still parents. But now we are onion bread.

Here we are hoping the world will accept this new recipe because we're still just not that sure. They remember the plain, uncomplicated bakery loaf. Some of them just don't want anything to do with such sharp flavors, which are completely new and unfamiliar. And some of them expect that, after all this time, surely she's had time to pick out all of the onion. They're still expecting the basic loaf. Or giving us time—and space—to continue picking out the onion.

Our loaves—our lives—are different now than they were before. But onion bread can still be good. It is just a heck of a lot more complex than the plain stuff.

All our life experiences add their own flavors. Rainbows, relationships, love—they all have potential to add sweetness. But the onion will always be there. One of the many ingredients in our lives.

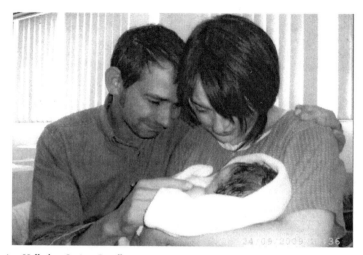

Saying Hello but Saying Goodbye

Amy Cartwright

Lorenzo's Island

Jennifer Massoni Pardini

*I*n a sparse waiting area at the Santiago airport, a mother and her baby boy sat down across from my husband, Ryan, and me. The baby laughed. I changed seats.

Lorenzo would have been about that age, had he not had a fatal congenital heart defect. In the alternate reality, he would be laughing. He would have all four chambers of his heart instead of only two. I would not have delivered him stillborn when I was nearly six months pregnant.

We were supposed to take this trip to Easter Island the year before as a "babymoon," a last chance to travel as just the two of us, as friends and baby websites suggested we do. Ryan hadn't felt the same urgency as I had. "The baby will always be there with us now," he'd said. At the time, I thought he wasn't getting how important it was for us to carve out this time together. Really, he already thought of us as a family.

Easter Island, or Rapa Nui in the native language, is the world's most isolated inhabited island—stranded at sea, out of reach while the rest of the world carries on elsewhere. As we flew overhead, it popped out of the immense Pacific like a green, triangular jewel. Its history goes back over a thousand years and is like any epic tale—one of glory and hardship, ceremony and destruction, oral tradition and misinformation. It is stitched with dirt roads, studded with grazing teams of horses, and outlined with high cliffs. There can be as much beauty as there is tension in a complicated survival story.

When we checked into our cabaña at Te'Ora, the owner shared its meaning: "the start of a new beginning." The bud of a flower. The first blush of a love affair. The color-streaked sky right before sunrise. After nearly a year of grieving our son and feeling as isolated as this island, Ryan and I were hopeful that we were also nearing a new beginning.

We took a tour with an older couple from Canada to see up close some of the nine hundred or so statues that have been discovered around the island. Called *mo'ai*, which means, "to be able to exist," they represent prominent ancestors and were sculpted from compressed volcanic ash before being transported from a central rock quarry to their final resting places along the island's perimeter. They were always faced inward to watch over their descendants. Only then were their eyes painted on, a final flourish to animate the statue with the spirit of the deceased.

When I held Lorenzo in my arms, his spirit would not animate his body. His eyes were closed, his heart stilled. He was gone. Ryan and I had spared him the suffering of a short, compromised life because we would not put him through the extreme and painful interventions that would have been required to prolong his life, but would not cure him or guarantee his survival. We accepted the pain so he wouldn't have to, because we were his parents. When I held my son, I told him how sorry I was and how much I loved him. I smoothed the contours of his face, which looked so much like Ryan's, and looped his long fingers over mine.

"Here, you can't rely on any one version of history," our tour guide, Marcus, said, standing among the ruins of a village close to the cliffs. He was Swedish; his blond ponytail flit in the wind like a horse's tail as we toured the archeology at our feet. He regaled us with theories of how the *mo'ai* statues were once toppled, either by a powerful female spirit or an intense tribal conflict or hostile settlers from afar.

We ducked our heads into caves where whole families might have been born, lived, and died.

"What brought you to Rapa Nui?" I asked him.

He squinted—he'd left his sunglasses in the van. "Love," he said, as if it was the only answer. "We just had a baby. He's thirty-five days old today."

"Congratulations," I said.

"Do you have children?" he asked, sounding hopeful to connect.

"No, we don't." The words fell flat and false against my tongue. I looked for Ryan, who was stranded in the same isolation I was. He was nearby with the Canadian couple, but out of earshot.

On the way back to Te'Ora, Marcus asked us if we'd like to stop by his home and meet his wife, who was from the island, and their thirty-five-day-old son. We drove up to a single-level, white square house, its windows opened wide. Unruly plants and propped surfboards surrounded the woman who stood on the front porch. Her dark hair was pulled up into the topknot we'd just seen on several *mo'ai*. She held a baby close to her chest, against a strapless cotton dress. Easy for breast-feeding. In the alternate reality, I'd still be breast-feeding Lorenzo.

Marcus made a round of introductions before turning to his wife to say, "Ryan also surfs."

A smile spread like a hammock hitched to her high cheekbones. "I teach the children here. They pile onto the front of my longboard. I always said that someday I'd teach my own kid," she said, looking down at the tiny boy.

Ryan had dreamt of teaching Lorenzo, and my heart broke for him next to all this. No one standing on the porch could know our own complicated history just by looking at us. We appeared young and happy, carefree even.

Back in the van, Joanne from Canada said, "Get ready. It's so tiring when they're little."

"Yes, he screams a lot," Marcus conceded.

I didn't know Joanne's history either, but I resented her attempt to tarnish the new parenthood we'd just seen, for complaining at all about a healthy child. As we bumped over potholes, I sat quietly in the back, dreaming of a screaming baby.

Fertility is central to Rapa Nui's imagery. On one of the island's three corners is Orongo, the crater of a massive volcano, filled in with water and moss and reflections of the sky. I stood a few feet from the crest of the remnants of a long-ago eruption in the middle of the ocean and peered into that vast emptiness. It was almost a year after my own body had emptied. I was still standing.

Long ago, Orongo was the site of the annual Bird Man Festival. Each spring, the first tribal member to return from the neighboring islets with an egg of the Manutara bird was named *Tangata Manu*, or Bird Man, and promised a fertile coming year for his tribe. I'd read about this race and wanted to see the stone petroglyph, *Komari*, a symbol of that fertility and creation. According to the map, it was by the edge of the volcano, but the section was cordoned off.

"Hop the fence," Ryan said, looking at what was little more than a low limbo stick dangling a sign of warning—*PELIGRO*.

I didn't want to disrespect the sign, the centuries beneath my feet, or the bountiful spirit I was here to conjure. But it was a man-made boundary dividing two sides of the same trail, so I hopped over the limbo stick and took a photo of the rocks, even though the symbols themselves were somewhere on the other side. To my left was a virtual drop-off—right into the crater of the volcano. *Peligro*. To my right were the neighboring islets. And somewhere in front of me were the petroglyphs. Ryan urged me to go further, to reach my hand out to those fertile rocks. We were trying to make a baby, a baby who would survive. But I felt close enough, so I stepped back over the short barrier and kissed my husband. "I think it's up to us to symbolize the love that's going to make this happen," I said.

On our last day, I swam in one of the swimming "bowls" carved out of the rocky cliffs. A sort of womb embraced me as I moved in parallel with a sea turtle, my husband off surfing the same waves that petered out and rolled softly over our backs, our shells, our ancient bodies. We had seen the unfinished *mo'ai* earlier, leaning in stages of incompletion at the quarry. Their eyes were never painted on, their bodies never animated by their spirits. They somehow looked more real that way, rooted in the landscape. They, unlike the others, gazed out over the ocean, a scene so beautiful and spare it could as easily have been from the end of time as the start of the beginning.

And Ryan was right—Lorenzo was there with us, the whole time.

Death of a Possum

Christina Melendrez

*L*ast night, I brought Murray with me for the thirty-yard walk around the house to throw away some trash. A big yellow dog is always good protection against bogeymen, grasshoppers, and ex-fiancés. I drop the bag in and head back to the house, and notice that Murray is crunching on something that sounds like bone and sinew. I can't get him away from whatever it is. I run inside to get a flashlight and then proceed to pry my dog off the dead animal. Black beady eyes reflect the light and the long tail wraps through the grass. His mouth is open—sharp little teeth bared in a postmortem snarl. I want to throw up. I want to choke. I want to cry.

By the time I drag my dad from bed and we shovel the critter into a garbage bag, and by the time I walk him to the trash can, my fingers pinched on the edges and the bag held as far away from me as possible, I am exhausted and I have no idea why. It's just a possum, ugly little beasts too dumb to move for a car. I mull it over and then I realize it might be because he had just been alive. And then he wasn't. Just like that, with one thrashing shake of the neck, the possum was dead. He was gone and something was then gnawing on his entrails.

I had seen one dead body, that of my grandmother, when I was five. I missed her a whole bunch, but I was equally excited about the fact that it was actually snowing in Hesperia. As I grew up, I went to several funerals, but none of them were open casket. I had never stumbled on a dead body or dissected a dead body or watched someone die—actually witness that last breath. And I had never touched a dead body.

Until Maddison.

Just like my furry friend, one minute she was alive and kicking, and the next, she wasn't. I missed that moment. I don't know how I missed that moment. Did she suffer? Did she know something was wrong? And most importantly, could I have done something? Of course, not at that exact instant when the umbilical cord had been closed off, but maybe I could have demanded another ultrasound. Maybe I should have left him sooner and prevented all of the stress. Maybe I could have grown a heartbeat monitor out of my stomach with the option of busting out an emergency C-section right at my desk. It's all speculation and nonsense.

I had loved being pregnant. My beautiful body stretched and shaped and blossomed with her life. I was so in tune with the rest of me with this little creature taking over, her needs my body's only priority. My heart, my blood, my lungs, my stomach—we all worked so hard to get her what she needed, straining to force it through the single artery in her umbilical cord. It wasn't enough. She barely grew. At birth, she was four pounds, eleven ounces, and seventeen inches long. So perfectly tiny—a miniature baby. I failed her. My only job as a mother was to protect her, and I couldn't. She slowly starved to death. She was born after a forty-three-hour labor, on November 10, 2011. I was later told that she had been dead for three or four days by the time I was able to deliver her.

There is this supremely surreal quality to life after the loss of a child. This can't be happening. Shock. Denial. Rage. Anxiety. The belief that now everyone else is going to start dying, too. I sat on my couch, day in and day out, wailing, aching. Alone. Not alone physically, but alone in my pain. Surrounded by love and friend-ship, but so disconnected. I remember going to Walmart a week after they released me from the hospital. I needed sports bras, Kleenex, and a new journal. And I remember walking through the aisles and thinking, as I dodged a little old lady, these people have no fucking idea what I'm going through right now. I'm not sobbing uncontrollably, and I'm responding to all of the social cues. I said hi back to the greeter, excused myself when I accidentally bumped into a shelf, and I remembered to look both ways before stepping into the hazardous crosswalk. I even smile occasionally. Yet every part of my body throbs with the pain of losing her. And these people have no clue. They don't know that I gave birth a week ago, that my daughter was silent and beautiful. They don't know that my breasts leak through these pitiful bras. They don't know that I cry when I step in the shower, blood running down my legs, my arms cradling the empty skin of my stomach. No one in this store has access to these intimate moments. My grief is my own, to bear privately.

When she was born, I remember experiencing this overwhelming fear of touching her, because I thought I would tear her skin. It was dark pink and like velvet, like soft suede. They asked me if I wanted to hold her. And I couldn't do it at first. I couldn't take my eyes off the umbilical cord that she wore like a backpack. She was so light and small and fragile looking. Delicate. My delicate baby girl. And she didn't breathe. I couldn't see her eyes. She made no noise. When finally I held her, she was still warm. She was swaddled, and I placed her right next to me. I wrapped around her on the bed and I wailed. I was empty without my little girl.

I tell myself that I should have known that something was wrong. But how can you know something that you've never known before? It's impossible. I mostly wish that there had been some kind of marker for her death. My little one had moved on, and I didn't know for two whole days, when my body started shutting down in response. In that one moment, the instant she died, my life changed. Not in a barely imperceptible way, but in an earth-shattering way, and I missed it.

That one moment had crept by quietly. Not like the possum. There was no violent shaking. No terrors in the night. No big yellow dog. She slipped away, stolen from my life.

It's like hearing a friend gasp and turning too late to see the shooting star. It has already fallen. Whenever I see a shooting star now, I think of you, Maddison. You are my brilliant glimpse of heaven, falling to Earth but then gone in a flash. Beautiful.

At the end of the night
All of the smiles have gone cold
The hugs have gone stale
I lie down on my bed
Just me and my grief
And my love for you.

Time-Warping for the Bereaved

Jessica Bomarito

It's like a weight,
or else a jigsaw
puzzle—
pieces everywhere.

It's like the world
stopped,
and instead of being
thrown by force,

you stuck
right in your place,
everyone else flying
beyond tomorrow.

On Letting Go

Jessica S. Baldanzi

*M*y yoga teacher is full of shit. I like her, but she's full of it. She's perched on her mat at the front of the room, her well-tuned voice telling us to relinquish control, to "practice letting go."

"I know how hard it is," she says, but provides no specifics as to what "it" is. Performance anxiety? Messy house? Or something more serious: domestic violence, breast cancer, the death of a parent or friend? Whatever "it" was, it all fell apart. She let go. It all came together. Now she's a much happier person.

The last time I let go, my baby died.

I was rolling on a gurney from birthing room to operating room, but it was my mantra that was really carrying me: It'll be okay. It'll be okay. Everything will be okay. I was floating, smiling—a magician's assistant on cotton-ball clouds. We were heading for the operating room because labor was progressing but the baby wasn't coming out. No one was worried—my pregnancy had been healthy, and although I had been hoping for natural childbirth, this move to a C-section was common enough, routine even. This was my first baby, but everyone around me had done this hundreds, maybe thousands, of times. We were in a hospital, among professionals, experts. We were safe.

The baby was limp when they pulled him out, but everything was still okay, of course. It had to be. It always would be. "Letting go" was the crux of my life philosophy, the best way to dissipate panic and anxiety. Stuck in the middle backseat with a driver tailgating at 85 mph? Let go. Airplane turbulence, oxygen masks dropping? Let go. No cry from a baby just freed from the womb? Just let go.

No one in the operating room was talking to me. No one was looking at me. Everyone was huddled around the baby. They'd moved him to a table at my left, they'd called more doctors in, and all of them were blocking my view. They took turns pressing on his chest, moving his legs up and down in infant calisthenics. "Is everything okay?" I finally asked the doctor, and she simply said, "No."

That "No" marks the line between who I am now and who I used to be. Am I wiser or just more wary—of luck, statistics, best-case scenarios? Of course I understand now what "letting go" really meant back then: not just that things would be "okay," but that they would turn out well, in one of the handful of positive ways I could envision.

At four the next morning I woke up after twenty-four hours of shock, of staring blank, at bawling family members and friends, of holding hands with my husband. I was staring again, this time at that huge, institutional clock across from my bed—the same kind they use in schools, in prisons—trying to figure out how to go forward. The clock's hands were moving forward. The clock made sense: all those tiny divisions of time, perfectly spaced. I was falling behind as the clock ticked ahead.

This was not happening. This was not part of the challenging but happy future that I had recklessly let myself imagine, that had expanded along with my belly over the past nine months. That life included kicking feet to fill the tiny socks from the baby shower, now washed and matched and folded, waiting in a basket by the changing table. That life included a warm baby on this cold September weekend.

Everything was now exactly the opposite of what everyone, absolutely everyone, had led me to imagine. After they gave up on reviving the baby, the nurses had spirited me out of the birthing ward and into the dark mirror at the other end of the hall, a wing they don't show you on the tour for expectant mothers. They made a plaster cast of his feet for us—they were old, wrinkled, as if a sad, heavy lifetime had already creased his soles. He was ice cold from the morgue. No socks could warm those feet.

I was stuck behind the glass of a clock moving backward, or maybe not moving at all—I couldn't hear a tick. The minute hand was circling the wrong way. Before four a.m. the previous day, my letting go had floated me through a life of grace. Now, with every silent click, another moment that used to add up to a charmed life became one mere moment of good luck, just one of the short black lines encircling that blank face of random circumstance.

Anything—anything at all—could happen next. Things wouldn't necessarily turn out well. Things could continue to turn out very, very badly for the rest of my life. For that matter, "the rest of my life" might not last the hour. I had neglected to acknowledge that luck could be both bad and good.

I have two toddlers now, two boys. My older son, almost four, has already lost a cat, so he often asks about death. I've told him about his older brother Christopher, as we named him, but mostly I avoid his more general questions about death. I tell him it's going to be okay, and I struggle to believe my own words.

Right now, right this very minute, it's more than okay. I love my two living sons and my husband with certainty, without the insubstantial what-ifs that can make people with safe, healthy lives long for something else. I never take anyone I love for granted. I never take my life for granted. Christopher gave me that gift.

But of course any or all of us could die at any moment, for any reason, bizarre to mundane. Christopher was a fluke, stuck on the wrong side of the statistics—one in thousands our doctor told us when we met again in the haze of the long, empty days after his death. But I can no longer trust even the most promising odds.

My younger son, barely one year old, is an expert hugger: he throws his arms around my neck, rests his curly head on my shoulder, and pats my back. I inhale the rich soil smell of his scalp as I return the hug. I practice hanging on.

Valentine
Bar Scott

My son, Forrest, was diagnosed with Stage IV hepatoblastoma in 2000 and died on February 9, 2002. He was three and a half.

Our house sits on the side of a mountain in upstate New York. Dense woods surround it on three sides, so the front yard is only visible from an airplane or standing on the deck that wraps around our second floor. When I lie in our hammock, I wave at planes flying overhead in case passengers or pilots can see me far below them. I love the thought that someone might be waving back at me. One time I was reading out there when I heard a helicopter coming straight toward me. I searched the sky, but I couldn't see it until, all of the sudden, it flew out from behind the trees and cut across my view. The men inside were so close I could see their helmets and dark glasses staring back at me. It was scary because it happened so fast. It's never happened again, but I still wonder what they were up to.

For my husband Peter's fortieth birthday, I hired a pilot to fly us up over our house to see what it looked like from above. Forrest used to say "up to the clouds, Mommy" whenever I pushed him on a swing, so he was excited to fly into the sky for Daddy's birthday. Unfortunately, he fell asleep as soon as the engines turned over. I'm not sure if he was sleepy or terrified, but he missed the whole flight.

As the pilot lifted our plane off the ground, Peter and I watched the Hudson River and Rhinecliff Bridge move away from us. It was a clear-blue day so we could see for miles. To the west, The Catskill

Mountains looked like an enormous bowl, and the Ashokan Reservoir shimmered like a golden puddle. Our plane cast a tiny shadow on the ground below us as we moved across the sky. Eventually we headed north toward Overlook Mountain and the town of Woodstock where we live. From there we found Plochmann Lane winding through the trees east of town, past Forrest's preschool, to Glasco Turnpike, and then West Saugerties Road cutting a straight line below our property. It was easy to see our land. It's a naked spot in the middle of the woods. Everything was quiet down there, and I could see my empty hammock on the deck. Behind the house, the mountains and trees seemed to go on forever. As we flew over, I could see that our life on the ground was surrounded by wilderness—something I'd never realized before.

So when it snowed hard on Valentine's Day in 2003, I wondered what our yard looked like from the sky. I often wonder that now because it feels like the sky is Forrest's new vantage point. When I looked outside, all I could see was quiet, undisturbed snow across our yard and the valley beyond. I'd woken early that morning knowing I wanted to send Forrest a valentine, but I wasn't sure how to do it. It had been one year and five days since he'd died, and I wanted to make sure he would receive my message. From our living room window, our snowy front yard looked like an enormous blank canvas, which gave me an idea.

I called the local florist and asked him to save any red rose petals he had left over from bouquets he'd made that day. I ordered a few bouquets myself, and then ran around to other stores in the area to buy whatever roses they still had in their coolers. When I got home, I pulled each rose from its stem, and carefully separated the velvety petals from one another. I put them all in a big plastic bag, pulled on my big snow boots and down coat, then picked my way through the snow to the center of our yard. For twenty minutes, I walked around and around in my oversized boots, packing down the snow until I'd made a heart-shaped valentine for Forrest that was fifteen feet in diameter. When I had it just right, I took the rose petals and spread them out evenly inside the huge heart. Their redness was soft and brilliant against the crisp white ground. I thought to sprinkle snow over them to keep them from blowing away, but when I rubbed my mittens together, the snow froze into tiny balls of ice. They collected like marbles in the bowl of each petal and quickly froze my Valentine's Day heart in place. It was perfect.

As I stood in the snow admiring my valentine for Forrest, I wondered if pilots flying overhead could see it. I knew if they did, they'd probably understand.

When I finally got back inside I felt good. My Valentine's Day plan had worked, and I was full of loving Forrest. I'd discovered over the previous year that expressing my love for him out loud was a good habit even in his absence. Something about believing he was there and could see or hear me replaced my loneliness with love. So periodically throughout the day, I went to the window to look at my valentine. It was so beautiful out there in the snow. Late in the afternoon, though, I looked out and was stunned. My valentine was gone. I didn't know what to think. But then I saw something that made me laugh. Leading up to and away from my rose-petal heart was a single track of deer prints. That deer had eaten my valentine!

A few months later, my friend Lisa called out of the blue. I'd met her the year before. Her husband Teddy had been killed in the World Trade Center attacks, so she and I had a strong connection because of our mutual grief. In a moment of curiosity and desperation, she'd gone to a psychic that morning. She told me that about halfway through the session, the psychic suddenly paused and said, with some confusion, "Who is Bar? What is Bar? Could it be Barb? No, they're saying 'Bar.' Do you know who Bar is? I see a little boy. He's holding a man's hand. They're saying something about a deer and some rose petals. Does this mean anything to you?"

I laughed again and shook my head. Then I told her about my valentine.

Adapted from *The Present Giver*, self-published in 2011.

Miscarried

Kristin Camitta Zimet

I have no place to lay you down,
my quiet one, gone without enough
living. No round-bellied jar
to fold my hands around, glazed
with soda ash that stings the fingers,
scalds the surface with a pock of tears.

No stopper to hold in this little
heap, this dry dissolve: skeletal
roses, brittle fern, baby's breath,
scent purely imagined. No matter
what I curl my mind around, this
ribbon unties. I turn and turn

and have no nest to settle in.
I cannot keep air enough under
my feathers, or form a cove
around you. Angels swerve away
from this unripe annunciation,
this shut ground. Only my beasts,

in their diminishment, are trying.
The dog with his crooked back
inches his wolf skull underneath
my palm. The deaf cat digs
her way up, licks my cheek
with a flesh-clearing rasp.

First published in *Quiddity*.

Lost Friends and the Big Lie

Mike Monday

One of the great things about the *Return To Zero* project is the blog on the movie's website, which contains some of the most heartfelt writing I have ever read. I suppose that should be expected, as parents would naturally be moved to eloquence when sharing their stories of loss with a community that empathizes and cares. The blog is a remarkable forum to help accomplish the mission statement of the movie—to break the silence that surrounds stillbirth.

My blog entry from January 2013—written at the request of the film's director, and my best friend, Sean Hanish—was something of an exception in that I am one of the few posters who had not experienced the loss of a child. I wrote of my experiences of knowing Sean and his wife, Kiley; of attending the memorial service for their son, Norbert; and of visiting the movie set. My purpose in writing was simply to encourage others like me—friends and family of those who have experienced a loss—to be present and available, and to listen when our loved ones want or need to talk about what they are going through. Given the content of the other entries, I expected mine to pass with little or no notice. However, after it was posted, it actually garnered a few comments on the blog page and on Facebook. Beyond the fact that it caught anyone's attention at all, I was surprised by the content of several of the comments, which said, in effect, "Thanks for sticking by Sean. I lost a lot of friends when I lost my child."

I was incredulous. Who would turn away a friend at a time when support was needed the most? I figured the behavior described in those few comments had to anomalous. But a little further reading and research, along with some anecdotal evidence, revealed that abandonment by friends is a fairly common occurrence under these circumstances.

I couldn't get my head around that at first. After all, isn't this what friends suit up for? Let's face it: most of a good friendship is pretty easy. It's hanging out laughing. It's grabbing a pizza at 1 a.m. It's going to that movie/concert/game that you both want to see. Those shared experiences are supposed to be the foundation for something, aren't they? And if it's not being there for each other when things get tough, then what is it? Friends are supposed to be the family that you get to choose.

But then I remembered something that I thought about during the aftermath of Norbert's death, when I reflected on the conversations I had with Sean, and with mutual friends after Norbert's memorial service. I found that I heard the same phrase over and over again. I said it myself, I heard others say it to Sean and Kiley, and I heard the guests say it to each other. We used the phrase so often, I didn't stop to question its veracity until later. But when I really thought about it, I realized we were all telling The Big Lie. The Big Lie can take many forms, but it almost always starts with the same three words:

"I can't imagine…"

I think I first told a version of The Big Lie to Sean on the phone when he told me they had lost Norbert: "I can't imagine what you're going through." I know I heard several versions of The Big Lie during or at the memorial service: "I can't imagine how they feel" or "I can't imagine what this is like." Often, the three words stand by themselves, and the sentence remains incomplete, but we all understand what it is that the speaker ostensibly can't imagine.

But it's a lie. Can those of us who haven't lost a child really know or experience the pain of parents who have? Of course not. But can we imagine it? Absolutely. The truth is that it's not that we *can't* imagine it, but rather that we *don't want to*. As you would expect, most of the guests at Norbert's memorial, myself included, were contemporaries of Sean and Kiley, which meant that many of us were parents of young children. What would it take for us to imagine ourselves in their position? All it really takes is to sit down and try to conjure up an image of losing one of your children—to try to convince yourself, even momentarily, that a child that you love more than life itself was taken from you before it ever got a chance to breathe or eat or laugh.

The human imagination is a limitless resource, and one could easily tap into it to better sympathize with the parents of a stillborn child. Understandably, though, most parents would never let their minds voluntarily go that dark of a place and try to capture the feeling of losing their child. And so instead, we tell The Big Lie and pretend that the experience is so alien, so beyond our comprehension, that it surpasses our ability to even imagine it. In doing so, we put an emotional distance between ourselves and the tragedy, and we let ourselves feel secure that this horrible thing has happened to *them*, and it can't happen to *me*.

Around the time of Norbert's memorial service, I confronted The Big Lie a couple of times. The first wasn't by choice. Knowing they would be unable to get out the words, Sean and Kiley asked me to deliver a eulogy for Norbert that they had written. (A greater honor, I will probably never know.) As I read their moving words, I couldn't help picturing myself trying to write something similar for one of my own kids and, for whatever reason, I thought of having to come up with a eulogy for my son, who was then just three. The second was on the plane ride home after the service. While thinking about Sean and Kiley, my mind raced back to the day my then twenty-two-month-old daughter was born. Minutes after her delivery, she stopped breathing and needed to be resuscitated by the attendant medical staff. I remembered the abject terror of waiting to hear that she would be okay, and began to wonder about the alternate universe in which she didn't pull through. In both cases I quickly became overwhelmed with emotion and had to purposefully steer my mind away from the thoughts of any harm coming to my children. My imagination was taking me places I didn't want to go.

Which brings me back to disappearing friends. While I certainly can't condone the abandonment of a friend who is grieving the loss of their child, I'd like to think that it's not because those people are callous or indifferent to the suffering. Rather, I think it's an extension of The Big Lie. Some must take "I can't imagine…" to the next step, which I suppose is, "I won't even deal with this." It's human nature to want to dodge pain—be it physical or emotional. By avoiding the situation entirely, these people can live in the phony world they've constructed, where terrible things only touch other people's lives, and can't invade theirs. To an extent, I can understand the desire to do that. We all want to believe that our children will be safe and that we can protect them from any dangers. But a stillbirth is one of those events that cruelly demonstrates to us that, sometimes, we have zero control over what happens to our loved ones, no matter how careful we are. By avoiding the parents, these former friends can shut out one reminder that tragedy can befall any of us, with or without warning.

Parents who have lost a child have taken up residence in a town that no one wants to visit. While staying away reveals an astonishing failure of character, I don't think it makes those people evil. It simply makes them afraid, flawed, and all too human. That's why it's so magnificent that a community has built up around *Return To Zero*. That community is a place where parents can share their similar but unique stories; where they can be assured that they are not alone no matter how much they may sometimes feel they are; and because of the shared experience of almost everyone there, where no one ever has to tell them The Big Lie.

Bella's Story

Paul De Leon

*T*oday is Thursday, or so I'm told. Mommy must have been really busy today, because we were moving nonstop. Right when I would get comfortable, she would take off again. She told someone she was *going to work* earlier. I could hear music and the laughter of other children for most of the day. I wonder what her work is.

Time has been going by so slow. I just want to meet her. I don't know how much longer I have to wait, but it seems to be getting closer. I've been growing like a weed the last few weeks. I'm pretty sure I put on at least a pound in just the past few days, in fact—though that's not all my doing. Apparently Mommy loves chicken nuggets. I do, too, I admit.

My hands and arms are long now, and I can reach so far in all directions. Sometimes, for fun, I extend my entire body and let out a long stretch. When I do that I hear Mommy giggle, and it makes me smile. I love her laugh. Her voice is what soothes me when I'm scared or uncomfortable. Sometimes I hear another voice nearby when Mommy laughs, too. That voice is deeper, but caring. He seems just as pleased with my stretching and kicking as Mommy is. I wonder who he is.

I'm ready to meet them. I know they think they have been waiting for me, but I know I have been waiting for them even more. I know it will be soon. I can just tell. I've started twisting and turning, getting myself ready to enter the world.

It's the end of the day, and the house is quiet now. All the sounds are gone. My eyes are getting heavy. Mommy is comfortable now it seems. Her soft snoring tells me she is asleep. I think I will join her and get some rest.

I twist and turn to get comfortable and finally find a spot that I like. My eyes shut, and my heart beats a little slower. I am so tired that I barely notice that I'm a little bit uncomfortable in this new position. I drift off to sleep—deeply, comfortably, resting.

Something bright is making me squint my eyes. I can only have been asleep for a few minutes—what is this? I try to open them, but I can't.

"Bella." A deep voice is calling my name. It startles me at first. I stretch my arms and legs, and that's when I notice that my surroundings are different now—quite different. There's nothing to kick at now. The walls that held me before are no longer here to push against.

"Bella." Again the voice shakes me. It's a deep voice, but not like the one I'm used to hearing. This voice smiles constantly. It is caring and happy—but if I strain a bit, I can hear a hint of sadness in it, too. *What is there to be sad about? I'm entering the world now. I'm about to meet Mommy; I'm about to meet everyone!*

That thought excites me, and it makes me open my eyes at once. Again the brightness is overwhelming and my eyes try to shut, but this time I push them open again and try to take in what is around me. There is only beauty. I know no other words to describe it. I feel myself smile. I feel my feet warm against the ground.

I looked down and see that I'm standing. *How?* My toes stretch apart and wiggle in the green blades between them. The ground is soft and cushy. I notice my hands. I bring them up to my face and tickle my nose. I laugh at myself. *What is all of this?*

"Bella." This time, the voice comes from right beside me. I turn and see that someone is standing to my right, but I can't see his face, only an intense brightness. I don't fear it. I look up into brightness. "Mommy?" There is no answer.

I step closer and peer into the brightness. Suddenly a man's open arms and hands are bending down toward me. I reach out and place my small, round, chubby hands into his massive ones. Still, no fear overcomes me. After a moment, his hands leave mine and reach up under my arms. In one swift motion, I am light, and I am gliding toward him.

As he pulls me in closer, I finally see his face. His eyes are radiant—a color not yet discovered. Warm and loving, they display his joy at holding me. My pouty lips attempt a smile and succeed. He smiles back at me. More brightness comes forth. He pulls me even closer to his face.

"My sweet Bella."

"Mommy?" I am still confused.

"No, sweet girl. It's not Mommy." That hint of sadness I detected earlier spikes as he says this.

A small feeling of emptiness sets into my stomach, and as I watch his face, a tear forms in his eyes and drops majestically down his smooth skin. In that instant I notice that I, too, am crying—and I realize that I won't be meeting Mommy after all.

As if he has read my mind, he quickly pulls me in and embraces me. The warmth of his broad shoulder soothes me beyond anything I could have ever imagined. The sadness I felt a moment ago transforms into complete joy. I know I will be safe from now on.

After a long time, he places me back on the grass, and I sit down. He sits down beside me and holds my hand.

"So I'm not meeting Mommy?" I ask, pulling at the green landscape.

I don't see him smile, but I feel it. He squeezes my hand. "Yes, child, you will meet her."

I perk up. "I get to meet her?" I nearly yell, overcome with excitement.

He laughs and nods. "Yes, you will."

"Oh, when? When, when, when? I want to meet her!"

"One day, I promise. You will meet Mommy, and Daddy, too!"

Daddy. That's the name of the other voice I used to hear. The deeper, caring voice. Enthusiasm fills my entire body, and I dance with glee, hopping, skipping, and rolling around on the grass.

He laughs heartily. "Bella."

I roll once more before coming to a stop on my back. I tilt my head up and look at him. "Yes?"

"Before you meet Mommy and Daddy, there are a few other people I want you to meet."

I feel my face form a question. "Other people?"

I stand up and walk toward him. He takes my hand and we make our way to the street, which is made of gold, and he extends his hand and points. My gaze follows its direction. Just on the horizon there stands a large mass of people—faces I somehow know, faces with smiles just as bright as the one on his face.

"You are home, Bella."

I look up at him and agree with a nod. But before I walk toward the people on the horizon, for the first time since I arrived here, I look back over my shoulder. My eyes dig into the street and beyond the grass. I strain to see her. And for a split second I get a glimpse.

There is Mommy, lying in the hospital bed. The caring man, Daddy, is sitting next to her, holding her. They are both crying. I can tell that the tears they are shedding are not of happiness, but from a broken heart. They're crying because I'm not there.

I try to get their attention. I want to let them know I'm okay, that I am perfectly safe, and I call out—but they don't seem to hear me. As I watch them hurt for me, I realize how much they love me, and I realize that maybe I was wrong; maybe they were waiting for me more than I was waiting for them. I want to cry, but instead a smile forms, because I remember what he told me: I will get to meet them. Our meeting is just going to be delayed a little bit longer, that's all.

I blow them both a kiss and turn back toward my new family. With one step, I am instantly surrounded by the large group of people. Laughter, hugs, kissing, and smiles start, and to be honest, I don't think they'll ever stop.

I'm okay, Mommy. I'm okay, Daddy. I'm home.

"So Tell Me About Heaven. . ."
Bobby Richmond

Address Book

Meagan Golec

"**Y**our address book will change."

In the aftermath of losing my first child at 38.5 weeks gestational age, this is one of the phrases that stuck out. My address book will change? Who cares? My baby just died and the last thing on my mind is how my social life will be affected.

I soon learned, however, that losing your child is only the first bad thing that happens. As awful as your child's death is; it is. It is a complete act. Finished. There is nothing you or anyone else can do to change it. There are decisions about funerals to face, the physical act of delivering a stillborn child, the phone calls to make, the hearts to break, the hopes and dreams to destroy. And these acts are overwhelming in their unfairness. But your brain has its defense mechanisms in place that allow you to get through the next second, the next minute. You can function because you have to. And once the choices have been made and the arrangements have been set, it is then that the real work begins.

I could tell you all about my son. His name. That he seemed to like bean burritos and action movies. That he was beautiful and perfect. I could tell you about the fear when he stopped moving. That I convinced myself that he had just run out of room, that nothing could actually be wrong. I could tell you about lying in bed at night willing him to kick me. I could tell you about the sound the world makes when you hear the words "Your baby has no heartbeat." How still everything gets. How you hear the ocean in your ears, only it is not the ocean, it is your own heartbeat. I could tell you how you hate the sound of your heartbeat because it reminds you of the other heart that is not beating. I could tell you about the emptiness he left behind. The confusion about my identity as a bereaved mother. The tears. The physical pain of grief. The days that stretch out in front of you when your dreams for the future are shattered. And I could tell you about the day you allow yourself to smile or laugh, and the guilt you feel about finding anything beautiful in a world that killed your child. I love my son, and I am still figuring out what that means. I will likely be figuring that out for the rest of my life. But this is not what I want to tell you about.

What I want to tell you about is how your life changes in the ways you don't anticipate. How you learn to navigate the world again. How support comes from some of the least-expected places. And how your address book really does change.

When we first lost Anderson, my husband and I were amazed at the response from our community. We both work for the same youth-services organization and were touched when the office closed early on the day of the funeral so our colleagues could attend. One friend immediately began a Facebook group where others could post messages of love and support; sixteen months later the group still has over two hundred members. We were loaded down with meals and offers to help paint the house we had bought for our growing family. We felt loved, even though we didn't know how to feel anything through the shock.

The first indication I had that my social world would in fact change was a couple months after Anderson died. I was at a dear friend's house. We had been close since college: we were in each other's weddings, and I was her son's godmother. She was the person I shared things with. And then the moment came when she looked me in the eyes and said, "I hope this doesn't change you."

I hope this doesn't change you.

As if the death of a child is something that can leave you unchanged. Something you can get over, bounce back from. As if it doesn't completely redefine how you view the world, yourself, your relationships, morality, religion, family dynamics, ambition. As if the death of your child doesn't tear you from where you were, rotate you ninety degrees, and put you back down, so you are looking at the same scenery but seeing it all so differently.

In retrospect, I think our friendship always had an expiration date. It was one of those unbalanced relationships that are amazing when you have the time and energy to put in the effort, but quickly fizzle when real life happens. Anderson's death was just a catalyst, speeding us along to an inevitable ending. We tried for a while, but my lack of energy to reach out was interpreted as withdrawal. The resources I e-mailed and posted in social media about how to help grieving friends were not read. (I assume. We never discussed them, and future conversations led me to believe that she had not looked at them.) To be fair, she had many of her own worries to juggle (finishing school, starting a new job, raising a special-needs child). Neither of us had the capacity to be what the other needed.

I found this to be true in other areas of my life as well. My relationships shifted. Some faded into the background. Some went through painful seismic shifts, and I am still waiting for the dust to settle to see where I stand with those friends. Some sprouted up from the least-expected sources and became a soothing balm. The common thread determining the future of our relationship was the other person's willingness to witness me going through the grief process without trying to interfere or tell me how I "should" feel. The people who asked me questions, let me talk about what Anderson was teaching me, did not assume they knew what I was going through—these were the people I craved. My tears may have made them uncomfortable, but they held me or handed me a tissue instead of turning away or changing the subject. They cried alongside me, letting me know they also grieved this little boy we were all robbed of knowing. They did not say "he's in a better place" or "you can always have more children." They understood that I wanted THIS child and that there is no better place for a baby than his mother's arms. And they understood that those phrases, no matter how well intended, tell a bereaved parent that there is no space here for their grief. When they did not know what to say, they said, "I don't know what to say," instead of offering Hallmark platitudes. They recognized that none of us are experts in this and that the process of working through grief is necessary. And healthy. And the only way I have left to honor my child. And they participated in honoring Anderson by holding space in their lives for him.

Now, sixteen months later and just five days before we hope to welcome Anderson's little brother, I am reflecting on just how many of my relationships have changed. There are some that I mourn, a kind of secondary grief. Some I probably don't even realize are gone. And some that I rejoice in. Losing my son clarified for me what is important and how I want to spend my time and energy. Anderson has taught me (and is still teaching me) about perspective, and about intentionality, and to see things for what they actually are instead of what I wish they were. In the strangest ways, losing my child has brought me peace that I never expected.

There are some amazing people who have come into my life since Anderson died, and there are some amazing people who no longer fit in my life. My address book changed when my son died, and the relationships that remain are the greatest gift from my little boy. I will forever be grateful to him for that.

Baby Maybe

Deborah C. Linker

Suddenly I bent over, sweat dripped from my brow, and I tugged at the elastic on my pants as a wave of nausea hit me. *If I could just breathe. What did I eat?*

As I sat on the concrete curb, I felt a little stronger. I took a deep breath and looked out on the construction of our new building—a place where my new office would be. I looked up to see my husband quickly surveying the building site. "I can't believe these incompetent subcontractors," he grumbled. "We are already behind, and now they're giving me grief about laying down a sleeve for the electrical line. I'll just do it myself. Can you help me?" He hurried off to find a shovel.

I managed to do what I could without a word that I was not feeling up to par. *Something is wrong. Maybe I am coming down with the flu. Maybe it's just the stress of working full time while this building project is going on.*

God knows, it was stressful enough just working with my husband. He was the boss, the owner of the company, and he never let me forget it.

Later in the week, I had lunch with a friend, who shared the excitement of her first pregnancy. "I know I am not showing yet, but my breasts are already so tender," she explained. "My bladder is so active, I look constantly for a bathroom."

As she talked, I thought to myself, *Wow, my breasts have been very sensitive lately, and I've been getting up several times in the night to go to the bathroom. Am I crazy? I must be having sympathy pains.*

As I told my friend good-bye, I started to think about her symptoms, my symptoms, the tiredness, the nausea. I stopped at a drugstore on the way home and bought a pregnancy test.

Later that night I sat alone in the bathroom as I watched the little stick turn pink. I slipped silently into bed next to my husband. Adrenaline ran through my body. *I'm pregnant. I tried before, but nothing. Now with my new husband of just two years, I'm pregnant.*

Several years before I was told by doctors that the chances of me having a baby were pretty much zero. I accepted the fact and went off birth control to avoid the nasty side effects. Little did I know the biggest side effect would be a baby.

The next day my ob-gyn confirmed my pregnancy of twelve weeks. "Do you hear that?" as he ran the ultrasound wand over my tight belly. "It's the heartbeat of your baby."

"Oh God, I am pregnant," I said, shaking my head.

The nurse came back in the room. "We need to know which hospital you choose. Since you don't have maternity insurance, we need a deposit. And do you think you will breast-feed or give the baby formula?"

What was she saying? How can I answer these questions? My head was spinning as she led me in to sit in the doctor's office.

"Mrs. Linker, due to your age of forty-one, we highly recommend amniocentesis to rule out genetic abnormalities. The test cannot be conducted until you are in your eighteenth week. This means that if there is a problem you need to make a decision immediately following the results." Without missing a breath, my doctor asked, "If the results are positive, what is your decision? Would you want an abortion or would you want to have the baby?"

I knew what amniocentesis was, and I certainly knew what genetic abnormalities were. I have a master's degree in speech-language pathology and had worked with numerous handicapped children. I also knew from my studies that when a woman is in her thirties, she has a one in nine hundred chance of having a Down syndrome baby, and when she is forty her chances increase to one in one hundred. I looked at my doctor and said, "I cannot bring a mentally disabled child into this world."

"Okay, then I'll schedule the test," he replied without further discussion.

When I announced the news to my husband, we both sat in disbelief. Then I asked the weighted question, "We don't want to deliver a disabled baby, do we?"

He quickly responded as I knew he would: "Of course not." Tom had a degree in special education and had worked with handicapped children many years ago. We both agreed that a disabled child brings heartbreak to all involved.

Over the next six weeks, we slowly grew used to the idea of a baby. We shared our news with friends and family, made plans, and chose the name Andre, as we were sure it was a boy.

During the amnio a small amount of amniotic fluid was extracted through a needle inserted into my navel. Then it was over. I went home, cooked dinner, and remained upbeat about my upcoming motherhood.

Then the doctor called and said those words I will never forget: "Trisomy 21, Down syndrome." I took a deep breath and focused on what the doctor was saying, "Tomorrow morning, 7:30 a.m., Mount Sinai—elective abortion."

How could this be happening? After all these years, I had finally convinced myself that I was content without children in my life. Then this surprise pregnancy turns my life around, and now here we are on our way to Miami, like two dazed zombies guided to do some unknown deed.

Since I was so far into my pregnancy, labor was induced so that I would actually deliver the baby. The room was dark. I was cold and confused. I was given so many drugs, I lost track of time, fading in and out, with so many people coming and going.

Tom complained. "I'm freezing, and this chair is so uncomfortable I can't sleep. I have to go home for a while." How I wanted him to stay with me—I was scared, but as usual I didn't say no to him. He had another baby to tend to, his business. The truth was he had to meet an inspector to get a certificate of occupancy for this new building.

The next few hours were a nightmare. I had drug-induced labor pains, and when my water broke, I had no idea what was going on. My knowledge of delivering a baby was what I had seen in movies: boil the water, get the clean towels, scream, breathe, push, and voilà—a baby.

"Push," I heard someone say. "Push again, harder, breathe." *Is that my doctor's face? Why is the room so dark? Why am I wet?*

Finally, after about two and half days the ordeal was over, and I delivered a baby. By the time Tom returned, I was sleeping. When I awoke, I was angry, hurt, and confused.

"Why did you leave me? I needed you," I cried. "Why is your company always more important than me? We just aborted a handicapped baby, and we should have been together for all of it. You should—"

I was interrupted by a nurse who said, "Do you want to view the fetus?"

My mouth fell open, and Tom and I looked at each other. Neither one of us initiated discussion; we just nodded yes. *How would it look if I said no—if I said, I don't want to see the baby, take it away.* I remained silent.

They brought the little boy embryo into our room all wrapped in a blue blanket. I felt a rush of mixed emotions as I looked at him—anger, betrayal, sadness. We could see, even at this early stage, signs of Down syndrome: the lowered ears, upward slanted eyes, the strange-shaped little hands. We said good-bye to our baby.

As I dressed to leave, still in a drug haze, I saw that I was wearing a maternity top that I had designed and sewn. As I made the long walk from my room to the elevator, I thought, *I'm so humiliated, how can I wear a maternity top? I'm not pregnant.*

At home, I walked by the stack of dirty dishes piled in the sink, threw my maternity top in the trash, and crawled into bed in a state of lone depression. Tom did what he did best—he went to work. In retrospect, work was his escape, his way to deal with the pain.

Since abortion stirs up so much emotional turmoil, we told our friends and family that I had lost the baby. So, I couldn't share my feelings with anyone. My depression lasted for months. I walked down the baby aisle at the grocery and burst out crying. I received a teddy bear in the mail from a formula company and lost control for hours.

Years later, I cannot look at a Down syndrome person or watch one in a movie, especially a child. I just close my eyes. Seventeen years later I am plagued by a recurring dream of an infant that I just keep forgetting—either the baby is on the beach by the water, or I realize I haven't fed the baby, or I will look and see the baby just lying unsecured in the backseat as I drive the car. The baby in the dream has no identity, no face—it just appears, and I awake in a panic.

No one recommended a therapist or counseling group. It would've been comforting to know that over ninety percent of women caring a trisomy 21 baby choose to terminate pregnancy. If it is so prevalent, then why don't people talk about it? Why did I feel I couldn't share this experience with anyone and perhaps get the help I needed?

Do I regret my decision for an elective abortion? No. Instead I am sorry that I did not produce a healthy baby, and I'm further saddened because of the silence that followed.

Slowly, I poured myself back into work. Tom and I briefly discussed trying for another baby or adopting, but as time went on, we just fell back into our daily routine. Only it was never the same.

Spare Me

Jane Blanchard

Don't tell me that I'll have another one.
I must still mourn the life just lost. I know
That there's a lovely little girl to go
Home to hold. But I haven't yet begun
To get beyond the pain of what was done
To me these past two days—the aching, slow
Dilation—the quick mask and gas that throw
Oblivion over memory lest it run
From sanity—the reluctance to return
To life and feel the emptiness within
The awkwardness of greeting visitors
The worry how a soldier will soon learn
His child is gone—the sudden anger when
A friend, who tries to help, just makes things worse.

First published in *The Stray Branch* (Spring/Summer 2012).

4 a.m.

Jane Blanchard

The dream recurs
often enough
to be unsettling
except that the infant,
sometimes a girl,
sometimes a boy,
is always
so calm,
so comfortable,
in my arms.

Is this the one
lost in the womb,
held only as a longing
in the early morning?

First published in *The Seventh Quarry* (Summer 2013).

The Hatbox

Kelly Smith

The air was thick with the smell of sweet summer wheat as my daughter Halle and I rummaged through old items in the living room closet. We were moving in just a few weeks and this was the last "room" to be tackled. I'd saved it for last because it was the catch-all of the whole house and a complete disaster. Board games, craft supplies, and old boxes of baseball cards were all bulging out over the edges of overly burdened shelves. Beads of sweat pearled at my nape as I shoved things aside and tried to group the chaos into piles that made sense.

Halle's breath caught, and I turned to see her gaping at something she'd just pulled from the back corner. A padded hatbox covered in thin, gauzy fabric, it was certainly intriguing, especially so to a little girl. Against the green stood gold-leaved tulips embossed deeply, frozen forever in perpetual bloom. The rounded shape of the box brought to mind the fine ones of old; the kind that made you wish you had a stiff brimmed hat to put inside, maybe one that was tall with a luxurious flower placed just so, pink silk ribbons trailing down the back. The kind of hat Rhett would give Scarlett; just the sort of thing a little girl could appreciate. Thick gold ribbon lined the base of the lid, drew the eye, and begged the casual passerby to pause, even if just for a moment, to lift the lid and have a quick peek inside.

I ran my hand gingerly over the fabric, tracing the glittering threads that ran around each meticulous flower. I closed my eyes, my hand trembling upon the box, my heart racing, palms wet. Unlike my daughter, I knew very well what was buried inside.

"Can we open it, Mom?" she asked breathlessly, excited about the goodies she was sure we'd discover.

"I'm not sure this is the time, sweetheart," I said carefully, watching her face fall with disappointment and knowing even then she wouldn't be dissuaded. "Maybe Daddy can show you later. There's nothing exciting inside anyway," I told her. "Just some stuff that belonged to your brother."

"That's okay!" she said, brightening. "I still want to open it!"

There was a time when the sight of the hatbox could turn my blood to ice. A time when I hid it from myself just so I wouldn't see it by mistake. I was always moving it, always hoping the new spot would afford me a reprieve and that, this time, it was truly hidden. But there'd been more than a handful of times when, standing on tiptoe to shuffle things around on a dusty attic shelf, or lying face-down on the floor to stretch underneath the bed frame in a perpetual search for that one basket that was just the right size or for the stupid Christmas wreath that hangs on the front door, I'd been unexpectedly surprised by the box sitting innocently behind broken picture frames and high school band instruments. It was always a sucker punch to the stomach.

I suppose if I'd really wanted to, I could have just refused her, made up a story, or changed the subject. Trains of thought are not so hard to derail in five-year-old minds. But I was tired: tired of hiding from the box; tired of moving it only to have it find me again; tired of being afraid. I smiled at her then, nodded, took the box from her, and placed it on the floor. We knelt down in the small closet, the box between us. I held my breath and pulled the lid from the top.

Carefully placed inside were the small pieces of me that I'd boxed away years ago. They'd sat quietly in their dark coffin all this time, strangled for breath, anxious for the light of day. The sweet and antiseptic aroma attached to them was instantly in my nostrils, thick with memories, laced with heartache. Halle peered expectantly over the edge. The items themselves were just as I'd left them, just as they'd been when I'd last peeled away the lid.

A knit hat. The kind they put on babies right after they're born. The one with the pink and blue stripes, made from waffled fabric designed to contract and expand, to fit snugly onto fat, pink-cheeked babies. A miniature medical bracelet, cinched unimaginably small—small enough to slide onto my thumb. The perfect size for the ankle of a baby at twenty-five weeks gestation.

An infant blanket, images of baby carriages dancing softly across brushed flannel, a small stain still on the corner. A book given to me in the hospital that fall day in 2003 titled *Empty Arms: Coping After Stillbirth*. I'd taped a piece of paper over the cover art—a mother's empty arms reaching in vain for her child—almost as soon as they'd given it to me. That image made me crazy. Running down the hallway, screaming at the top of my lungs crazy.

A white envelope, the edges worn soft from the opening and the closing, filled with the only pictures I'd ever have of him, hat still on, blanket wrapped round, hospital bracelet in place. A tiny blue onesie, an exact replica of the one I'd ironed and delivered to the funeral home so I could remember what we'd buried him in. And finally, the announcement card onto which they'd pressed his perfectly still hands and feet, laden with black ink.

Halle happily removed all the treasures. Together we lifted them, touching and smelling, breathing in a moment past and always present. After everything had been explored and she was satisfied, she planted a kiss on my cheek, wrapped her tiny arms around my neck, squeezed with all her might, and then skipped away in search of yet another adventure.

I sat quietly for a while, memories spread about me like a fan, my hands buried in a grief too old for my thirty-three years. I picked up the knit cap, pressed it to my nose, and breathed in the scent of the hospital room, somehow perfectly preserved in the tiny hat. I closed my eyes and smiled; saw myself holding him quietly again, my lips pressed to his forehead; could feel again the nervousness of the nurses who stood alongside my husband and me, waiting patiently for us to say our good-byes so they could take him away.

Six years. Had it really been six years since the world fell apart? It was true, I didn't think about him constantly anymore. I'd moved past spending every waking moment wondering what I'd done wrong or how such a terrible thing had happened to me. The true bottom for me had come and gone years ago and now, for the most part, I could navigate my way through life normally again. And yet, the box could still bring back that familiar and sharp stabbing sensation in my middle—the feeling of having been run through by an unseen enemy who walked away, leaving me doubled over and groping at my stomach, the question on my face.

Sometimes it still seems like the fog of one of those relentless dreams that repeats itself, over and over, night after night. When I wake, just for a second I feel the relief of having been asleep; the fleeting joy at having thought it was a nightmare. They are priceless: the quiet, sacred first breaths upon waking when all is at it should be and I am whole again.

I laid the knit cap down, placed the lid back on the empty hatbox, and pushed it aside. Slowly, methodically, I packed each of his things into an empty cardboard box and sealed it with packing tape. Then, in permanent black ink, I marked it simply, "Elijah."

"Where is the Other Baby?"

Jessica Killeen

"Wake up, Maggie, I think I've got something to say to you!" I was belting out Rod Stewart as loudly as my now squished lungs could manage. My two-year-old daughter, Molly, giggled as I grabbed her hands and twirled her around our living room. My nine-months-pregnant belly prevented me from attempting anything too acrobatic, so we contented ourselves with mini rotations and elaborate flounces. My husband Joseph and I were just a week away from meeting our own "Maggie May," and I happily indulged my need for sentimentality. In my giddy excitement, *Rod Stewart's Greatest Hits* had been a permanent fixture in the CD player. I imagined myself singing this tune to my baby girl every night as I rocked her to sleep. It would be her special song, I decided.

Instead, Maggie died, unnoticed, on a Thursday. Or at least, that's when she died to us. It seems likely that she passed away early sometime the previous morning. That Thursday we arrived at our obstetrician's office buzzing with nervous excitement for our final routine checkup before the due date. When our doctor struggled to find Maggie's heartbeat, despite her calm reassurances that the baby was probably just "hiding," my own heart leapt into my throat. But it was not until the nurse wheeled in the rickety old ultrasound machine, kept for emergencies, and we all saw Maggie's completely still and lifeless body, that I felt the sensation of a cliff crumbling beneath my feet. The doctor took my hand, and I reluctantly met her gaze, the weight of inevitability unbearable: "I'm sorry...I'm just not seeing what I need to see." The words were unreal, unleashing a wave of sickening shock. I barely noticed anything else going on in that little room, except Molly leaning over the bed and stroking my hair: "Mumma...Mumma," she murmured.

It wasn't possible in that moment to make sense of what had happened, from a medical or emotional standpoint, so we carried on with the new plan of action. Did we want to deliver her today, or wait a while? Is there anything we want to do first? It always seems easier to assume a role or task, rather than delve into the bottomless pit of pain and grief in situations like this, so we agreed to make arrangements for Molly, grab our hospital bag, and proceed with the delivery. I felt utter dread at the thought of birthing my dead baby—how could I possibly find the strength to do it? I loved her terribly, but things had gone so completely wrong. It just wasn't supposed to be like this.

Still reeling from shock and the sucker punch of emotions, we somehow made it home. Staggering into the bedroom, I grabbed the neatly packed hospital bag and emptied out its contents, strewing nursing bras and baby blankets across the room. I was possessed with grief, determined to weed out every last piece of baby paraphernalia. The drive to the hospital was sobering, allowing us a moment to brace ourselves before facing the next stage of the ordeal. "I can feel her moving now!" I wailed as we turned into the parking lot. My body had deceived me; with each waddling, reluctant step, I could feel Maggie's body swishing and floating, graceful limbs and hands moving in rhythm. These sensations had become familiar to me over the past week, yet it was only then as we passed through the sleek sliding hospital doors that I realized how mistaken my perceptions of my own body had been. In that moment, I was convinced that the innate, primal mother-child connection that every pregnant woman is supposed to possess had malfunctioned. Even in my belly I had failed my child, and there was no one to hold accountable but myself.

Walking into Labor and Delivery less than two years ago to deliver our first baby, everything seemed happy: the pleasant receptionist and the jolly maternity care coordinator who waved and remembered us from the preadmission appointment. We were greeted like old friends. Even the walls seemed welcoming in their soothing tones of peach and eggshell. Now, everything about the place seemed cruel: the obnoxious front desk clerk engaged in some kind of hilarious exchange on the phone. Didn't she know what had happened? I glanced at the insipid framed watercolors on the walls, images of mothers cradling newborn babies. We were supposed to look at them and smile knowingly with the glow of expectant parenthood, which, I now understood, quickly becomes intolerable to anyone whose baby has just died. Today, the maternity care coordinator was busy spreading jollity to another pregnant couple. *That was us*, I thought bitterly as we scuttled past.

Everything was ready in our room: a cap, gown, and tiny diaper were laid out in the crib. A baby is going to be delivered here today. Will they dress her and put a diaper on her, I wondered, or just wrap her lifeless body in receiving blankets? There was comfort in dwelling on the minutiae of the situation, rather than confronting the impending wave of grief, fear, and guilt that threatened to break at any moment.

The silence of a stillbirth is deafening. It is the absence of everything that should be—the sounds of a baby's first breath and cry; the tears of relief and joy from mother and father; the jovial chatter of doctors and nurses tending to mother and baby. Even if I had been able to forget that the baby I was delivering had died, the silence in the room at the moment she emerged was engulfing. Instead of sighs of relief, I was sobbing and wailing like a wounded animal. Maggie didn't wriggle or splutter as nurses swathed in blue gowns swooped in and whisked her away to the warming area. That day, the usual hustle and bustle of nurses carrying out the necessary cleaning, measuring, and wrapping of the baby was more like a respectful murmur. There was no haste; everyone trod gently and spoke quietly. Someone asked if we wanted to see her. Yes, we wanted to see her, so she was prepared in several layers of soft blankets and handed to us. Her beauty, despite peeling skin and blood-tinged lips, was undeniable. We were left alone, just the three of us, to talk and snuggle. We told her we loved her, and how much we wished she could stay with us. I hummed "Maggie May" and rocked her in my arms. Then we said good-bye.

At home several days later, I was struck again by how dysfunctional my body seemed, as my now useless breasts began lactating. I cried, I leaked milk, and I cried some more. Forced to retrieve my previously discarded nursing bras, I stuffed them with breast pads in disgust. What kind of cruel joke was Mother Nature playing? Could there be any greater slap in the face to a grieving mother than spontaneous lactation after the death of her baby? We can't switch off the natural, hormone-driven urge to nurture and nourish our babies, even when our babies die; as women, so we're told, mothering is at the very core of what it is to *be* a woman. But I already knew the mother-child connection was broken somehow; my body had failed at the most critical moment, in what should have been its most natural function, supporting and growing a new life.

Yet I needed my body to cooperate. In the midst of intense sorrow grew a fierce determination to not be conquered by fear. I wasn't angry at God, or my doctor, or anyone else involved in this tragedy; I was angry at fear itself. I was angry that the fear of intense grief and pain might throw my life off course, and I really would never feel okay again. I wanted to converse with my child without a torrent of tears when she asked questions like "Where is the other baby?" Eventually I did feel okay, and two years later we were hopefully, cautiously retracing our steps, returning to the hospital where we met our two girls for the first time and said good-bye to one.

The unlikely gift that comes with the death of someone you love is the realization that love does not go away when they are gone; in many cases it grows stronger. The terror of reopening the wounds of loss and grief was ever present, sometimes even oppressive. It took a determined effort not to succumb to that fear, but the profound desire to give birth to and nurture a healthy child, coupled with our determination that this tragedy would not define us, carried us through a new pregnancy and the birth of our beautiful, screaming baby boy. The depth of pain we felt when Maggie died proved to us how unfathomable a parent's love for a child can be—a gift beyond description.

What to Do When They Bring You Your Dead Baby in the Hospital

Elizabeth Heineman

*T*ouch him.

Touch his face, his narrow cheeks, his hard brow. Use the tip of your index finger. Cradle the back of his head and move your hand down to feel the curve of his skull. Trace the hump of his chin, starting from the tape that holds the intubation tube in his mouth. Continue down his long throat to his collarbone.

As you support him with your left arm, use your right hand to pull the blanket away from his chest. Fill your hands with your baby. Spread out your fingers, making your hands as big as you can. One on his back, the other across his chest. Your hands will not meet, because this is a big baby.

Try another hold: one hand on each side of your baby's head, fingers overlapping at the back. Now you have a feel for your baby's head and your baby's torso. Your hands will want to remember those proportions.

Unfold the rest of the blanket. See the stump of your baby's umbilical cord, brown, with a piece of gauze held in place with a clamp. See his small uncircumcised penis, his wrinkled, dark scrotum. Notice how fat his thighs are, and turn him around to see if the buttocks from which they extend are equally fat. The lower legs look slim in comparison. Be careful of the pegs protruding from the shins, the pegs that were to deliver drugs directly to the bone because the veins were too small. His feet are wrinkled and crusty with meconium.

Hold your baby under his arms so his feet rest on your lap, as if he were standing. You'll have to support his head.

Notice that his eyes are half open. He looks like he's looking at you. Meet his gaze. Tell him with your eyes how much you love him. Lean your brow against his brow, your nose against his nose. Close your eyes.

Breathe in. Smell your baby's smell. It is earthy, bloody, unwashed. Lift your baby higher, until your nose is buried in his neck. Smell him again. Inhale deeply.

Sit your baby on your lap. Tell him that he is your beautiful, beautiful baby. Tell him that you love him, and that you will always love him. Caress his cheek and tell him the same thing. Kiss his face and say it again.

Invite your baby's Daddy over with your eyes. Hold your baby up so Daddy can take him. Watch how Daddy cradles him as he stands, how he looks down at him, biting his lip.

Talk about your baby. About how big he is. About how his eyes are open. Let conversation falter.

Follow Daddy with your eyes as he sits down by your bed. You can hold the baby together. Put your face to your baby's face as Daddy does the same from the other side.

Close your eyes. Breathe deeply.

Pull back as Daddy takes your baby's hand. He will slip his finger into the hollow between your baby's curled fingers and the palm of his hand. Look at the wrinkles on the back of your baby's tiny fingers, the solidity and straightness of Daddy's big finger.

Take your baby back. Sing him a song that you make up as you go along, a song with few notes and few words, but which goes on a long time. Rock the baby as you sing to him.

Look into your baby's eyes. Realize, suddenly, what your baby's eyes are saying to you. He is asking why he has died. He is saying he had looked forward to meeting you. He knew your warmth and your voice from inside. He wanted to feel your arms and your lips once he was outside. He wanted to see you. He thought that coming out would be the beginning, not the end. You are his mother. He doesn't know whom else to ask.

His mouth is covered with tape.

Staring Death in the Face

Loni Huston-Eizenga

The first thing they did after Aisley was officially pronounced dead was hand her to me. I'll admit there was a split second where I was afraid. It pains me to think that for even a second I was afraid of my own daughter. In truth, it was death I was afraid of, the crippling reality of death. In that split second my daughter represented death and all the dread that comes with it.

They placed her in my arms. I stared into her face. I stared death in the face. She was the most beautiful thing I had ever seen. I couldn't understand how I could feel anything other than anguish in that moment as I held her lifeless body. The sorrow was still present, but I felt slightly different. Having her near me gave me a strange solace. It was as if she were consoling me. I smelled her hair, stroked her cheeks, and kissed her softly. I stared at her features as hard as I could, willing myself to memorize every inch of her. She had my exact mouth: a round button nose and a prominent little chin, just like me. From the nose down it was like looking in the mirror. From the nose up she looked just like my husband. She had his cheekbones and his round eyes. The tips of her hair felt as soft as feathers and smelled deliciously sweet; that indescribably soothing scent that only babies can emit. Her fingers were long and elegant. They didn't mimic average stubby baby digits; they seemed almost capable. She appeared long and sturdy yet simultaneously fragile. She was incredible. An overwhelming sense of peace and complete connection with her enveloped me. I never wanted it to go away.

I laid with her for what must have been an hour. I couldn't tell you because time stopped. The world stopped. My husband came over to cradle me as I was cradling her. He sobbed uncontrollably, moaning in a desperate tone I'd never heard before. The moan of grief. My tears had stopped. I was in limbo between a state of shock and a Zen trance. I couldn't comfort him like I normally would. All that mattered was my daughter.

Next thing I knew it was time for them to take her from me. The man was polite and apologetic, but I knew where he was taking her. He was taking her somewhere cold and sterile. They were going to cut her up like a science experiment. How could I hand her over to that? I felt like growling. I felt like ripping his arm off with my teeth like a wild bear protecting her cub. I needed to be with my daughter. I wanted to protect her. No one else could touch her. I never wanted to let her go.

But I did. I quelled my animal instincts and let the man take my baby. I collapsed in tears as he walked away with my heart.

A few days passed and we had the opportunity to see her again at the funeral home. I was very nervous but I longed to feel the comfort of being near her. I needed it. I had to pick out an outfit for them to dress her in. They told me to send them a hat as well, that I probably wouldn't want to see her head. I tried to banish thoughts of them cutting into her from my mind as I sifted through the tiny caps I'd bought for her. Knowing this would be the only time I'd get to select an outfit for my baby was devastating. I wailed like an injured animal as I waded through tiny colored clothes. The bright bubbly colors mocked my pain. I finally chose an outfit. I placed her little giraffe next to it so we could give that to her as well. I thought it might have been her favorite, but of course I'd never know.

I was still in tremendous pain from giving birth, but I was determined to make it to the funeral home. In reality I probably shouldn't have left my bed, but nothing could have stopped me from seeing her again. I rode in the backseat on my side, as I was still unable to sit. It made sense to me that my body felt destroyed. My outside reflected my inside.

After a short ride we arrived at the funeral home. We slowly made our way into the building. I've always hated funeral homes. I'd been to several, and they never brought me comfort. They were cold and eerie. They frightened me. Again I realize that it wasn't the building that made me feel that way, it was what it represented. Death was cold and eerie. Death was frightening. The fact that my daughter was there was almost unbearable. Death had no business with her.

The funeral director gave her condolences and pointed down the hall to the room Aisley was in. She walked us toward it and stopped at the door. "Take as much time as you need," she said. We looked through the door, and down at the end of the room, we saw a tiny white bassinet. A wave of anxiety rushed over me, my body trembling in trepidation. We grabbed each other's hands and inched slowly toward it, passing rows of chairs as we walked. It felt as if we were in slow motion; we were getting closer and closer, yet we were still unable to see her. I saw the head of her little toy giraffe. It sat next to her as motionless as she was.

Finally her little face appeared. I expected to feel the same peace and comfort as the last time I saw her. I expected that solace to return, but the first thing I thought was, "That's not my daughter." Her face was covered in makeup. In their attempts to disguise her pale-blue skin, they had given her a brownish-orange appearance. Her features looked different too. Her face seemed slightly stretched. I felt a pang in being reminded that her face had in fact been stretched. She was freezing cold to the touch and smelled strongly of formaldehyde. I couldn't pretend she was merely sleeping like before. It was painfully obvious she was dead. I wanted to pick her up but felt afraid. I was afraid she'd fall apart. Her little body had been through so much.

We went to ask if it was okay if we held her. The women said that we needed to be careful but that we could. I picked up her little body and she felt so light, so empty. She felt empty because she was empty. I kept thinking, "This isn't my daughter; this is just her shell." I wanted to be able to look at her and hold her, but it wasn't the same as before. It just wasn't her. The smell of formaldehyde was overwhelming. Every time I tried to gaze at her and connect with her a whiff of chemicals reminded me...she's dead. She's dead. She's been sliced and diced and she's dead. She's empty like a doll.

I tried to fight these thoughts. It was like being tortured. Reality was piercing through my fantasy. Taking the beautiful moment I wanted and gutting it. Cleaning it out with strong chemicals and handing it back to me. Laughing at me for thinking I could change it.

I wanted to be with my daughter like before but I couldn't. I kissed her and told her how much I loved her. I put her back in the bassinet. At first I felt like something was wrong with me, like I was rejecting her. I should be cuddling her body like before. But how do you cuddle a shell? I shouldn't have let the smell bother me. I shouldn't have thought about how gray her skin must have been under that paint. I shouldn't have let these things be morbid reminders of what they had to do to her. But it all bothered me.

Admitting this felt like the beginning of acceptance. Accepting that she died. I love my daughter more than anything; I just couldn't get rid of that voice in my head that said, "That isn't her."

A sudden sense of closure came upon me. If that isn't her, then maybe she is somewhere else. Maybe her energy or spirit left. Maybe she crawled out of her shell to be reborn. Maybe that wasn't her lying in a cold bassinet, stitched up and empty. Maybe she was okay. I felt a different sense of peace. I kissed her again, told her good-bye and that I loved her. This time I said it to the air around me. I left that funeral home feeling unexplainably better. Deep down I knew that I wasn't leaving her there in that cold, eerie building...she wasn't there after all.

Mute

Courtenay Baker

I took the phone call ordering me to the hospital while standing in the dairy section, my cart full of produce and meat. I fumbled as I grabbed some cream cheese and somehow levitated through checkout and to the ER, where I was directed upstairs to the cancer ward. My feet fit nicely in the recurring pattern on the carpet; my right foot stepped on a mauve flower, my left on a leaf, all the way down the hallway.

"I'm sorry, there are no patient rooms available, but here is a family lounge. Wait here and I'll be back with your injections."

I nodded.

The room was tiny, barely larger than a laundry closet. There were two faded armchairs, at least four boxes of tissues; on a counter a soundless TV was tuned to an episode of *The Fresh Prince of Bel-Air*. This was the room where they told families a loved one has died. This was the room with heavy curtains and thick upholstery designed to absorb mourning. This was the room where my first pregnancy ended, not with a birth, not with a failed D and C, but with a shot of Methotrexate in each of my hips.

I stood there in the path worn between the window and the door, the path debrided by the endless pacing of many. Through the window I saw cars speeding home from work, picking up kids from soccer practice, racing for dinner. My own groceries were melting in the trunk of my car.

The nurse returned and asked me to drop my pants. I braced

myself on the counter as she swabbed me and stuck me with the first shot. On TV, Will Smith jumped over a couch.

"Was this your first pregnancy?"

I nodded as Will Smith mugged for the camera.

"I'm sorry."

She stabbed me with the second needle in my other hip.

"I'm sure you'll have another baby."

I nodded again.

She made a note in her chart and gathered her things as I pulled my pants up. "You'll need to wait here for about twenty minutes or so to make sure you don't have a reaction to the drug. Why don't you have a seat? Here's a box of tissues, if you need them."

She disappeared, closing the door quickly behind her. Will Smith was dancing, gloating about something. Whoever had put this show on didn't know how to mute the TV, so though there was no volume, there were also no closed captions. Even in the silence, I knew what was happening.

Twenty minutes later, the nurse returned to find me sitting delicately on the edge of the chair; I was unwilling to commit to the room. She checked my vitals and decided that I was not having an allergic reaction to the noxious concoction, so I was free to go.

I stood and picked up my purse.

"Good luck next time!" she chirped.

I nodded and Will Smith laughed.

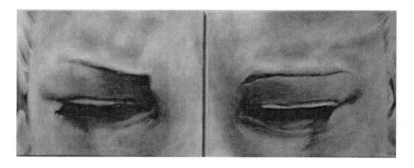

Split Wide Open
Franchesca Cox
Oil on canvas, diptych, 2007

Split Wide Open

Franchesca Cox

I am *split wide open*
My heartache is on display
My mask is coming back slowly
But some days it's difficult to fake.

How important my life used to seem
All the dreams that I hoped for one day
Art school, grad school, painting was my life
The colors have all faded
Into tones of gray and white.

I thought I knew heartache
a few years ago,
but I realized the preface
could not compare to this empty hole.

I have a scar that just won't heal
It takes time, they say
But do they know my pain runs deep
that reminders hit me every day?

My mind used to think in colors,
and create murals of landscapes in daydreams
I have been changed, wanting ever to escape
From the dry reality around me.

And in all my heartache
I can be thankful that my time with her was real
I am better for having her visit my world
She graced my life gently, briefly,
but still she was here.

I am split wide open
I want this wound to be healed
I know the scar will always be there
For true love can never be concealed.

Ghost Child

Jessica Null Vealitzek

Six weeks ago, I had a beautiful girl we named Clara. So it might seem odd that the memory of my miscarried child has come to surface now more than at any time since it happened two years ago. I often think of it as I care for my new baby.

My first child, Henry, was eighteen months old when my husband and I were surprised to find I was pregnant again. Though we wanted a second child eventually, this felt too soon. But after initial hesitation, we embraced the pregnancy wholeheartedly. In the way of many moms, I felt strongly that I knew the gender: a girl.

My eight-week appointment went well. I saw the little bean on the screen, the heart fluttering away like a down feather. A few days later, the doctor's office called me back in to recheck the placenta on an ultrasound. The doctor was worried I might have a condition—I can't even remember now what it was—that would mean I'd need to be extra careful during my pregnancy.

So the possibility of bed rest was on my mind as I lay on the table and looked at the familiar bean. Only, I saw no rapid flutter this time. For a moment I was confused, and then I saw the look on the technician's face.

Several days of visceral sadness followed, the kind of emotion you do not have to think or talk yourself into. It just was—when I awoke in the morning, during playdates with friends, while I talked on the phone with the cable service. It wrapped itself around me like a wool blanket. Hardest was the moment I'd never imagined: lying on a hospital bed, filling out the standard paperwork for a dilation and curettage. I was happy to have something to do while I waited, something simple, but slipped into the middle of the mundane was the question, "Would you like to take the remains home for burial or would you like the hospital to dispose of them?"

I felt apologetic about my sadness. Miscarriages happen all the time, right? There must have been something wrong; it was nature's way. And after all, it was only nine weeks. Imagine the pain of miscarrying once you've felt the baby inside you.

But—nine weeks. Since my husband and I found out as early as possible, at two weeks, that means I had seven long weeks of imagining my baby smiling at her older brother, imagining the peach fuzz along her cheeks and the cooing of her voice. She was not a bunch of cells to me. She was my child. Though I never met her, not literally, I carried her, and that is an experience unlike any other. The bond grows fiercer the longer the pregnancy, but it is strong from the beginning.

A friend of mine had a miscarriage, too, followed by the birth of her daughter. My friend feels that the miscarried baby was who eventually became her daughter; she just wasn't ready to come at that time. For me, it is a bit different. She is sort of my ghost child, an absent older sister, the one who came before. She never quite became a part of the family, but she will never leave it. I feel my ghost child in Clara; she is a part of her, but not the same.

My miscarriage has given me deep gratitude as I watch my sweet baby girl sleep, delight in her cries for milk, and cradle her head in the crook of my elbow. In a very real way, Clara is an honor to her, my first girl.

A version of this story first appeared on the author's blog, *True STORIES*.

Red Ant

Rebecca Patrick-Howard

Six weeks before I found my son cold and blue in his bed, we had a picnic in the backyard. The air was hot and thick and took your breath away as soon as you stepped out the front door, but there was relief under the maple tree. We were broke and had cabin fever and our three-year-old wanted to do something fun.

Toby, only a week old, was unimpressed with the whole thing: minutes after going outside he promptly fell asleep in his daddy's lap, his spindly little legs dangling over my husband's knees. It occurred to me that our babies always started out skinny enough, yet we still find ways to fatten them up until their checks puff out and their legs became rolls of sweet, plump skin.

We had no sooner spread the food out on the blanket, than I caught a glimpse of something red out of the corner of my eye. Upon closer inspection, I saw it to be a rather large, scary-looking insect, covered with fire-engine-red fur. Neither wasp nor ant, though having characteristics of both, this intrusive stranger marched over to our blanket with purpose. Barefoot, I grabbed for a cola can and gave it a good whack. The ant/wasp appeared stunned for a moment, but then it stopped and I could have sworn it stared at me. Afraid for both of my babies, I hit it again. It barely moved.

After what felt like an endless amount of time, the ant/wasp turned away and marched off into the grass, fading away as a patch of red among the scraggly brown.

Having never seen such a creature before, I quickly excused myself and ran to the almighty Google. A few quick strokes informed me that it was a red velvet ant, also called a cow killer. They were usually found in sandy areas. Having neither sand nor cows, I was perplexed. I had lived all of my thirty years in the region and not once had this wingless wasp made my acquaintance.

Their sting was said to be a powerful one and could cause nerve pain and trouble for weeks. Thankful that it had left us alone, I went back outside, promising myself that I would be more cautious about letting the kids go barefoot in the future.

I washed my hair and applied my makeup while my son lay dying or dead just thirty feet away.

Something should have felt off about that morning: the sun was too bright, the temperature too perfect for an August day, and the sky too blue. I should have been suspicious. I wasn't even concerned about the stillness that enveloped the house.

Instead, I was glad for the quiet. As the first one up, I was happy to have some spare minutes to myself. Taking a shower, brushing my hair, actually taking the time to pick out the clothing that I wanted to wear for the day and putting some thought into the decision—these were luxuries that I didn't often have with a three-year-old and an infant to parent.

I was not a woman filled with maternal instincts. I loved my babies, but I had never played house as a child, never longed to have children, and always thought that I would be perfectly happy to live out a carefree, child-free life with my husband—one full of travels, wine, and the occasional bouts of solitude. Sometimes, I was afraid that I was inherently selfish and lacked that motherly feeling that other women claimed to feel so naturally. I was pleasantly surprised when

I found out I was pregnant with my oldest son, and had loved him from the start, but there were moments that I felt a strong amount of guilt and shame for the quietness and aloneness I craved.

But Toby was different. I didn't want to let him go.

Quiet and not the least bit demanding, he was happy as a lark to lie in his jungle-themed swing with his diaper full at the seams and his milk bottle empty. He fell asleep like a champ and at seven weeks old was already sleeping five to six hours at a time. When my oldest son was that age, I had yearned for a time when I could have put him down. With Toby, I often held him for no reason other than to feel his little soft body in my arms.

I was worried that the bonding between the two would be difficult, but it wasn't. The weekend before, we had gone to Cracker Barrel and had sat at a table, eating breakfast and coloring. People stopped and smiled at us—a happy family of four with no worries. Back in the car, my oldest son had called to me. He had slipped his blankie over both of their laps. "Look at us, Mommy," he said proudly.

"Us." There was already an "us."

I couldn't remember the night before. It had been a tough day, and I had spent most of it on the couch in the living room, Toby wrapped in the bathrobe with me, watching reruns of *The Golden Girls*. I think he found my quoting endearing. I didn't even manage to get dressed, although I had put him in a summer romper that matched his soulful blue eyes.

During one of Rose's St. Olaf stories, I quoted her monologue word-for-word. At the end, I touched his nose to mine with a grin. A gurgle had erupted from him, deep down inside, and his little mouth had formed a perfect smile. It was his first laugh. I knew it.

That was the last thing I remembered.

With my new skirt and top on, my makeup applied, and my hair freshly washed and combed, I headed down the hallway to his cradle, ready to wake him up and get him ready for the day. Both kids were going with me and I looked forward to feeling good and showing them off.

But he was gone.

His normally pink-flushed face was blue, with patches of white where the apples of his cheeks had been. His hands, clutched into tiny fists, were cold. The scream that came from me was not human.

I breathed into his nose and mouth and pumped his stomach while the shrills of the ambulance filled the driveway. The sounds of the paramedics thundering up the stairs and the 911 operator's voice were not real. The only reality was that Toby was inches from me yet he wasn't there at all.

My baby had died while I slept, maybe even while I brushed my hair.

The service was over, and the small yellow casket had been lowered into the ground. We had all placed something inside. From me, my treasured gold "Mom" necklace. I had worn it the day he was born and wouldn't let them take it off of me during labor. Now, it would go with him. From my husband, a small flashlight so that he wouldn't be afraid of the dark. From his big brother, a stuffed monkey so that he would have something to play with. His grandfather had given him a five-dollar bill so that "the lad could buy some ice cream when he got to Heaven."

The first thud of dirt that hit the casket was a bullet through me. It stung as though the dirt was filling my own lungs, taking me lower into the ground myself. A friend came up beside me, wrapped her arms around me, and kissed my cheek. She began singing to me as a way to drown out the noise of that dirt—a sound that seemed to echo through the hills.

I sat with my head on her shoulder, the sun beating down on my black dress, my shoes forgotten somewhere between the grave and the hearse.

How many minutes had passed? Ten? Twenty? Sixty? Did it matter? What was time anyway? Toby had lived his entire life in seven weeks. A body can be pushed underground, cast off from everyone else, in less than ten minutes. One minute, I was standing in the doorway, looking at his cradle, ready to get him dressed. In the next minute, my life as I knew it was over—as was his.

The dirt might as well have been covering me up, too. I was dead. I would never be the same person again. My innocence in believing that everything works out for the best had been ripped apart. I would never again look at a sleeping baby and marvel at the peacefulness of their shallow breathing and still body. For years to come, I would wake up first on a beautiful Saturday morning and immediately feel those chills of dread, checking first to ensure that my husband was breathing and then flying down the hall to my oldest (only) son's room.

And then the ant came back.

It couldn't have been the same cow killer. We were hours away from home. Yet there he was. Slowly, he walked toward me, his red fuzzy back glowing in the afternoon light. A few inches from my feet, he stopped and stared at me.

This time, I didn't shoo him away. What was the point? I had already been stung.

Pinwheel

Janet Lynn Davis

For Jonathan

Stone not yet placed, but weeds
fill in. New home, extra room.
Crib unused, still up and dressed.

Earlier, the breeze unseasonably
cool. Now, melted sun-pelts splash
across shoulders, drizzle down backs.

See the family ringed around
the site, fingers intertwined,
prayer whispered:

One who carried him into
the world for three seasons.
Another who carried him out
in a tiny white case.
Delicate daughter, able
to comprehend.
First son, tow-headed
two-year-old I think I must be,

Who, moments later, will run off
to twirl a pinwheel. Will scoop up
the small American flag blown loose
onto a narrow hallway of grass,
then wait for feedback.

First published in *The Penwood Review* (Vol. 9, No. 1, Spring 2005).

Eternity

Susan Miller Lawler

We routinely count our minutes, days, and years. The concept of time itself, however, we don't count: it simply remains an abstract, human-made construct that exists because we observe it and make it so.

Time only matters because we make it matter.

In early 2007, while round and full of baby, I taught English to adult immigrants and refugees at a nonprofit organization. For months I showed up in their lives every Monday through Thursday evening as a consistent and stable authority of the English language. I also appeared to them as a woman about to become whole, to have my desire—the presumed desire of every woman—fulfilled; that is, to finally have a child of my own.

I smiled at the students' faces, full of approval. And initially believed that I was some kind of an imposter, because although I wanted this child more than anything I had ever wanted in my life, every evening that we met to practice English and that they acknowledged my upcoming status as mother, I would pretend that all was well. Privately I carried the knowledge that upon delivery from my womb, my baby would die.

I had only known this devastating fact throughout the last trimester of my pregnancy. Not long before winter quarter began, at a routine ultrasound my husband Steve and I had learned that the fetus, our baby Frankie, had a condition which rendered him—as the medical professionals chose to put it—incompatible with life. His chance of living outside my body was zero percent.

Zero percent, in no uncertain terms, no chance for anything else. I felt sorry for myself. I felt regret, and stupid that I'd waited so long to try to have children. I questioned my worth as a woman. I was deficient, faulty. Why couldn't I do anything the usual way? How could I not do the most natural thing in the world, to procreate?

Most of my students had children, and they were proud. Two, three, five, six; sometimes even more. Most of my students had also experienced huge loss, with stories that my fellow Americans knew in the abstract only, the stuff of history, newspapers, and fictional movies: religious and political persecution, bombings, extreme hunger. I would rarely hear them talk about their trauma, because most of them were taught to not do so. You pick up the pieces and move on.

This idea sounds similar to what the doctors told Steve and me after delivering the news of our baby's diagnosis and prognosis. *After the pregnancy is over*, they said, *then you can get on with your lives.* They had presented us with three options to handling this situation: Go to a clinic to have an abortion. Be induced and deliver our baby, who could do nothing but die once outside of my body. Or simply wait until I naturally went into labor once I was full-term.

We answered that we would have them induce labor (why put off the inevitable, prolong our pain, when our baby was going to die anyway?), and the doctors had expressed their approval. *Yes*, they had said, *so then you can get on with your lives.*

Get on with our lives. Not my specific objective really, or one I even felt was possible.

This phrase echoed. As we waited for the induction, I considered the sense in this. I would maintain the same joy and pain whether I was carrying my baby inside my belly or in my heart and mind.

So I changed my mind; I would carry my baby boy until his natural end. The pain would be present no matter what—but I simply wanted to *be* with our baby, even if he could only survive inside my womb. Steve was relieved that I felt that way; he had been independently contemplating the same things.

I reported our thinking to the doctors, who scratched their heads at our decision to carry to term.

After making this decision, I still grieved heavily for our impending loss. Each morning, I needed hours to get myself up out of bed in order to get on with the day. By afternoon I was able to pull myself together enough to fashion a simple lesson plan. By evening I was able to stand before the students, trying not to cry but rather to help them.

I stood in front of the students, somehow managing to focus on their needs. Many evenings the students said enthusiastic things to me about my growing baby, such as: *Teacher, you are so strong to come to class this big!* (I took this as a compliment to my baby.) *So it's a boy? Wonderful!*

In class the students knew nothing of my pain. Just as they lived their lives from one day to the next (no dwelling on pain of the past), they were not counting the days until my baby's death, but were rather—innocently, with no agenda—expressing to me joy for his current life.

I listened and took in their enthusiasm. I pretended their remarks fit my situation. Eventually, I quit confusing the pregnancy with the trauma, and I began to believe their comments. I felt joy for his life right now. I did not line up the days and months to count him into a bona fide baby as people do. Rather, once I let go of the mental constraint of Time, I was free to love him as deeply as eternity would allow.

Two days before the end of the quarter, I went into labor. I called my supervisor and told her I wouldn't make it to class. I imagined the students smiling when a substitute teacher would arrive to take my place, because they would envision my being bestowed the greatest blessing to them of all; that is, to have a child.

They were not wrong. My son was born into eternity, beyond Time, and for that long will he be my child.

Their Names

Julie Christine Johnson

*E*ach of our children has a name. Each name is derived from an ancient language, lovely to the eye and gentle on the tongue.

In those early, giddy days of our first pregnancy, I recalled a name from a beloved novel. I researched the name's origins and meaning and said it aloud to Brendan one spring morning.

"This is her name," he said, working his mouth around its flowing Gaelic syllables. "This is our daughter."

I can name the children who began their lives with such promise, whose hearts beat in tandem with mine. But I have no name for the rage, bewilderment, and unfathomable grief of losing a baby.

Our first pregnancy was unexpected, yet desired and celebrated. We began trying to conceive in 2002, when I was thirty-two. I followed the natural fertility method by charting my cycles and calculating our best dates to conceive.

After a year of failure, we each underwent a battery of fertility tests. A diagnosis of unexplained infertility was rendered, followed by the usual advice: relax, let it go, and you'll probably get pregnant; consider adoption—and you'll probably get pregnant; accept your infertility—there is more to life than children.

A long period of anger and grief followed the diagnosis of infertility and our decision not to adopt. Following each announcement of a pregnancy by a friend or colleague, I would implode. I wanted someone to take the blame for my inability to conceive. I wanted someone to hurt as much as we were hurting.

Moving on wasn't a conscious decision, not at first. Two years passed, and we began talking about living overseas again. That first seed of excitement—the idea of radically changing our lives—blossomed into a plan. We became determined to live a life of joy and adventure, even if it wasn't the life we had envisioned.

In 2006, we moved with newly minted visas to New Zealand. We lived in a bungalow in a tiny village by the Pacific Ocean, and we worked side by side in the vineyards of North Canterbury. It was a life less ordinary, one many dream of having the chance to live.

Our family of two began to feel just right. We were content with our *now*, and we embraced a country that surrounded us with creative energy and natural beauty. We remained in New Zealand for two years before returning to the Pacific Northwest to be within easy reach of aging parents.

Early in June 2009 I sat on my yoga mat during a predawn class, wondering if I'd make it in time to vomit into the trash bin just outside the studio door. The nausea passed. Two days later—same time, same place—it returned. Suddenly, I knew its cause.

Hours later Brendan and I stood at the counter of our neighborhood medical clinic, crying in wonder as we learned I was several weeks pregnant. The next two months passed in quiet joy.

Our baby died during my eleventh week. "Spontaneous abortion" is the notation in my medical file. The ob-gyn assured me that nothing I'd done or neglected to do caused the miscarriage; first trimester miscarriages are very common. Despite all indications that the fetus was developing normally, our baby was simply not strong enough to survive.

My physician recommended I undergo a dilation and curettage (D and C), a procedure to remove the fetus by scraping or vacuuming it from my uterus. In my grief, I was determined to hold on to my child as long as I could. I rejected the D and C.

It took three agonizing weeks and two rounds of Misoprostol, a drug used in lieu of surgical abortion, to complete the miscarriage. Brendan felt so helpless. My body was beyond his reach to heal. The most he could do was hold my hand and support me.

I'm not certain how we functioned in that time. Friends came for a weekend visit in the middle of our ordeal. We showed them around Seattle, which sparkled in the August sunshine, without saying a word about the pregnancy and miscarriage. Neither of us missed a day of work. I started running again.

Late one afternoon I filled multiple sanitary pads with thick, ropy blood. I lay curled on the living room floor, my belly roiling with cramps. After one final trip to the bathroom, I knew it was over. She was gone.

We healed slowly and unsteadily in the year following our miscarriage. Our wounds reopened often, such as when we learned of a friend's pregnancy, conceived after her husband's vasectomy, or when friends who didn't know of our miscarriage or years of struggling with infertility proclaimed that Brendan and I would make great parents. "You've been married so long! Don't you ever want children?" They'd ask.

Three years, nearly to the day after we learned we were first pregnant, I quietly purchased and took a home pregnancy test. We were shocked to learn we were pregnant again—we'd long since given up hope.

It was impossible not to give in to joy, not to allow our hearts to swell in anticipation of meeting the life we had created. It was impossible not to name this child. Yet we tried to prepare ourselves for heartbreak. The wounds from our miscarriage in 2009 reopened, and we admitted our deepest fears. We proceeded with caution, telling no one but our parents and handful of close friends.

In a moment of twisting around to look at a less-dark side, I said to Brendan, "When we lost the first baby, I wasn't writing. I wasn't creating anything. I had nowhere to voice my grief and rage. But now, if the worst happens, I have a voice. I have a place to go that gives me hope and joy and meaning. At least, if the worst happens, I have that."

A few weeks later I attended my first writers' conference, an event that filled me with purpose and confidence. Late Saturday afternoon, just before the final session of the conference, I dashed into the bathroom for a quick pee. I pulled down my panties and saw what I hadn't felt.

A streak of bright-red blood.

I sat on the toilet with my head between my legs as the world went gray.

When I walked into that bathroom, I was ten weeks pregnant. When I walked out, I was...

Empty.

The cramps began that evening, not long after I returned home. They were bad. Then they got worse. By the next afternoon I was writhing on the living room carpet, crying and gasping as my uterus ripped itself apart.

I refused to let Brendan take me to the hospital. Women have been giving birth to life and to death on their own since the beginning. These were the only labor pains I would ever know and it was pain I would own, pain I would remember, because I had nothing else. At 10 p.m., I finally crawled into bed, my body no longer sharing space with another.

I wasn't pregnant long enough for those first ultrasounds to reveal either baby's gender. Yet we claimed and named those children who I hoped would have my auburn hair and musical inclinations and their Daddy's chocolate-brown eyes and sweet temperament. I am aware each winter of their due dates, each July of their deaths. I still whisper their precious names. And I write, because writing is how I create life.

Brendan took me in his arms when I returned home from the conference, in the quiet moment before the pain thundered through me.

"It's going to be just the two of us," I said.

"That's fine by me," he replied.

And we cried, because nothing was fine.

But it will be again, someday. We have accepted the presence of sorrow and realized that within the sorrow are moments of incomparable bliss.

The Broken People

Robyna May

I am one of the broken people.
The people who are hollow.
The people made of glass.
The people made of sorrow.
You might not know it—
think me the same as you.
But look a little closer—
you will see straight through.

I am weightless, groundless.
I am battered, I am broken.
I am bruised, I am tired.
I am words left unspoken.

I am acting when I›m smiling.
I am pretending even now.
Appearing to be living,
when I have forgotten how.

I go through the motions.
I wake up every day.
Do the things that need doing.
Say what I am supposed to say.

But this vessel is broken, empty.
It is cracked beyond repair.
And sometimes when you see me,
I have vanished into air.

I am living on the outer,
each breath hangs by a thread.
I am halfway between the living.
I am halfway to the dead.

One day I'll find my feet.
Feel the earth and remain.
But even when I make it there,
I'll never be the same.

Because now I am so fragile.
Heart shattered on the floor.
And though I am made of glass now,
I am somehow stronger than before.

Diary of a Wimpy Mom

Keleigh Hadley

Pre-pregnancy, I was great at ~~lying~~ imagining what type of mom I would be.

I wondered if I'd be Earthy Mom—a vegan who breast-feeds, co-sleeps, and uses cloth diapers. She is so carbon-footprint-free that she hovers, wears the baby as an accessory, and serves organic meals on Fair Trade plates woven by Ugandan women. But I had a special place in my heart for burgers and leather sling-backs, so Earthy was out for me.

Sporty Mom is skinnier after pregnancy, has playdates booked months in advance, runs around town pushing a $900 jogging stroller, and joins Baby Gym, Gymboree, Baby Yoga, and Baby MMA. I prefer the mental workout of a good book vs. actual sweating, so I wouldn't be Sporty Mom.

There is Crack-the-Whip Mom, who is no-nonsense, no frivolity, "no wire hangers!" She carries a well-worn copy of *Battle Hymn of the Tiger Mother*, insists that her newborn will rise to meet her expectations, disciplines other children in the grocery store, and side-eyes mothers who coddle. I practiced my "Don't you even think about it" look in the mirror but couldn't keep a straight face. Frowns give you wrinkles.

I didn't fit any of those types, but I wasn't worried. I'd be warm and firm. Loving and strong. I'd have the chef skills and craft finesse of Martha Stewart and the enthusiasm and endurance of Mary Lou Retton. Plus, I'd be artsy and smooth like Lou Rawls. I'd be a Black Martha Lou Rawls.

I envisioned myself as Warrior Mom, clad in thigh-high boots and a Spanx-lined utility belt (packed with an iPad, Purell, and lip gloss), with my baby in a sling and a blinged-out *W* on my chest.

D-day came, and my robust son was delivered via natural childbirth. Daily I awoke to a new purpose, a new passion, and a baby on my boob. Life was good, everything seemed rosier, sweeter, glossier—*insert record scratch here.*

My son was two weeks old when my husband said, "Imagine if Jireh had lived. We'd have two boys."

I nodded my head and murmured, "Uh-huh." On the outside I was calm. But inside a horrifying thought resurfaced. One that I thought was dormant. *Babies die.*

Old people die. Sick people die. Drug addicts die. Not babies.

Six years before, I had suffered the loss of my first child when I was ten days from my due date. It was a Sunday, and when I woke up, I immediately knew something was wrong. We needed to go to the hospital. I was seen by a nurse who did a sonogram. Her face remained impassive, and her tone was remote. She would find a doctor. Two more nurses came and did sonograms. Same reaction and response. I felt like I was drowning in a frozen lake, and each person that walked through that door, with the passive expression of a serial killer, pushed me further below the icy water. The doctor finally came and performed a sonogram, tried the heart monitor that produced a resounding silence, and gave me the news. For some inexplicable reason, my son had died.

I delivered a physically perfect stillborn. I still have no clue as to why he died or what went wrong. I couldn't bear the thought of an autopsy, so we had a memorial and buried him in a ridiculously tiny, white casket. I could finally answer the question, "What is more painful than childbirth?"

I couldn't attend baby showers, seeing kids at the mall made me burst into tears, and I *hated* the thought of people pitying me. I would forever be the girl whose baby was stillborn. But it didn't really hit me until the first anniversary of his death that I had lost a son. I fell into a paralyzing depression. Yet, as time promises, my wounds healed, and I grew strong.

Six years later I was ecstatic to find out I was pregnant again. Sure, I had anxious thoughts while I was pregnant, especially as the due date approached, but my doctor reassured me. He went above and beyond, taking all precautions; my son was induced two weeks before his due date, and emerged healthy, loud, and strong.

But I was not the same woman from six years ago. During my first pregnancy the possibility of a stillborn was not on my radar. Now, I knew the SIDS statistics of every state west of the Mississippi. I clucked my tongue at any mother who didn't know vaccination side effects. I was armed with knowledge, and dangerous.

But the biggest change within me was not my fascist stance on breast-feeding, but my incessant feelings of worry, fear, and weakness.

Although my son slept through the night by the time he was six weeks old (don't hate), I gave myself insomnia worrying about SIDS, colic, autism, and the notorious flat head syndrome.

I even worried that I worried too much. I thought I was going crazy, like, grab-a-cop's-gun crazy. I was on a cycle of worry, weakness, despair, worry, weakness, despair. The cycle was exhausting, and I retreated more and more.

After a night of staring at the video baby monitor, it occurred to me, "I'm not a Warrior Mom. I don't deserve the blinged-out *W*. Or better yet, that *W* stands for something else. I am a Wimp." I had discovered my mom type now. I am Wimpy Mom.

Frustrated by this revelation, I sought out the advice of other moms. Did they use a meat thermometer to check the bathwater? Did they pay for background checks on their doctors? By the raised eyebrows and one, two, three, steps taken back from me, I took that as a no.

When my son was eight months old, I overheard my mom talking to my brother on the phone.

"Don't forget to call me when you get back from your trip. You know I worry," she said.

I had one of those long, stretching-hallway moments. After thirty years, my mom still worried about her adult children.

I nearly slapped the phone out of her hand. "Mom will you ever stop worrying about us?"

She looked at me as if I had just grown two heads. "Of course not. My cause of death will be Worry/Disappointment."

I gritted my teeth and ignored the last part of her statement, because she just gave me a glimpse of my future. A future I wanted no part of.

My next move was to garner spiritual, timeless truth to free myself of a possible life sentence of weakness and worry.

I googled "Worry scriptures."

That is why I take such pleasure in weaknesses, insults, hardships, persecutions, and difficulties for the Messiah's sake, for when I am weak, then I am strong.

—2 Corinthians 12:10

ISV

Ah, so, the wimpier and weaker I am, the stronger I become?

I needed more clarification.

I read the verse that preceded verse 10:

But he said to me, "My grace is all you need. My power is strongest when you are weak."

—2 Corinthians 12: 9a

Then I read one that tied it all together in my mind:

The LORD is the everlasting God,
  the Creator of the ends of the earth.
He will not grow tired or weary,
  and his understanding no one can fathom.
He gives strength to the weary
  and increases the power of the weak.
Even youths grow tired and weary,
  and young men stumble and fall;
but those who hope in the LORD
  will renew their strength.
They will soar on wings like eagles;
  they will run and not grow weary,
  they will walk and not be faint.

—Psalms 40:28–31

I finally understood. It's not about some caricature of a super-woman who can leap Lego buildings in a single bound. It's about acknowledging my weakness, faults, and imperfections and allowing something greater than myself to be strong when I am weak.

Fast forward four years and now we have added a bouncing (literally) baby girl, McKenna Drew, to our family. She falls off slides, chairs, stairs, and people, and brushes herself off and moves on. She once swallowed dog kibble and dog poop within the same hour. I didn't make her down a bottle of Ipecac or disinfect her mouth with Listerine. I simply checked poison control online, and obeyed when they advised, "just monitor for signs of discomfort."

She is a happy ball of energy that needs to test the limits of play-ground equipment and gravity. I still carry Purell, but I use it more on myself than on the kiddos. Their immune systems are as solid as my faith. I now rock my blinged-out *W* shirt, and I no longer care what my Mom Type is. We are all a part of the sisterhood of wimpy, warrior, weird, wacky, wonderful, and altogether worthy Moms who know where our true strength lies.

Heavy as Grief

Mercedes Yardley

I'm holding a baby in my arms as I write this. She's three months old and fresh out of NICU. She isn't used to a quiet house; she's used to beeping and buzzers and terrible alarms. She would lie in her bassinet alone, unheld until it was time for nurses to feed her. My husband and I saw her as often as we could. It wasn't enough.

She was a triplet. We called them Winken, Blinkin, and Nod, after the little ones who fished the stars. We were charmed and delighted and anxious about rocking three little babies at once.

I stayed up nights, sick with worry. I stayed up nights, eyes bright with dreams. I stayed up, my hand on my stomach, thinking that my heartbeat was no longer a singular thing, but one of four. One of *four*.

Then the doctor called, saying we needed to schedule another ultrasound. I had so much hope at first, so much faith. In my body. In divinity. When they told me that one of our babies had died, that I was carrying around the remnants of my child, something broke inside. I lay there on the table while the tech deftly finished the ultrasound. Like everyone else, he focused on the living.

"There's the head," he said. "There's the rump. You have two busy little babies."

I didn't care. I wasn't looking at them. All I could see was the form of the one I had lost, that it wasn't moving, that it was smaller than the others. I cried without making a sound. The tech handed me a tissue and carefully looked away. He would be the first of many to do so.

The pregnancy progressed. The remaining twins were both beautiful, beautiful girls. I pictured rosy little toes and matching dresses. We thought of names. We planned the nursery. Two children were less than three, and I felt the loss, but I also felt the sweetness of the remaining girls. It was enough to get me through.

But the doctor called again, and it was devastating. One of the twins was struggling, suffering from a severe genetic anomaly. Incompatible with life, they said. If we were lucky, she would live long enough to be born, and then die.

Born to die?

I didn't know what to pray for. That she'd live? I'd get to meet her, hold her, snuggle her, and love her, but then I'd have to watch her pass away. Could I do that? Would she suffer? Or did I hope that she would slip away quietly, too early to feel any pain? No pain, but my arms would feel forever empty.

"If she dies in utero," the doctor told us, "there is a very real possibility that the physical trauma could be too much for your body."

"What does that mean?"

"It means that you could spontaneously abort the final, living baby."

Lose all three? Unthinkable.

I became ill. At first, too ill to leave the house. Then too ill to leave the bed. Too ill to feel like a functional mother. My other two small children played on the bed beside me, napping and reading stories. I didn't know how to feel. Excited. Terrified. Full of grief and sorrow and joy and expectation. We bought a crib and a casket on the same day. My husband went out and found two tiny matching white dresses, one for a blessing, the other for the funeral that we knew would come.

They came unexpectedly, two months early. Beautiful. Tiny fingers. Tiny ears. Two enchanting girls. The nurse put them together and took a picture of them side by side before they whisked them off to their separate NICU units.

The eldest died in my husband's arms. We had time to hold her, to smile and tell her how much we loved her. We oohed and aahed over her tiny bent legs, her exquisite face that was put together in all of the wrong places. I knew she was gone even before my husband looked at me and whispered, "She's beginning to cool."

We were forced to leave our remaining daughter in NICU while we drove home for her sister's funeral. She was buried on a sunshiny day; that's what I remember. After the service, we drove four hours to see our surviving baby. She would be loved ferociously, always. We promised her this.

Our last, the one I hold in my arms right now, she doesn't hold one-third of our hearts. Sometimes when I look at her, the sadness washes over me because she is surrounded by the ghosts of her sisters. But usually I see her simply as herself, as my precious little one, and she makes me smile.

It's time that I take a cue from those around me. I'll never forget, and I'm not expected to, but it's time to focus on the living instead of being haunted by the lost.

Still

J.lynn Sheridan

In the Joy,
while waiting for you,
I lost your heartbeat.

In the Mourning,
I lost
your name.

Sometimes, I try
to whisper it
to give you
voice.

At night
I try.
In prayer.
In the deep comfort of dreaming,

You are the northern lights,
the silent splashes of watercolor
chasing the sky. You are Indian paintbrush
rushing through heaven's prairie.

In the pinks of dusk I think I see
your yellow hair; it's reflected
in the indigo frosts of winter and
the cherry blossoms in spring,
in the tide, in forlorn feathers
awash on the beach, in the summer
grass, and you smell like honey and
wind and poetry and...

I lost
your heartbeat.
I didn't know
when it last shuddered.
A mother should know.
A good mother.

That night we sang lullabies to soothe
our sorrow borne during the stillness.

My December hands caressed a bouquet
of fresh baby's breath. I planted it while
your heart still beat against mine.

Today, I untied the ribbon and sprinkled
the petals
upon the garden.

Called to Motherhood

Stacy Clark

*E*arly on an April morning, I sat beside my four-year-old daughter on the couch. She nestled close, her legs not quite reaching to the edge of the cushion, her pink-socked feet waggling in anticipation. I told her a baby had snuck inside my tummy. Her eyes went wide like a child, then wise. She placed a small hand on the curve of my stomach and said, "Mommy, it's Hannah."

Children know things. Or they only imagine them. Maybe both. This child had an uncanny way of clomping out in her plastic dress-up shoes and telling me the world was not as it seemed. Regardless, when she called the baby inside me Hannah, the name stuck.

Being pregnant is like carrying the future inside you. This collection of cells spinning into life was not merely the tiny blurred body on the sonogram, it was all the things this baby might grow to be: the little blonde girl who looks like her sister; the toddler who stumbles forward on shaky legs; the kindergartener and the college student, the bride, the CEO. Imagination melds into reality the instant the pregnancy test reveals two pink lines. Suddenly, we were a two-child family underway. My husband and I bought a minivan and picked out a crib. We held hands and said prayers at dinner. Often our daughter would close her eyes and add softly, "Please let baby Hannah be safe."

When the sonogram technician asked me, "How far along are

you?" I knew. It was the wrong question. A tear slid sideways down my cheek. My husband sat to the side smiling, unaware. Deep inside, I knew this child had left me.

I also know "sneaking in" and "leaving" are not the right words, but this was the language of the experience. I had the odd sense of my body being entered and abandoned. Not pregnant and miscarrying.

There were endless weeks of mistrustful hope. Then one night I awoke to a piercing pain in the small of my back. After a rush of minutes on the toilet, I spent long hours staring at the moonlit shadow of the window on the ceiling, feeling the echoes of emptiness.

Miscarriage is a tenuous sorrow. There is no child to hold. Yet the future is lost.

When, again on the couch, I told my daughter about our loss, she nodded gravely and slipped down to the floor to play. Nights later at the dinner table, she took her father's hand and mine in hers, closed her eyes, and said, "Please let baby Hannah be safe."

Oh no, I thought. *She does not understand.* I would have to explain better. My husband and I held her hands tighter. I told her again, more precisely, our baby was gone.

"I know," she said and smiled. "Baby Hannah flew off on vacation, like we do Mommy, and she'll be back."

Children know things. Or imagine them. Maybe both. Hormones and tears can skew a mother's perspective. For whatever reason, I began to think my baby would be back. Though I did not think *this* baby could return, I felt determinedly certain a child would come to me.

More than a year later, I still was not pregnant. Every month I felt crushing disappointment. I tried to have a positive outlook. *Things*

happen for a reason, I told myself, *even if we can't see the bigger picture.* I could see only the small, sad part that left me with the feeling something—someone—was missing.

One June day, in a cranky act of surrender, I stomped across the bedroom, and shouted up toward the ceiling: "I quit. If you've got a better idea, well I'm open." It was the bratty, arm-crossed stance of frustration. I did not expect an answer.

An answer came.

In July, I got my period. Again. While seeking the consolation of real caffeine at the coffee shop, I bought a plain, ceramic mug. The mug came wrapped in tissue paper. Script scrawled across the tissue reminded me life is full of "Secrets and surprises" and promised "The unveiling of the unexpected."

In early August, I had a thought: *I could adopt a baby from China.* An odd thought for several reasons. This was back in 2003. I knew nothing about adoption and had no connection to China. I knew no one who had done such a thing. I would not have known where to begin. The thought evaporated.

Two days later, I met a freckle-faced woman on the elementary school sidewalk. She was the proud mother of a new kindergartener. When I asked if this was her first child in school, she whipped out a photo. One child looked just like her, the other two girls looked Asian; as it turned out, they were Chinese.

"I may want to talk to you sometime." I said only that. She looked me up and down, pulled a grocery receipt from her purse, and wrote the number of her adoption caseworker.

As I walked away, I knew. As sure as I knew one soul had left my body, another was on the way to my heart.

Why China? I had no idea.

Things happened quickly after that. My husband agreed effortlessly to the idea, as did our daughter, when I asked her that same night. "Mommy, yes!" she said. "Let's go adopt baby Hannah from China."

The mounds of paperwork required for an international adoption, the interviews, exams, and background checks rapidly ensued. Our dossier was completed within six months. The process was not without its crises of confidence. But each time I veered from the path, a whisper of coincidence would steer me back on course. I dreamed of this child on the other side of the skies waiting for me as I waited for her. I could not picture her, but could feel her like a phantom limb, a part of me, only lost. Six months after our paperwork landed in China, we were matched to a baby girl with deep, soulful eyes and big, adorable cheeks.

While awaiting our invitation to travel to China, my now six-year-old daughter and I went to the bookstore. Pouring through a stack of books, we made a list of baby names, starring our favorite one. As we walked to put the books back on the shelf, she smiled up at me and said, "Mommy, I think Baby Hannah is going to like her new name."

I surrendered again, this time with joy. Though I insisted we change the spelling. *Hannah* went from "Grace of God" to *Hanna*, "Goddess of Life."

On a warm October afternoon, nearly two and half years after my miscarriage, I met this baby we would name Hanna in a nondescript building in Nanchang, China. She sat on a polished, wooden bench and stared up at me with those deep, brown eyes, her lips pursed. I stared back, whispering hello in a language she could not understand.

Though we were strangers, when I lifted her warm body into my arms, it felt like she belonged there. Like when I first held the daughter I birthed, yet different. This child did not come from me, but to me, borne on random chance.

I carried her out into the sunlight and onto the bus that would take her to her new life. She sat silent and still on my lap, grabbed onto my thumb, and held tight the whole ride.

In spite of those first quiet moments, this child and I did not take to each other right away. She cried for hours every night in China and during the first months home in America. When I tried to comfort her, she pulled back, pounding her face with her tiny fists. Any fantasy of belonging withered away. I worried if I had done the wrong thing for her, for us.

Yet, in the daylight, she was curious and gentle. I was patient and open. Our bond grew. She stumbled on toddling legs while holding my hand and planted sloppy kisses on my cheeks. I loved this child deeply. I would catch her watching me with a look that said she felt something of the same. Her trust began to last through the night.

When Hanna grew old enough to talk, she would sometimes answer questions I did not ask aloud and understand things I could not explain about how she came to be my daughter. Be it knowledge or imagination, I played along. I did not really care how she arrived, as much as that she was here.

One afternoon, when Hanna was nearly three, she sat at the kitchen island eating breakfast, chatting.

"Mommy, 'member when I was a baby, I was in China, and I called you to come get me?" she said. She put a thumb to her ear and a pinky to her lips, mimicking an old phone.

"Oh, yes, Hanna, I remember."

"Why did it take you *so* long?" she asked.

"I came as fast as I could."

"Did you run?"

Cuisle Mo Chroi
Amy Grebe

Trinity

Barbara Mulvey Little

The life and death of my infant granddaughter fundamentally changed who I am.

Death, and its trappings, marked me early. My grandmother's death on my first birthday assured many birthdays included cemetery visits. Life/death, joy/sorrow entwined.

Later my infant nephew's death shook my faith, shifted my interests, and challenged my understanding of the world. But it was my granddaughter's death that reverberated like an earthquake through my soul.

Two Sisters, Two Pregnancies, One Death

In 1980 my sister and I were both pregnant, due only weeks apart in February 1981. The day after Christmas my sister suffered a placental abruption. Her once healthy son, delivered lifeless, was revived hours after the placenta bled out. Joseph suffered massive brain damage.

My son followed on February 26, exactly two months later. Pure joy—and gratitude in his safe arrival—enveloped me. Yet as I celebrated, my emotions were tempered by my sister's pain. Her son, still in the neonatal intensive care unit (NICU), had a grim prognosis. When Joey died again on May 21, just five months after his birth, he'd lived his entire life in the NICU. That he didn't have to suffer any longer was small consolation to the devastation of his death.

Over the years I coped by becoming a hospice volunteer and spiritual director as my son grew into a robust, joyful, gentle soul despite (or maybe because of) the tears his mother, aunt, and grandmother shed during every major life event that celebrated him. Again life/death, joy/sorrow entwined.

Joey's death stung less intensely as the years passed, but the emptiness, the sadness for the missing child, lingered. A generation later, the lessons learned from Joey's death about integrating grief's sorrows into life's joys would be applied again.

Two Siblings, Two Pregnancies, One Death

On February 13, 2011, my daughter gave birth to a healthy baby girl. On February 14 my son and his wife had an ultrasound to learn they too carried a baby girl—but their daughter had a genetic anomaly that was, as the doctors pronounced, "incompatible with life." Offered an abortion, they immediately realized they "could not do harm" to their baby. She was alive and safe in her mother's womb, and she would remain there until nature took its course. Their choice to safeguard the baby's life guaranteed their own intense emotional suffering, but for them it was the right choice. The only choice.

And so, as we celebrated the life of one healthy baby girl we began to wait—and grieve—for the child whose life would be so incredibly brief. The unknowable was whether the baby would miscarry early, be stillborn at term, or die within hours or days of a live birth. The outcome took five months to unfold. Five precious months of what turned out to be a pretty normal pregnancy—except it would end in death rather than life.

Anticipatory Grief

Powerlessness compounded and complicated my grief. I grieved both for my child and for his child. My son and his wife suffered through the shock, pain, and terrible reality that their first child would grow and live only in the womb. At first I listened to his questions: What did I do wrong? *Nothing*. Did I do something to deserve this? *No*. Could it have been prevented? *No*. I held him as he cried. Then I marveled at his acceptance, his love for his wife and daughter, his strength, his grace. I learned from him. I was inspired by him. Joy, always one of his strongest traits, remained. He celebrated small moments, singing to his baby, kissing her hello and good-bye, and feeling her kick. Grief couldn't diminish the awe that his child was growing in his wife's womb.

Growing up with joy and sorrow entwined had prepared him well. He'd become an amazing husband and father. He lived "Joey's lessons," the most important of which was: the present is all there is; embrace its joy, accept its sorrow, and love regardless.

My son and his wife named the baby the night they found out she would die. Naming her made her real. Trinity.

I sought ways to honor Trinity, her parents, and the journey. A private website enabled them to communicate with far-flung family and friends while they managed their need for seclusion and calm. A moment of inspiration created a communal ritual: family and friends were invited to send a small bead infused with their thoughts and prayers. The beads were gathered and strung on a pillow that went to the birthing room as a tangible reminder of the circle of love holding them all. Gifts of beads, prayers, and more came over many weeks offering immense solace and support.

Trinity died in her mother's womb on June 22. She lasted longer than expected, but she never took a breath on this earthly plane. She came from stardust and returned her essence to it in a swirling ball of energy before presenting her lifeless body in the midst of an unusual lightning storm that lit up the night sky.

Owning Grief

During the months of pregnancy we all reminisced about the healing and grace that followed after Joey's death. We talked about facing hard emotions head-on, not recoiling from the visceral earthiness and messiness of grief. We kept the website updated with news, photos, and many of the prayers and poems sent. We made arrangements with a funeral home and county governments so that when the time came we had choices that worked for us. My daughter-in-law couldn't bear the thought of her baby alone in the hospital morgue so we arranged to transport Trinity's body ourselves.

Special ultrasound appointments enabled us to see the baby alive. We put great energy into living in the moment and enjoying a pregnancy that so progressed normally. However, I couldn't escape that when I was supposed to be planning a baby shower, I was learning the legalities and paperwork needed to transport a dead body, and talking to a funeral director and getting measurements for a coffin-cradle that my husband would build for our granddaughter.

After Trinity was delivered, she came home for a wake. Family and friends gathered. An impromptu funeral ritual began after sunset; we read the prayers and scripture sent with the beads, sang hymns, and then Trinity's parents placed her shroud-wrapped body on a bed of fresh red roses that lined her tiny pine cremation cradle. Flowers, prayers, and mementos then filled the space around and above her. Her body was ready for cremation, her spirit already set free.

Two days later, we took an impossibly small box containing her ashes to the river her parents loved. Sunshine. Numbness. Warmth. Tears. Dozens of yellow swallowtail butterflies joined us. A message? We smiled.

Journey into the Abyss

After Trinity died, I realized neither hospice work nor spiritual direction prepared me for the depths of bereavement. I tried to hold on to the faith that had sustained me all my life but its rituals felt hollow and meaningless. Prayer was empty. Unable to relate to the ordinariness of daily life, I kept to myself. I was lost. Dispossessed. An alien in what had been my world.

Some of my pain came from "God reneging on the deal" I'd made when Joey died—as in, I'd willingly suffer any of life's tribulations if you, God, would spare my babies. I'd suffered my share of troubles, faced them with a faith borne of my certainty in the nature of God and the universe. Still, my granddaughter was dead. I raged. Not so much at God but at my own naïveté. My faith wasn't nearly as mature as all my study, certifications, and devotion should have made it.

Recognizing the Light

Trinity's life, measured from conception rather than from birth, was full. Though tears still flow so easily, I can now point to lesson after lesson learned, grace upon grace found, insight upon insight revealed. The pain of Trinity's death remains and it marks a turning point in who I am and how I encounter the world. My belief in God remains, but my concept of God has changed. Expanded. Deepened.

Rituals continue to be a vital way for me to encounter the Sacred, but once life-giving Catholic rituals remain hollow. While I still believe the essence of what I learned from traditional religious teachings, Trinity's death has opened me to a different way of understanding faith, religion, and life. I feel like I've woken up. I don't quite fit into my church anymore. This is a huge shift in my identity.

I am grateful for Trinity's death. I'm not glad she died, nor am I glad for the pain her death wrought. But I am grateful. Through her life and her death I learned how to live in a way that is more truthful, less fearful. I learned not to cling. I embraced that I am One with all that is; that love is timeless. Trinity is gone, yet eternally with us.

Life/death.

Joy/sorrow.

Entwined.

Waiting

JS Nahani

We leave our pasta half eaten, move directly to the bedroom, and undress each other like new lovers. Seven years into our marriage. Nineteen years after our first date.

Are we crazy? I ask.

Maybe, he says, laughing.

Are you ready? I ask, laughing now.

Why not? he says.

We fall asleep in each other's arms. He goes back to work the next day. I do the dishes, make dinner, look for a job, talk to the dog—tell her soon she might be a big sister. Days pass into two weeks, when we can take the test. He reads me the instructions while I pee on a white stick. Two pink lines show up before he gets to the second sentence.

Holy shit! he says.

I thought so! I say.

We curl up on the floor like a soft pretzel, look into each other's eyes, acknowledge that there's no one in the world we'd rather parent with more.

We drive up to visit old friends, share our news as if we'd known all along. As if the words "pregnant" and "parents" had been part of our own vocabulary all these years. Like the words "joyful" and "enthusiasm"—we're only just learning how to form them, but there they were, waiting.

We spend winter evenings listening to the rain, under soft

blankets, with the dog nestled nearby. She cocks her head in that big sister way as we read about eyelids appearing, lungs forming, arm buds developing.

I eat lots of cereal for a while, then—anything but cereal. Each night, I pop a prenatal vitamin and don't even miss my antidepressant. We meet cousins from LA for lunch at the water. On the elevator, in my red jacket, hiding the new bulge, I turn to him and say:

I haven't felt this happy since I don't know when.

And I mean it.

We make love again, I bleed a bit afterwards, and call the advice nurse.

Spotting? she asks.

That's common, she says.

Still, she sends us to Urgent Care, since it's a Sunday. So we go wait for hours in a room with windows. I feel calm, even as tears flow. The nurse has the name of my grandmother.

Your cervix is still closed, the doctor on call assures us. We keep our growing love tucked away, tied to our heartstrings, voicing it only to our inner circle.

We wait for the first week of the New Year, when we can finally go meet our midwife, see the heart beating. When we can confirm the cause of strange new eating habits, swollen breasts, bone tiredness. Our eyes widen as we witness the fast beating for the first time.

Our baby. We toss the words around like magic.

We go for our next appointment, a new midwife this time. We want to meet everyone so we will recognize the face of the one who will catch our baby. She comes in smiling, says usually she has to tell women at least one thing they need to work on.

But all your numbers look great, she says.

Keep up the good work.

This time, we *hear* the heartbeat. She tells us little kids like to guess at what it sounds like. I nod when she shares the ones most guessed.

The ocean, she says.

Or horses' hooves, galloping.

I start to pull on my pants.

What's that? asks my love. His smile turns to quick concern. I look at the table just as I feel a rush of fluid between my legs. I am bleeding through my clothes. We call to the midwife.

Please come back. Her smile is gone. A nurse escorts us to a desk to set up an ultrasound.

Stat, she says. *Stat*, the word does somersaults in my brain. We guess it means emergency. We wait.

The chairs are different in this waiting room. We look for a magazine, talk about nothing while holding hands. Shift our weight in the brown and purple seats. Finally a woman comes to get us. I notice the stark white of her lab coat as she ushers us back, puts the tool to my sticky belly. She is without words.

She's measuring your cervix, and now the baby, Mike says to comfort me. *Right?* he asks her.

Yes, that's the heartbeat, the white-lab-coat woman says, then asks: *Is someone meeting you now?*

The midwife said to come back, I say.

Mike lets go of my hand as I get off the table, pull on my blood-stained pants. The technician tells us nothing.

It's her job not to comment, he says on the elevator. I hug him as we travel up to the third floor.

Back upstairs, we sit in a new room. Eventually our midwife pops in again.

Still no results, she says.

Why don't you go home and rest? I'll call you.

I lie on the couch, the phone within arm's reach. Mike goes back to work. Nothing. He calls them and leaves a message. Nothing. I call them and leave a message.

After another restless night of sleep, I start calling around.

Results, I say. I am looking for answers.

It is midday when someone calls back. By now I have eaten a burrito—the craving of the week—talked to a friend, tumbled through what happened yesterday. Trusting that today is a new day, I return to the couch.

Take it easy, she'd said.

I set up an appointment to go see a doctor. New day, new ultrasound. My feet in stirrups, she leans on my knees as she forms the words: *I'm concerned*. Her expression is grim. She is shaking her head. I like her eyeglasses. She ushers us into an empty office to wait while she gets the genetic counselor. The roller coaster ride is just beginning. We have just pulled the bar onto our laps, begun the slow incline up, up.

Three weeks pass. I wait on the couch, in the bed, at the table. Wait as we walk on clean, wide sidewalks with our dog. Talk to her raised ear: *You might not be a big sister quite yet.*

She tilts her head, like she already knows.

They smell pheromones and sense pregnancy right away, the vet had told Mike.

And now, does she sense that we are dangling on a thread of uncertainty, slow dancing with grief? Does she sense the fluid around the baby growing?

We keep busy while we wait. Busy with the early amnio, busy with blood work and bile, busy with dreaming and sleeping. Screening supportive phone calls, movie marathons to escape our own story. Wading through the days, waiting through the nights, walking hand in hand. Hugging a lot.

Two hundred forty hours pass slowly when waiting to hear news about chromosomes and genes, about whether our baby will be our baby, about next steps.

The test results come back. They come back negative; we try to stay positive. Try to keep believing in something. We put one foot in front of the other, keep walking toward the answers.

Soon we come to learn the problem—rare and random, this condition: *cystic hygroma.* We mix the words like strangers that soon become fast friends. A fluid growing, a fetus growing, a body's wisdom, telling us that this is not going to end okay. Mike finds a website, a chat room, some horrific stories, some hopeful ones. We tune into our own story.

A dream one night: I go into labor. My water breaks; we are in this together. But the baby, the baby has a problem. The baby is not going to make it. Something with the lungs, something about the Spirit staying for one hundred days. I wake up nodding.

Our next ultrasound will be the last.

I'm so sorry. The perinatologist half smiles. Her hands are soft. Compassion fills the cream-colored room. She points out the increased fluid engulfing our little baby. It is the silhouette of a heart, which somehow warms my own.

No room to kick, she points at the curled legs.

No way to make it to birth, she continues.

One hundred percent certain, she says. *I'm actually surprised the heart is still beating.*

Silence, before I hear myself say: *So, we'll terminate today?*

And next time… Mike starts.

Next time should be fine, she says.

We came to hear this. We waited for the moment when the specialist would tell us what would be and we would know what to do. Our little trooper, brave little one, heart still beating in the middle of a flood that would overtake her at any moment.

So we leave to eat some lunch, take the dog for one more walk. Stand together in the kitchen, touching my belly, hands over hands, before we get into the car. Just outside the clinic, under a cloudless sky, we spot a lone man on the sidewalk, holding up a sign: *Abortion Kills*. We turn into the parking lot, enter the building, and wait for them to call my name.

Carrying Ashes

Latorial Faison

In an eight by two
Decorated with thick, pink
Ribbon and young tears

They're everywhere
Except alive in live arms
Or Grandma's dead ones

Mentally buried
'Neath sands of untimeliness
Lie stolen childhoods

She, too, longs for the
Precious pitter-patter of
Firstborn happy feet

To light the darkness,
Complete her chaos, give life
To this make-believe

Refuse to Lose

Rachel Libby

When Oliver left, the last nine months of my life left with him. Nine months of joy and laughter and discomfort and so much expectation. You can't admit the good. Because of how it ended. And you can't talk about the misery either. Because of how it ended. You can't be grateful for the late-night internal dance parties, because it hurts so much to remember. You can't celebrate the ability to sleep on your own stomach again. Because you'd trade it all—you'd sleep uncomfortably for the rest of you life—for your baby to still be here.

The first days after he died, I could talk freely. I could talk about Oliver and nothing else for hours if I wanted. I could cry and everyone knew why. I was surrounded by people who were acutely aware of exactly how much pain I was in. Or at least they could imagine how much pain I was in. Gradually, time has passed. And now people look at me sometimes, if I'm staring off into space or I look a little lower than usual, and ask, "What's wrong?"

It takes a lot of self-control not to respond, "My baby is still dead."

(That very fact still surprises me. Every single day.)

I understand that people move on; they move forward with their lives, and while they still remember the pain of losing Oliver, their wounds heal. Mine is still fresh, raw, and wide open. I'm still acutely aware of how much pain I am in.

But I do get it: the world must go on, which seems impossible at times. And I'm going on with it, which seems even more impossible. I have let myself be reintroduced into society, back into the real world.

A world of unavoidable land mines, of new healthy babies and pregnant ladies and salesmen who ask, "Do you have any kids?" A world of strangers, of new acquaintances who didn't know me then, people who don't know that the whole world changed on April 10, 2012.

You see, I still want to discuss Oliver with frequency, with immediacy, but as time has passed, my audience has changed. Physically, a new cast of characters has emerged. People who don't even know about Oliver. And even if the people are the same, they've moved on, some of them growing their own little ones inside. I no longer feel it's appropriate to be recounting every heartache, every instance that reminds me of my boy.

And like I said, some of the people in my world are in the best time of their life; they are in the midst of cookin' a bun in their oven. And I tell you, I'm so, so happy for them. But I feel as if, here I sit, the cautionary tale. Their worst nightmare. And I'm caught betwixt my head and heart, wanting so desperately to let out the constant Oliver newsfeed that's running through my mind but so wholeheartedly not wanting to cause them any worry, stress, or anxiety.

I want to throw in my pregnant two cents; I want to commiserate about swollen ankles and deciding on a name and being consistently punched in the rib cage by the boxer inside. But I can't. Or rather, I won't. Because of how it ended. Because who wants to hear about my cravings and bizarre pregnancy dreams and epidural experience? I can only imagine what they would think if I were to join in—how they would compile a list of what not to do. (I know it's not my fault, but still I can think of million things I would have done differently.) So I could understand why one, full of another life and hope and expectation, would not want advice from someone like me. Because of how it ended.

Three months after Oliver died I was sitting at a friend's house—a very pregnant friend—listening to her talk about her current situation. I sat there listening and I wanted so badly to say, yeah, I know what you mean. I know what that's like. But I couldn't. For her sake. Because of my head-heart battle. And because there was a stranger in the room. By stranger I mean, acquaintance who may or may not know my sad song. It's hard to start a sentence with, "When I was pregnant..." if you're petrified of answering the possible and probable follow-up questions.

The thing is, obviously, I don't mind talking about Oliver. Life without him is my constant existence, so it never feels like a shocking secret to let out. It is what it is. But I fear for the poor unsuspecting folks. I hate to bring them down. (And after having had my first instance of unleashing my truth on an unknowing innocent, I know how it feels, for me and for them. It. Feels. Awful.) I mean, I'd like to think, oh well, it's the truth, and if I have to live it every day, who cares how they react. But, I also believe people have the right not to be blindsided by dead baby talk over fondue.

Maybe it's one of those things that will get easier with time. With practice. Or maybe it won't. Maybe it will always be the battle between wanting to honor my time with Oliver (for the good and the bad) and wanting to protect those around me from my tragedy.

Perhaps that's why I'm writing this, though. To give myself permission to keep those nine months. I've already lost Oliver; I can't lose the only time I had with him, too. I don't want to forget what it was like to have him here with me. I want to recount the numerous times I sent Daniel out, demanding macaroni and cheese or Hawaiian pizza. I hope I'll always remember listening to my students propose names like Shiny and Fruit Bar and Fire Lord. I can't forget Daniel feeling Oliver move. I refuse to forget what it was like to be that happy. To be that full of joy and laughter and discomfort and expectation. No matter what I've lost, I still have that.

And I know it can be done. That kids gone too soon can still be a part of the present life in a way that is joyous and loving and real. And I have to believe it will get easier, that my armor will strengthen and I'll be able to talk about Oliver with family, with friends, and even with strangers, releasing myself of the responsibility for their feelings and reactions. I'll be able to tell his story, our story, and ensure that he is not only his death. He is his life.

The Raven

Angie M. Yingst

I am wearing a pink gown, the opening in the front. I am grateful for that small gift—back openings makes me feel so vulnerable and undignified. There is a paper blanket covering my legs. My shaking hands fumble with the thinness. I tear a hole in the thigh. It is not meant to keep me warm, I remind myself. There is a blood stain on it already. I lean back on the table. There is a skylight over the stirrups. The rain falls like a war drum, hard, without rhythm, but persistent. The wet leaves cover the bottom of the skylight.

Nature keeps falling, water and leaves. Dead things that look alive. I stare at the counter. Purell and ultrasound gel. A Pap smear kit, and non-latex gloves. A black bird flies over the building. It looks like a shadow of a happier bird, something predatory but special. I know the baby is dead before he tells me. I have imagined the baby dead in all the moments I am not actively thinking she might be alive. But I wait for him to say it aloud.

The doctor tells me it looks like a miscarriage. I am twelve weeks pregnant, but the lab work and the bleeding and the ultrasound without a heartbeat suggest an empty sac. The baby is gone—perhaps it was never there. A paradox I may never unravel. My uterus growing and believing, even while I am stunted and cynical.

The doctor convinces me to go for another ultrasound because of the trauma of Lucy's death. He thinks I should see there is no heartbeat again. He said, "Just so you know, deep within you, that we did not make a mistake." And I tell him steadily without tears in my voice that I held my dead baby and I still thought it was a mistake. Her skin was torn and growing colder, and I thought she would live again. She was six pounds, and twenty inches long, and I was in labor. Not early labor. Not false labor, but the labor of full-term babies. I thought there was some system-wide error when they couldn't find her heartbeat. She could still come back, if someone did something other than mourn and dim the lights. I thought I could puff my lungs up, cover her nose and lips, and breathe life back into her, as though the doctors and nurses hadn't quite thought of that yet. "She just needs some air," I wanted to explain. "We just need to remind her to breathe."

Sometimes I still think that perhaps we cremated her too soon.

I watched a hawk chase a raven, diving and attacking. It was a spectacular show above us as we hiked through the woods to a waterfall. We all stopped and gawked. I bent over in the first bangs of unbearable cramping. The ravens have been around me all this month, waiting for the death in me to escape. The ravens swoop low, cross in front of my car, reminding me that I can lose once, lose twice, I could lose them all. It has been an unkindness of omens—dead baby birds on my front steps, and ravens stopping me in the street, daring me to hit them. Maybe I should call the nevermore baby, Raven, the blackness, the hole within me.

I received an e-mail from another woman who lost her only son. Stillborn like my second daughter Lucy. It arrived just as I began bleeding. "Your life is beautiful, so beautiful now. You have another child, a son, like my son. And your older daughter. Do you appreciate it? I think you do. I appreciate it, but I can't bear it. I have to look away. It is painful how beautiful your life is." It is beautiful, even though our daughter died, even though the last child is dead now. I made something else out of her death—a life I always wanted to live. I understand if someone can't bear it. Joy reminds me of grief too. Happy reminds me of sad. And besides, two children is something, I get that. Two living children cover the holes where the others were. You'd never notice if you didn't search for the spaces where others were supposed to be, if you didn't read our stances and our smiles. It would be hard not to believe the lies we are telling in our photographed smiles. My dead outnumber my living now, but still two children is not all of your children dead. I do appreciate it.

What I wanted to say, though, is that we still suffer. We have a beautiful life, but we still suffer.

They search my womb, and they don't find the baby. The technician says the baby is dead, even though she is not supposed to say it aloud. Words I needed to hear. In moments, I begin the process of miscarriage, passing clots and tissue. As though my body was holding on to her until someone could speak the truth that she died. The little dot inside of me that was growing once is gone now. The children would ask me how big she is every day. And I would tell them the size of an olive, the size of a lime, the size of a peach. But she was no size—just my womb grew, making space for an unkindness. She is an empty space now. A hole of what could have been.

I thought I could slip under the radar with one more quick baby, like Fate could turn her attention somewhere else for a quick nine months. "The last time. The only time. One chance," I said to my husband. "One more chance at one more child, then nevermore."

I know what I know and I still got baby greedy. I still thought somewhere in me that things would end differently. I am not ranking my sadness, but this is a small grief compared to Lucy. Lucy died, and I held her. I felt like I knew her—she was in my womb for thirty-eight weeks, nary a thought of life without her. I never imagined her dead in those thirty-eight weeks. But my little raven died, and I only ever imagined her dead. (It didn't help the pain.)

Perching on the fence in my backyard, like the raven, Grief waits for the physical pain to subside to invite himself into our home again. I reacquaint with Grief, another stodgy old raven wearing black. He is silent, never flitting, still is sitting, still is sitting, sitting by my office door, whispering, "Nevermore."

This piece was originally published on the website *Glow in the Woods*, May 2012.

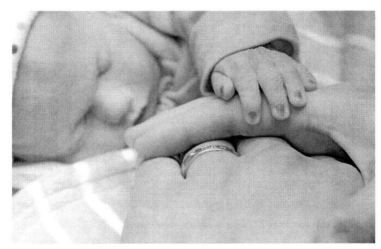

Forever Held
Jen Hannum

Ash

Colleen Lutz Clemens

I remember the last thing I said while my baby still sat inside me. "I'm not a doctor, but I think you are supposed to wait."

I lay on the operating table. Earlier, the kind nurse warned me that the room would be cold. Goosebumps popped on my arm as the mean nurse wheeled me into the operating room. I had been spared a D and C after the first miscarriage. This time I needed the surgery. She, big-boned and brusque, wanted to take my blood from me before the anesthesia took effect. The kinder pre-op nurses all had tried and failed. My fertility doctor, whom I had now known for three years, decided I had endured enough and ordered that the bloodletting wait until I was adequately numbed. My new nurse, annoyed and impatient, didn't like to be told what to do, but did wait until I counted back to ninety-seven from one hundred.

Looking back I wish I had said, "Can't you let me have this last minute with my baby? Why not shove that needle into my hand since nothing can hurt more than what I feel?" But instead I remained silent and lay on my back, hearing the machines beep and staring at the white, sterile room until I didn't see it anymore. I awoke with no baby inside of me, and a hematoma on my hand. I wonder if that bruise wasn't payback for my back talk.

The first time I heard the heartbeat inside of me, I imagined a little girl. I saw her long hair at her first birthday party. I saw her riding a horse. I saw her going to the prom. Before her heartbeat stopped, I imagined an entire life with her. The doctor needed to take her from my body to figure out why she didn't make it, to try to make sure the third time would be the charm.

Minutes before the surgery, I had signed a stack of forms. In a sea of legalese, one form was memorable: the burial form. It asked for the signature of the parent—that was the first time I had been addressed by that title by someone other than myself. I had only seen her in my imagination. I was always out of view. But her mother would be there at the birthday party, the horse lesson, and the pre-prom hours.

After two years of fertility treatments, I was finally a parent—a parent of a dead baby, but a parent all the same. The burial form asked us whether we wanted to be notified when her remains had been "taken care of." The parental consent line sat empty. Was it ridiculous to know when the ashes were buried? How many ashes could that little being make? One or two. Something that would float by in the air and one may not even notice. A fleck. A piece of dust. I wanted that piece of dust back inside me where it could grow into something bigger. But she was already gone.

I can understand the people who choose not to know about the baby's remains, who make a vain attempt at forgetting their trauma and moving on without thinking about that ash. But I checked the "yes" box. I imagined the day when I would open the mailbox to find the card that told me our baby had been buried, her ash mixed in with all of the other dead babies' ashes, making the saddest pile I can imagine. I imagined that moment would allow me to move on: the moment of closure when I could finally rest, finally be able to live again in a world where babies are born and statistics can also work in one's favor.

But that day never came. It took months for me to give up thinking the letter would arrive; one day I just didn't steel myself in front of the mailbox. Its hinge squeaked as I pulled open its metal door like a normal person would, expecting to find only Lands' End catalogs and credit card offers, not the death announcement of a much-wanted, much-worked-for baby. Sometimes I still ask myself: is my baby in limbo? Sitting in a jar somewhere? Rationally I know that isn't possible, that she was all heart and not much else, a loud noise that filled the doctor's office the week before and then silence. There weren't fingers and toes, but there was a heart, and it beat and beat for weeks until it didn't beat anymore.

I never called the doctor about the notice. I didn't want to seem like a desperate Gothic woman with crazy ratted hair wandering the halls waiting for a phantom sign from her dead baby. I didn't want to explain to the person on the other end of the line what that card would mean to me, that I would put it alongside the single "Happy day! You are having a baby!" card, all sherbet colors and glitter, as a bookend to the baby's short life. It would honor that she died. That she had lived and died, and lived dead inside of me for many days before she came out into the world. That she was then made into ash, and no one ever told her parents—her mother—what happened to her.

Silent Miscarriage

Marina DelVecchio

A few hours after I had begun spotting, I found myself in my obstetrician's office. Dr. Sylvia Becket scoured the sonogram machine's screen for traces of life.

"I'm sorry," she said, her voice empathetic but practiced. "We call this a 'silent' or 'missed' miscarriage because the mother-to-be does not know that the baby has stopped developing in her uterus until she has a sonogram. You're supposed to be eleven weeks pregnant, but from the size of the fetus, it looks like it stopped developing at around eight weeks."

I felt my husband Joe's fingers grasp mine tightly, affectionately. His gray eyes peered at me, willing me to look at him, to share the loss with him, but I couldn't meet his gaze. I knew if I did, I would begin to cry, right there, at the doctor's office. I surrendered my hand instead, letting it rest limply in his own larger one, but I couldn't look at him. Not yet.

I was eleven weeks pregnant, but there was no life inside me. There was only death.

Three weeks earlier, we had been vacationing at the beach. I had posed happily for pictures, touching my hands over my accentuated belly with pride and joy. Joe and I had decided on names and focused on moving rooms around the house to accommodate the new and tiny addition to our family. We had been making plans, family plans, while death had occupied my insides.

I had been informed by two pregnancy sticks and a blood test at the nurse's office that I was pregnant, and I never thought that this positive would result in nothingness. Even my body stubbornly clung to the thought that it was still pregnant, continuing to produce progesterone long after the fetus—*my* fetus—had stopped developing.

"What do we do now?" I heard Joe ask my doctor from a muffled distance.

"Well, you're spotting now, so it can take a few days to a week before the fetus comes out on its own. All you can do is wait and allow the miscarriage to take its natural course." Dr. Beckett gave us a slow, sympathetic smile, and patted my hand.

Slowly, I moved to get off the table, sensing Joe's eyes on me. I knew that he wanted to talk to me, to console me, and for me to console him. But I avoided his gaze, his disappointment, the coldness he must be feeling as I cast him to the side, cocooned by my own misery. He let go of my hand, deliberately, waiting to see my reaction. I withdrew my fingers with an immediate force that shocked even me, and I felt him take a solid step away from me, neither of us realizing that this wide shift away from one another would create a chasm so deep it would take years to fill again with love and trust and hope.

As Joe moved away from me, giving me the space I needed, I moved deeper into myself, surrendering to the dark folds of loss and death and rage that enveloped me. There was nothing for me to do now but wait for the fetus to detach from the warm womb that had once nurtured it. And I had to witness the bloodbath, like a spectator, in ways that only women who miscarry are forced to experience such a loss—helpless to do anything about it.

For the next two days, I continued to bleed, and it wasn't until the third night that an immeasurable amount of pain stabbed my insides. I doubled over, hands clasped tightly around my middle. It was like having contractions, like giving birth, except there was nothing breathing, living, or crying that would rush out to be placed in my arms. I braced myself for the stillbirth.

For what seemed like hours, I bled into the toilet, and even though I didn't know what to look for, I surveyed the clotted and bloodied contents that spewed from between my thighs and splashed into the toilet water, searching for answers, for something meaningful in the experience.

As the contents of my dead insides forced their way out of my body, there were no words. No answers. No conciliatory meaning. There was only the sound of red jellylike tissue as it leaked out and broke the surface of the water. That was the only sound: the impact of death sinking into the depths of a crimson, watery grave.

With a moroseness that I had never encountered before, I scrutinized every single gelatin-shaped matter that I could scrape onto the toilet paper.

I touched it with my bare fingertips, moving around the tissue for signs of my lost baby. I didn't know what to look for, what the size would be, or how it would appear to me. And for every bit of matter I examined, I couldn't decide what it was, or if it was what I was searching for.

"Why are you doing this?" Joe asked with an incredulous tone when he came upstairs at one point and found me crouched over the toilet bowl, which was now lined with blood and unidentified clumps. "This is sick," he whispered in a thick, low voice.

I did not answer him. I didn't know myself, but I kept examining, nonetheless, shutting Joe out. I didn't even notice when he shuffled away, weary, shaking his head with disappointment.

I didn't know what I was searching for exactly, but I had the notion that if I looked hard enough, I would find something related to my loss. I needed proof of life. Proof that something tangible had in fact grown inside me, making me sick and proud and joyful all at the same time. If nature compelled it to be flushed out, to be aborted, I wanted to be there to catch it, to cradle it, to whisper something softly to it. To say good-bye.

After an hour of cramping and bleeding, a sharp, biting pain in my lower abdomen propelled me atop the toilet again. As soon as I squatted, I felt a soft, rounded form squeeze out of me, and heard a loud plop as it crashed into the bloodied water of the toilet. I knew instantly that this was what I had been waiting for, the last part of my fetus as my body expelled it; it was the remains of the baby I had been nurturing inside me, the baby I had been dreaming of holding, but would now never get to place in my arms. I bent beside the bowl and looked into it, but whatever fell was now blanketed by bloodied liquid.

Compelled by a force stronger than myself, I placed my arm inside the toilet bowl, past the red surface, and reached for the gooey remains of the life that would never be revealed whole and live to me. About three inches long, I held in the palm of my left hand a C-shaped mass of flesh. It was soft, long, rounded in the midsection, and outlined by red matter that I couldn't make out. It didn't look like a baby, but by the size of it, and by its shape, I knew that I was looking at the baby I had lost three weeks ago. The baby that had remained inside me with a willful conviction that equaled my own, both of us rooted to each other in silence.

I cradled it in the palm of my hand and looked at it longingly, saddened by the sight of something so small and helpless and undeveloped that could not locate in me the strength it needed to survive and become something more than a seedling.

Leaning my head against the cool surface of the bowl, splattered with blood and fatality, I began to weep until there was nothing left. Until, eventually, I knew that the only thing left to do was place the small mass back in the bowl and flush it into my neighborhood's sewer system, as if it was fecal matter, waste, and not something that had been growing inside me for the past few months, full of potential and vigor.

Crouched there, my knees resting upon the cold surface of the bathroom floor, I felt something rise from deep within me; it was a low, guttural exhalation that escaped from somewhere unfathomable and obscure, passing through my clenched lips against my will. It was the hushed sound of a sigh that claimed the final passing of my undeveloped, unborn child. And then there was nothing—nothing inside me, and nothing around me.

In the end, I crawled into my bed and stayed there for two days, not moving, not sleeping, but simply escaping the clamor of life as it persisted around me. I wanted to disappear and be as silent as my miscarriage had been, for in the end, all that remains is the sound of an aching silence for which there are no words.

After Stillbirth

Kate Roper Camp

"How are you?"
 She barely heard the question,
 For the keening wail that whirled within,
 Scouring her insides smooth like the pale lining of a shell.
 It echoed through the hollowness tapering into every curve,
     every limb,
 Rattling her empty womb,
 Vibrating to a pitch that roared through her ears and sinuses
 And pulsed in her fingertips.
 It beat at the back of her throat.
 She spoke through numbed lips,
 Words passing through the wail,
 And was surprised to hear her calm voice reply,
 "I'm okay."

Love of My Life

Ashley Kimberley

In Loving Memory of Walker Kimberley, born July 5, 2009.

*T*hat woman who I don't know walks to the end of my hospital bed. I feel barely alive. She slides her hand up inside me, checking my cervix.

I remember her. Two years ago I watched her deliver my nephew here. She rushed in, still pulling on gloves. Frantically she pulled out a vacuum extractor and commanded everyone to step aside. She delivered my sister's baby as his heart rate plummeted. My nephew's head emerged from his mother's birth canal; a few seconds felt like minutes as this doctor used a bulb syringe to pull fluid from his throat and nose and then used her gloved hands to pull him from his mother's body. He had cried loud and strong, the way healthy babies do when they are born, and the room was filled with relief and celebration.

Now the woman looked at me with tenderness. "You're ready. It'll be really quick," she whispered firmly, removing her hand from inside me. She is the doctor on-call this holiday evening and desperate to give me some encouragement. She's willing me to be able to birth my son. She doesn't usually show such tenderness. But tonight she is kind. She'll take care of me and then try not to think of us again. She introduced herself earlier in the tiny triage room seconds before confirming he is dead. No one said anything, and finally it was me who whispered, "He's dead," in the way that I often make a statement when I am really asking a question. "Yes," the woman had replied, her eyes full of pity. I went numb, looking away from the ultrasound screen. Tyler sank into the chair beside me. Fear and pain I'd never seen filled him, and sobs shook his body. My world began crashing in around me in slow motion.

It's after two in the morning on my husband's birthday. We squeeze each other's hands with whatever strength is left. I nod to the doctor and try to keep breathing. My nurse, Caroline, touches my arm, trying to give me strength or comfort. She has been quietly caring for us, making sure no ill-mannered residents come by to prove themselves at my expense. I plead with God again. In my head I know my baby must be dead. But in my heart I have a glimmer of hope. I am praying and begging God for a miracle. Maybe he will come out living. I feel foolish for clinging to my hope, but I can't help it. If I have ever needed anything from God, I need this miracle. If I have ever put my hope in anything, it is in willing this child to be alive. If ever I have been faithful, it is in this moment asking God for my son and putting my hope in Him.

I am full of fear. I will hold my baby boy in a moment. Will he really be dead? The stirrups and a disposable sheet are in place. Tyler is trying to hold me. The two women are gently drawing forth my strength. "Okay, Ashley, now. Push, honey." Silently I push with all my courage until they tell me to stop. A few seconds. I don't have time to think. "Again. You're almost there." I am pushing, pushing, pushing. Through the epidural I can feel his body emerging, and I feel my womb empty.

Silence.

She is bringing him toward me all in one motion, setting my baby on my chest. I can hear only my own sobs as I get my first glimpse of his perfect, beautiful face. I'm trying to breathe, desperate for him to breathe. Walker's bald head is cradled in the crook of my right elbow. I gasp for air between sobs. "Oh, honey," I plead. "What happened to you, baby? Wake up!" I beg him. She is grabbing at my abdomen, careful not to stab me as she forces the scissors through the umbilical cord. She clamps the end of the cord dangling from

Walker's belly but doesn't bother cutting it down to the start of a proper belly button.

We are staring at our son. I've loved a child like this before. The familiar feeling of being consumed by passion and adoration for my newborn baby floods my heart. Stroking his cheeks and head, I can hear the nurse and doctor crying for us quietly. Walker is warm and wet, the way a newborn should be. His little body feels good against mine. His back is the softest thing I've ever felt. I am shocked at his beauty. He is perfect, and I am overwhelmed with love and grief. How can he be so perfect and dead? How can he be beautiful and dead? How can I love him so much but not get to keep him forever, or even for a day? Walker looks like he is sleeping the most peaceful sleep. I keep nudging him, trying to wake him. "Wake up, baby!" I plead. I run my fingers down the side of his adorable face, from the top of his head down his cheek to the tip of his sweet little pointed chin. I kiss his bald head over and over. I kiss his nose. I kiss his lips.

My love for this sweet little boy who is mine tricks me into moments of joy that are promptly snuffed out by the depths of sorrow. I can feel the ache of my broken heart consuming all of me. I am proud to be his mama. I think my heart will explode with love and despair. I want him with every morsel of my soul. I am ravaged by pain and a depth of aching that makes me desperate and sick. I want to cuddle and kiss this little perfect dead body. I want to look at every little inch of him. I examine his ears. They are small like mine, with little attached earlobes, and I beam with satisfaction that he is mine. He is fucking adorable.

Tyler is eager to hold his son, so I let him. The nurse wraps Walker in a swaddling blanket, and I watch my baby cradled in his daddy's arms. Tyler adjusts the blanket and peaks at Walker's big chest. He kisses his forehead and his cheek. I love to watch this man I love hold a baby. He does it with such confidence and tenderness. He cradles Walker like he's trying to protect him. Tyler's face cringes in pain, riveted with sobbing and sadness that I've never seen.

The nurse takes our baby in her arms. She unwraps him. We notice his hugely swollen little testicles, and we smile at each other. She sets him on the scale: eight pounds, eight ounces. His chest is full, and his body is stout. He looks like a little ox with a perfect angelic face. He is so familiar. He looks like my dad, and his auntie, and our daughter when she was tiny. He has his sister's chin and Tyler's beautiful full lips. His feet are huge. The nurse dresses him in a nightgown with a bee on it. I wish we had some of his things from home. I don't like the nightgown; it isn't what I chose for him. But it goes on easily and his skin is so fragile. The bumblebee reminds me of my sister whose middle name is Be. Caroline sets him down in the glass hospital bassinet, leaving the sides of it open. It bothers me, even though I know he won't wiggle and fall out.

I gesture that I want him back, and Caroline carefully passes him to me. I hold him against my chest and cheek. His body isn't warm anymore. With every ounce of my humanity, I try to warm him. I wrap the blanket more snuggly around him and pull it up to his chin. I put my cheek against his, and I try to keep him from getting any colder. It is torture to feel my son growing cold. I have no idea that I will long for this moment with him over and over. I don't know if I will survive this, but I have a daunting feeling that, mercilessly, I will. I am sick with shock. We haven't yet told anyone he is dead. It seems like admitting it will make it true. We haven't wanted to ruin Fourth of July for our families, and now it's the middle of the night.

We are beginning a long and miserable journey through hell. I don't know what it means, but in darkness and disillusionment I vow not to sacrifice my life for my grief and love for Walker. And I vow not to deny the depth of my despair and love for Walker. My world is crashing, crashing, crashing in on me. It's sunny and bright, but I am trapped in hell.

The Coin

Sarah Elizabeth Troop

*I*t's one of those things that you never hear about. The chances of it happening to your child are so small; it isn't something you will ever need to worry about, because it isn't going to happen to you. At least that's what the doctors say. However, someone has to be the one percent. This time, it's me.

My baby was diagnosed with a very rare genetic disorder. A "fatal prognosis," one nurse called it. Another doctor actually handed me a prescription slip to take to the hospital's Labor and Delivery department. On it he refers to my little one as a "lethal anomaly."

The doctors, all five that I have seen, tell me the same thing. I can carry my pregnancy to term, but my baby will die. I can be induced and give birth now, but my baby will die. I can undergo a surgical procedure to end the pregnancy, and...my baby will die.

No matter what I do, the result will be the same. My baby...my future, my heart, my hopes, my plans...will die. It feels as though I, too, will die.

At the hospital I sit at a desk while a nurse asks me questions as part of the intake procedure. I hear shuffling and commotion outside the rooms and pick up bits and pieces of conversation from the medical staff. A girl has been brought in. I cannot see her; I can only hear her heart-wrenching sobbing. Someone brought her in because she was trying to kill herself.

I can hear everything now, as there are just thin partitions between she and I. A doctor is in with her now, informing her that she is pregnant. She cries harder and claims she didn't know. The doctor questions her sternly: How could you not know? What did you think was happening to you all these months? The doctor informs her that she is just a few weeks away from giving birth and like it or not, she is indeed, going to have a baby.

The girl is screaming through her sobs. Saying again and again, "I don't want it! I don't want it!" It is terrible to hear someone in so much pain, but she is only voicing what I cannot. The unbearable pain, the heartbreak, the desperation. We are two sides of a terrible coin this poor girl and I. One who desperately does not want her baby and one who desperately does.

I feel myself beginning to rise out of my chair. I have every intention of circumventing the partitions to find this invisible stranger who has everything I want, to comfort her and tell her not to worry. I will take her baby.

That isn't what I want, though. I want this baby. I want my baby. I want none of this to be happening right now. Not for me, not for my baby, and not for this girl.

Simultaneously, nurses come and take each of us away to rooms where I can no longer hear her. I wonder how either of us is going to live through the coming days and months. Me with my empty arms and hers full with a baby she does not want.

It has been a month since I have been without my beloved baby. Much of the time, even the effort to breathe or get out of bed seems overwhelming, but I do try my best. I do.

Most nights I dream of the girl. I embrace her, stroking her hair and drying her tears. I speak in gentle tones, telling her not to worry and that she should be strong for her baby. Someday, everything will be fine. I hold her baby and wish it were my own. I wake up.

So Much Love, So Little Time

Erica Danega

Dashed

Anne Phyfe Palmer

"Look, Lily, do you see the baby?" Bez asked softly and pointed to the screen. She lifted her head from focused drawing and squinched her eyes to concentrate on the lines—more random than the ones she'd been drawing herself. Lily's head tilted to one side as she filtered the patterns on the screen to make sense of their alignment.

"Oooh, lookit, Papa, I see a foot!" Shiny little bones rippled at one corner of the screen. Above them a long straight femur wavered then disappeared.

Patricia lifted the ultrasound transducer out of the substrate of gel and wiped it on a paper towel. She smiled warmly and left us to get the radiologist. "You can take a trip to the restroom if you need to," she told me. "The doctor will be right in to take a look." I swung my feet around and reached for Bez's hand to heave myself off the table. A stool helped me to navigate the extra foot or two of height, my midsection already weak with expansion. I had a sweet little belly, just big enough at eighteen weeks to feel genuinely pregnant. I pulled my shirt down and wrapped the long cardigan sweater around this pronounced bump. Self-satisfaction combined with love hormones exploded every time I reflexively pulled one side then the other across and tied the knitted belt. It was both a swaddling of my midsection and a message to baby: "There you are little one, safe and sound."

What seemed like forever passed before the radiologist came in, nodded kindly, and went to the machine to linger, as the technician had. Little did we know that he had been watching all along, like the Wizard of Oz behind a curtain.

I smiled sheepishly at Bez as this man I'd never met ran the thick white wand over my bare belly. My sweet and introverted husband lifted his eyebrows and smiled back. I tried to take deeper breaths and enjoy the time off my feet while the doctor continued to explore. The image on the screen was so hard to understand, the moiré patterns constantly changing. It was hard to really imagine a baby within all of these lines. The doctor was quiet, and focused, until he finally spoke.

"See your baby's heart?" the doctor asked.

The lack of warmth in his delivery was my first clue that something was amiss. This was not a compliment on my child's organ structure. Instead of nodding an answer, I froze in place and held my breath to stop time and move it into reverse. My own heart surged with a galloping syncopation.

I saw the heart. It was beating. It looked perfectly fine to me.

So I stalled, silent. There was nothing for me to say, no way to take back what had been revealed. The doctor had discovered something that I could not see, or feel. We learned that there was something fundamentally wrong with the heart of our perfect little baby, this sibling for Lily, the completion of our family. We left the building in shock, our lives forever changed.

A week later my phone rang. I stared at Jennifer's name on the display for a few moments before answering. She was calling from New Orleans, a faraway place where most everyone we grew up with went to church, had lots of kids, and favored right-wing politics.

I sat down to accept the call, reluctantly. I always pick up when my sisters call, but I didn't want to bring Jennifer into our situation. It could open the door to possible judgment, advice, or concern that would conflict with our nascent decision to terminate.

Breathing deeply as I answered, I placed my hand over my belly, as though it were a totem, and braced for Jennifer's rapid-fire accent. I had a hard time understanding her over cell phones now that I was far removed from my mother tongue.

But today she was quiet, and curious. She knew about the ultrasound, that we were in the midst of a medical calamity. Neither of us brought it up at first—not my baby, or the baby she wanted more than anything. Since high school, Jenn had been waiting to get pregnant. Now that she was newly married, they'd been trying for a year. I no longer asked how it was going—the fertility project. I knew I'd be one of her first three phone calls the minute the tides turned and she was with child.

"So, well, what's going on with your pregnancy?" she finally asked.

"The testing is taking forever with everyone on vacation for the holidays."

"What are they testing for? Don't they know what is wrong?"

"They want to see if it's genetic."

"What does that matter?"

"They want to know if it's more likely to happen again, or just a fluke."

Jenn was unusually quiet on the other end, but I could hear her brain calculating, ticking away.

"You want to know whether it will happen again to know if you should keep the baby or not."

"We…" I started, hiding behind coupledom.

"You aren't going to keep the baby, are you?" she spurted.

"No."

No, I'm not going to keep my defective baby. No, I'm not going to be that parent who dedicates her life to the care of her sick child. I'm taking the easy way out. I'm a bad person.

A decade earlier I had found my true home in bleeding-heart Seattle, where more people fought for gay than fetal rights, where my yoga studio took the place of church, where you did your own thing and respected others' choices as their own, and where I already had one perfectly formed child. Talking with Jenn I felt defeated, exposed, wrong, but I wasn't willing to make the other decision, the one Jennifer would make without even thinking. She would take my baby, any baby, her longing acute and primal.

"Jenn, I..." I started to explain, but stopped.

"I can't believe you're not keeping it"—her voice broke along with her heart—"I just can't believe it."

I cringed, blocking myself from her words.

"I love you, Anne Phyfe, but I can't really talk to you right now."

A Modest Mouse song helped us explain to Lily what was happening. Ours was a "baby cum angels, fly around you reminding you we used to be be three and not just two." I asked Lily what we should name her brother/angel. "Dash" immediately came out of her mouth. I gasped and my eyes filled at the perfection of that word. He was dashing in and out, and dashing our dreams. Her accidental poetry came from a preschooler crush on the boy in *The Incredibles*, a Disney film about superheroes. This brother of hers was superhuman, not subhuman.

Every night, the bed brought forth the tears. It was an expanse of dark water I could sink into, the perfect environment for grief. I made it through those late-December days waiting for the velvet of night to fall. I had to stay present for Lily, for her process, to help her navigate her own feelings of loss. Once she was in bed, I would lean into the sadness for this ritual of grief.

It would start with a trickle, a tear, a grasping for release. I'd reach for Bez like reaching for a life raft. Once I had one hand on his body I could let the real tears come, the body-racking kind that would send me crawling backward under the covers into the safe tent-like darkness I'd sought out as a child. Once expelled, it unfurled into the sound of a child after a crying fit—the gasps of inhale, then one heaving exhale—until I found sleep under his arm.

I'd never experienced this before. I'd been sad, depressed, upset, lonely, heartbroken, homesick, dejected, and abandoned, but I'd never felt this kind of grief. It was all encompassing but it was clean, pure, single-pointed. There was no anxiety, no fear, no worry.

I knew that I could safely let it flood every crevice of my body. I wouldn't drown. I had Bez and Lily to swim up to when I was ready. I could go through this pain and come out the other side. I could move past my grief in ways I imagine would be impossible for a widow, or a parent who spent months or years with their child. Their memories would be stacked as evidence that this person was supposed to be alive. They would want what they had back. I had only weeks of bodily knowing, not snuggles, or embraces, or experiences.

Grief has a comforting cloak. It covers you completely and compassionately, opening your heart to deeper appreciation for what carries on. For me, plenty remains in my arms. Husband, daughter, and now another daughter, Coco.

Sometimes our family takes the short drive to Calvary Cemetery, where Dash is buried. Lily and Coco arrange toys around the stone marker that bears his name, one date, and the words "We Miss You."

A Touch of Life

Jessica Watson

After years of fertility treatments and a successful round of in vitro, our triplets were born at twenty-eight weeks. Twenty-eight weeks and five days to be exact. I was counting.

Early labor kept me from ever leaving the hospital, where I had lain day after day, staring at my feet and a calendar on the wall. *X*'s marked each extra day that the mix of medication and bed rest had given my babies to grow. After the threat of delivery at nineteen weeks, twenty-one weeks, twenty-four weeks, and every few days from then on, making it to my last trimester seemed a miracle.

I knew the triplets would be in the NICU, and I was as prepared as any soon-to-be mom of three could be. I had toured the unit, watched the babies born too soon struggling with life, quizzed the nurses and neonatologists, and researched feeding and bonding and every possible medical complication under the sun. I was ready. We could do this.

But when the time came, and my babies and my body could not wait any longer, all my readiness fell to my surgical-slippered feet.

Nothing could have prepared me for the delivery of three babies at once—the sea of hospital masks, the hum of machines, the buzz of anticipation encircled by the quiet of hope.

As the first baby came there was no calm before the next.

There was urgency, and there were monitors and calls for oxygen.

There were NICU teams and respiratory therapists and relays to incubators.

Baby A, my little girl, was brought near to me first, all two pounds ten ounces of her shocking me into the delicate world of mothering a preemie; though she was not as alarming as the one pound fourteen ounces of her brother, the next to wriggle his long pink limbs at my cheek. As the nurses brought them to me, one tiny baby at a time, I wanted to take in their every feature and hold them and love them—but it was not yet my turn. They needed intensive care, and I felt that need and urged the nurses along, fighting my yearning to trace every ounce of their fragile babyness. I would see them soon enough. Forever was ahead of us.

There were several moments between the delivery of Babies B and C, my son and my next daughter…enough for me to take in what was happening, settle into my excitement, and wait for her. As she came by, I adjusted my focus, trying to see her two pounds five ounces of features through the mask of oxygen already mingling with her labored breaths; and as I tried to move my hand to her face, she held me first. Her tiny pink fingers were white at the tips as they wrapped around mine. I did not feel that urgency to let her go as I did with her siblings. The nurse pressed forward before I was ready for her to let go. I wanted to keep her there, suspended at my cheek, squirming with new life, telling me she already knew who I was. My first touch from one of my babies who had endured the push and pull of life all those weeks was perfection. She was here, and so was he, and so was she. All alive and fighting, a testament to faith and hope and unending love.

This small moment, this first touch, was the clearest, tiniest, most profound moment of my life, of my pregnancies, of our seventy-seven days in the NICU, of my marriage, of my days as the mother of four living children, and the mother of one who is not.

One who stopped to tell me that she was okay—that I am her mother and always will be.

One who squeezed a moment of her short life into my waiting hand before she left this place for another.

Written on the Palm of My Hand

Faith Paulsen

Years later, across a table
at a charity fundraiser, an Indian palmist
cradles, dips my hand
in water, towels it dry.
At the corners of his eyes, no older than mine,
lines crease and uncrease.
He describes the palmists' map: *Mount of Mercury,*
Father, Mother, Upper Mars, Health,
Longevity, Continuation
of the Progeny. His finger traces
folds that curl around my thumb, lines
I've never noticed before.
And there it is, my private
truth, woven into the geography of my body,
a birthmark.
He counts, *Lines of Children,*
three strong,
two weak.

Violets in the Mountains

Brooke Taylor Duckworth

In memory of my first Baby Duck, Eliza Taylor Duckworth

> *I shudder with horror when I look on what I have suffered;*
> *& when I think of the wild and miserable thoughts that*
> *have possessed me, I say to myself, 'Is it true that I ever felt*
> *thus?'—and then I weep in pity of myself.*
>
> —Mary Shelley, *Frankenstein*

Six hours before my daughter would be born dead, I stood in front of my literature class to lecture on Mary Shelley's *Frankenstein*. We discussed the novel's preoccupation with issues of life, death, creation, parenthood, and childbirth. I mentioned that Mary Shelley's biography is intriguing to consider alongside her novel, particularly as she wrote *Frankenstein* not long after the death of her first child, a premature infant daughter. I remarked on how childbirth and mortality in the nineteenth century were connected in ways we no longer think about today. I then rubbed my eight-and-a-half-months-pregnant belly and said, "Thankfully!" My students and I all chuckled.

You see, I was confident that one hundred and ninety-two years after Mary Shelley wrote *Frankenstein*, babies no longer died. Well, some babies, maybe. Other people's babies. "At-risk" babies. Not *my* baby. Not Baby Duck, who was so very loved and so carefully planned. Not my baby, who was nourished with Mother's Tea and organic produce and healthy protein and yoga breathing and hypno-baby audio tracks.

None of my pregnancy books had told me that love and plans and the very best of intentions don't keep babies alive. Eliza Taylor Duckworth came into this world on December 6, 2010, beautiful, silent, and dead for no discernable reason.

In between the broken pieces of my life, it must be said, I found profound love. In my husband's white-knuckled hands clutching mine. In my mother's tear-filled eyes. In my dad's shaky voice. In messages from friends and acquaintances. Later, in life-saving connections with other parents who didn't need me to explain my unspeakable grief because they too had empty arms and shattered hearts. In a world altered by my changed perspective.

A few short months after Eliza died and was born, I went to lunch with a friend. He mentioned that he was going to visit an old Catholic cemetery in preparation for a class field trip. To fill the empty afternoon, I accepted his invitation to go along.

It was a dazzling spring day. The cemetery was as green and pastoral as I could have imagined. I looked around, and everywhere I saw dead babies.

William Tecumseh Sherman's nine-year-old son: "Our Little Sergeant Willie."

A baby boy named Otis.

An Eliza—someone's daughter, though this one died in old age—her resting place in a family plot.

Near her stone, another that read, "Here lies Ann, wife of Henry. Likewise their infant daughter Catharine." I held a prayer in my heart for Ann and Catharine, and vowed someday my gravestone would have my Eliza's name on it.

After we saw Kate Chopin's grave, my friend looked over the cemetery map and asked if I wanted to go up to the Shrine of the Infants, a grassy knoll bathed in sunshine and dotted with stuffed animals, flowers, and other impossibly inadequate tokens of love.

There were decades of baby graves on that hilltop. Some had single dates, many had hyphens separating dates just a few days or weeks apart. A few had birthdates that post-dated death dates. My throat ached with unshed tears as I thought about all the families who had walked this path—those who had literally stood here, mourning a child buried nearby, and those struggling each day to forge a life that goes on without their baby.

At the same time, the vastness of the cemetery made me feel like one small part of something greater than my own hurt. My loss can feel overwhelming, threatening to enshroud my entire identity. A cemetery full of centuries of strangers was a poignant reminder that we are each living one short chapter of a much longer narrative. In that cemetery, I saw the staggering evidence of generations of parents who have endured the loss of a child, their grief indirectly proportional to the size of those tiny graves.

My friend consulted the map to locate Tennessee William's grave. To get there, we would pass the Shrine of the Compassionate Mother. As I looked for a statue of the Virgin Mary that would mark the shrine, my friend pointed at the map and said, "Oh, look. Shrine of the Compassionate Mother. That's you."

He tossed the comment out lightly, an offhand remark that had just popped into his head. I almost made a follow-up joke about the likelihood of me being compared to the mother of Christ.

Instead, that comment filled up my heart in a way I can hardly explain. To know that he saw the word "mother" and automatically associated it with me—the grieving mother of a stillborn baby. As a mother robbed of all the ordinary opportunities to parent her child, I cherished the association. It astonished me that my pain hadn't scared this friend away; I was even more astonished, somehow, to discover that he viewed me as a compassionate mother. I hadn't been able to put any other adjective with the word "mother" in regard to myself except "bereaved."

But I hope his version is also true. I hope I can ultimately say that Eliza hasn't made me simply sad. I hope she has made me more aware and empathetic. She has made me less fearful about confronting broken places in other people, more willing to bring to light the pain and sorrow we often hide.

For so long, I felt loss had wrecked my life. My carefully laid plans were decimated, and I could scream for years about how unfair it is. But it occurred to me, as I walked among the graves, that Eliza could change my life in good ways, even without being here.

Tennessee Williams's gravestone has an epitaph that reads, *The violets in the mountain have broken the rocks.*

I read that line, and then I knelt and traced it with my finger. I thought about tiny, fragile, beautiful things and the enormity of their influence. And then I cried in that huge Catholic cemetery full of people I never knew, each grave representing someone's grief etched in stone. I cried because I miss my girl more than I can say, and because I know that loving her will make all the difference in my life. It already has.

The year *Frankenstein* was published, Mary Shelley's one-year-old daughter and three-year-old son both fell ill and died. Their heartbroken mother is now famous for creating a monster who grieves his lack of family. I've no doubt she would have obliterated that entire novel and the posthumous fame that went with it to save the lives of her babies. I know because for a long time I played the bargaining game and couldn't find a single thing I wouldn't trade to get Eliza back.

Eliza is so many things to me, but she never gets to be simply a sweet baby we brought home from the hospital whose diapers we changed and whose smile lit up our home. She is a precious symbol of unconditional love and devotion, she is our firstborn daughter and our Baby Duck, but she doesn't get to be what we wanted most: our little girl.

And yet, I can't deny the many gifts that Eliza brought us. There's the way she has connected me to other people, the way she has opened my eyes to the suffering that's all around us, the way she showed me that my capacity for love and compassion is beyond what I had ever imagined. If I am a better mom and wife and daughter and sister and friend, it's because of her. I know that my life now is richer and fuller and brighter and truer and fiercer than it would have been if I'd never loved and lost Eliza.

Intangible gifts and character improvements be damned, I still want *her*, my first baby, my sweet girl. I want my husband and I to have that other life, the one I was sure was meant to be ours, the one where we watch all our kids grow up and our heartaches are mundane, predictable, and far away. I want us to be parents who have never cradled a cold, dead baby, who never sobbed to the point of oblivion, who never tasted the metallic chill of shattering loss.

The truth is, I'll never fully know all that was lost and gained in the moment of Eliza's birth and death. I'm forced to accept that my life will never be what it might have been with Eliza here. Yet it will also, undoubtedly, be more—more of everything—than it ever could have been without her, Eliza, my first, sweet baby girl, and the abiding love that came with her.

Nesting

Laura B. Hayden

As Larry and I moved boxes into our fixer-upper, a mourning dove slammed into the front bay window, leaving a pinkish splotch on the glass. I recoiled at the notion that a dead bird was lying on the ground just outside. When I went out to remove the bird and its mark on the window, the bird was gone. It must have only stunned itself, revived, and flown away.

Chickadees, cardinals, and tufted titmice filled the pine tree in front of the picture window. I soon grew accustomed to their birdsong and occasional bump, as one mistook its reflection in the windowpane for another bird and flew into the glass to greet it.

Larry and I had been trying to start a family for years, but nothing was happening. In the midst of having begun fertility counseling, Larry suggested, "We should get a puppy." We had been in our new home a month.

I looked around at our house's faded exterior, worn rugs, and outdated tiled bathroom. But we had bought the house, like so many other things, for its promise, not its polish. Its fenced-in yard promised to provide a perfect home for a dog.

"A dog needs to be trained and cared for," I said, playing Mrs. Panza to my Mr. Quixote. I ended with the frequent plaint of the working wife. "I can't do it all."

"You won't."

Larry had his heart set on a Westie. He phoned a breeder, and we were invited to meet the pregnant pedigree, Jeanne, and her owner,

Judy. I wondered about a dog with a person's name, but when Jeanne greeted us, she was as licking, gnawing, and sniffing a terrier as she could be.

Judy the breeder greeted us with less fervor than Jeanne, but warmly nevertheless. A sweet face supported her thick glasses. She turned quickly staid over the business of choosing a home for one of Jeanne's impending pups.

Judy said Jeanne would be a mother on May seventh. She had mated in March. With dogs, fertilization was pretty much a sure bet. Sixty-three days later Jeanne would give birth to, most likely, four pups. My own temperature charts, infertility tests, and disappointing counseling sessions crossed my mind. I began to wish my name were Lassie instead of Laura. Maybe canine breeding odds would rub off on me.

"So you want a Westie?" Judy asked. Since I knew nothing about dogs, I tossed my head as if to relay the question to Larry.

"Oh yes. I want an exuberant welcomer, an intelligent learner," he said. "Had a Scottie once…Merlin," he continued. "Merlin was fun, but I've always liked the personality of a Westie."

Judy looked pleased. She shot the next question at me. "So you know terriers too?"

I hesitated. "Larry does. I…never had a dog."

"I see," said Judy. "And where do you live?"

This began to feel like an adoption screening. Larry quickly answered, "We just bought a home—with a great yard. Over half an acre."

Judy looked reasonably satisfied, so I added, "A fenced-in yard."

Her eyeglasses slightly magnified her widening eyes. "The entire half-acre?"

"Chain-linked," I said.

"Well, then," she clucked like a mother hen. "The litter'll be here in May. I'll call you then."

Larry put out his hand. "Thank you, Jeanne."

"I'm Judy," she said, shaking on the done deal.

Three months later we brought our tiny Westie home. We ministered to his first-night frights, encouraged his little body over steps, placed heartworm medicine down his throat, and rubbed his belly often. If a puppy is, like a man, what he eats, Piper—named for the player of Scottish pipes—perfectly fit his portion of eight parts dry Puppy Chow to one part canned Mighty Dog.

As weeks passed the Mighty Dog portion increased. I grew more and more uncomfortable with the smell of its moist, meaty byproducts mixed with the dry chow. Before long, a mere whiff of the dog's food nauseated me—which thrilled me! I made a special trip to the corner drug store and bought a pregnancy test. Actually, I bought three pregnancy tests, and within an hour confirmed I was expecting, once, twice, and then a third time.

"Guess what?" I asked Larry at dinner.

"We won the lottery"

"Better," I said.

"Reeeaally?" There were almost three syllables in his exaggerated articulation.

"Reeeaally," I imitated. "We're having a baby."

We celebrated that night, clinking chilled Perrier in crystal goblets. I just glowed.

"Good timing," said our veterinarian. There must have been a range of two octaves between Piper's yips as the vet administered four vaccinations and the guttural tones the puppy directed to the tabby in the waiting room. "A puppy in July, a baby in March," continued the vet. "If you keep him out of the nursery now, he won't resent the baby later."

Each week Piper napped less and played more, the way a

baby would. The most contented puppy in the world, I thought. Occasionally the thump of a misguided mourning dove on window glass drove him to a barking frenzy. And he obeyed our emphatic, "No," whenever he lingered by the baby's waiting room.

A misguided mourning dove smudges a window. A puppy accident on a rug. These became the least of my concerns

I was spotting.

Doctors and medical books offered no remedies for symptoms that my baby was about to slip away. Instead, they gave odds: a fifty-fifty chance that the pregnancy would miscarry. The books stated a lost fetus is a sick fetus. A sick fetus that would have developed into an abnormal baby.

My doctor ordered bed rest. Larry took on the kitchen chores. He served his first meals with panache. Fat garden tomatoes stuffed with chunks of tuna, backyard squash steamed to a still-crisp perfection, parsley garnishing it all. By week's end Larry would be heating frozen dinners.

"I'm tired," he said.

"I know," I reassured him, as we traded our private ironies: Larry, the weary, working househusband; me, exhausted, from bed rest and worry. At night we hugged hard, as if the tight embrace would keep our baby intact. Piper slept under our bed.

A trace of blood appeared on the sheets.

In a few days Larry opened the door to the nursery that, after the miscarriage, reverted to a spare room. Piper sniffed at its threshold and then curiously peered in. He let out a low growl.

"Good dog," I said, patting him.

Through the next few weeks we no longer talked of cribs and changing

tables. We didn't compare canary yellow paint samples to goldenrod. The ecru paint already on the wall would do.

Conversation remained in the present, avoiding the immediate past and any hopes for a future that would include a child. Larry went to work. I would have to wallow in more worrisome places at home, until my teaching job restarted after Labor Day. My body had healed, but the mind still oozed. I felt empty. I felt robbed.

One late August morning I let Piper out as usual. Thick pines, like the one outside the front window, lined the yard. Piper must have thought these trees were, truly, the boundaries of the world. He took his slow hop down the step. But, today, his sleepy walk halted. Ears up, snout frozen, Piper heard first, what I heard next.

A robin's sound.

My puppy hurled into a blurry, barking streak at the bird in the grass. This would not have been an unusual scene, except that the robin did not fly away. And quicker than I could distract Piper, the puppy was atop the helpless, hopping prey.

Growls overtook peeps. Then, in one striking snap, silence.

A community of birds screeched, their usual birdsong replaced by quick piercing cries of nesting baby birds. A long shriek followed the dual notes of adult birds sending out alarms.

On the ground the bird lay lifeless. What should have played out as an amusing scene—a dog pawing upward, dancing on its hind legs, a tiny bird safe in flight—turned into a natural catastrophe.

Piper rolled the carcass, sniffed the blood. Oak leaves swished like protesting placards against the sky. I remembered that even before the attack the bird could not fly.

In his scissors bite, Piper carried his prize and placed it, as if a gift, at my feet. I fell to my knees. Tears streamed down my face, some dropping on the dog's white muzzle. Twisting his snout, right to left, left to right, his eyes swept mine as if confused. Where was the pat, the treat, the praise for this flawless execution of hunter instinct?

"Good dog," I said, still sobbing. I placed my hand on his

stretched neck. I stroked down to his back and lifted my hand up again to his neck, over and over, acknowledging not his brutal act, but its message. Had the dear, yet flawed, fetus I carried a month earlier, survived, the baby, like the bird, would still not have been able to fly.

"Let's go inside," I told the dog, He trotted obediently in front of me.

First published in *Staying Alive: A Love Story* (Signalman Publishing, 2011).

Miscarriage

Jeannie E. Roberts

you left home

slipped away

a mere bud

a whisper

in white

perhaps

you passed

through

altered time

beheld

a better place

took root

in brighter space

thrived

in a finer womb

after your heart

set my heart

abloom

To Balance Bitter, Add Sweet

Shoshanna Kirk

Unable to hear a heartbeat, the midwife casts aside her Doppler and wheels out an ultrasound. I think of telling her not to bother—she won't hear it that way either—but that would be a strange thing to say, so I keep quiet. On ultrasound, the fetus measures small, far smaller than it should be. My husband and I are rushed to radiology for a closer look at my visibly swollen belly on more advanced equipment. Radiology confirms that fetal growth stopped weeks ago.

We listen, mute, to the options. I could have a D and C, or dilation and curettage—scraping. Except they don't really do curettage any more, the midwife explains. Now they use aspiration. Or, she continues, I could take a drug to induce the miscarriage, though at this stage, ten weeks pregnant, it might not work anyway.

Or I could wait it out. Eventually, my uterus will expel its contents.

In the silence, in which I am supposed to announce my decision, I chew the skin on my thumb until it is close to bleeding.

Bleeding is exactly what is not happening right now. It could take weeks to begin.

On the drive home, I study my husband's face. His jaw is clenched. The age lines that have developed since becoming a father three years ago seem deeper, longer. I turn to watch the road. *It will be fine,* I announce. *I've done it twice before. It's just like a heavy period with a few more cramps. I'll just get into bed, and before you know it, it'll all be over. I'm a tough cookie.* My husband nods and says nothing.

I want my body to do this naturally. After a Pitocin drip, failed forceps delivery, and unplanned C-section with my daughter, I've had enough of conventional obstetrics. I have no interest in a "procedure"—aspiration is a fancy word for vacuuming. Nor for drugs, for while said to be safe at this stage, chemical induction poses the single-greatest risk of uterine rupture for someone who's had a cesarean.

No—this time, no interventions. I want my body to be in charge.

We had already decided to do things differently with this pregnancy. At my daughter's birth, hospital policy had excluded my husband from the delivery room. After the surgery, the baby was taken away into a warmer room. The shockwaves of these separations have taken months and years to dissipate. This time, we decide, we will do whatever it takes to stay together. Given the reigning climate of anxiety in hospitals, staying together means giving birth at home.

One hour turns into another, and another, and then the days begin to pass. Each day feels longer than the one before. I abandon the book I'm writing about the year I was pregnant with my daughter, the year I gave birth to a real, live baby. I decide instead that knitting is a good way to pass the time, since there seems to be so much of it. I take my daughter to the yarn store, and we take turns touching the skeins. I splurge on white cashmere.

Since everyone I know seems to be pregnant, I will knit baby hats. The first is for a friend's baby due in just a few days. The pattern seems so small that after the first few rows I try it on my daughter's stuffed rabbit for size. It fits.

After a week, the on-duty nurse calls. *Just to see how you are doing.* She urges me to make an appointment for a "procedure." As a placeholder. I thank her for the suggestion.

The following week she calls again. She tells me she had a client who waited four months to start bleeding. Am I sure I don't want an appointment?

I am sure. At least I think I'm sure. Every day a little bit more of my life force disappears. Time with my daughter is a chore; I spend our afternoons watching the clock, waiting for bedtime. My husband's conversation is annoying and trite. Friends call, and I let the machine pick up.

One afternoon I pee and discover bright-red blood. I cancel all commitments and stack fantasy novels on the bedside table beside the half-knitted hat. Cramps come and go all evening. I am strangely excited. Soon all this will be behind me.

The next morning, the bleeding has stopped.

I remind myself that this has nothing to do with me. Most miscarriages are caused by genetic abnormalities—they are in fact proof of the body's wisdom, a way of letting go of aberrance. And yet I am so furious that I can no longer look at myself in the mirror, no longer rest hands on my belly.

I visit an acupuncturist, who creates a mandala of needles around my belly button. A homeopath prescribes envelopes of tiny sugar-coated pellets. I visit an herb store for something, anything, to kick my body out of its lethargy.

At home, I mix an herbal tincture with a cup of hot water as instructed. It is bitter, more bitter than anything I have ever tasted. I drink it as fast as I can and run to the sink to retch. My brother pads into the kitchen and opens a cupboard. "Here," he says softly, handing me a jar of honey. "To balance bitter, add sweet." I take a big spoonful and then lean on him to cry.

Sunday marks twelve and a half weeks. The day we should be calling friends and family to announce our news. I awaken with cramps. At breakfast, I snap at everyone and withdraw upstairs.

On the toilet something slips out of me, something warm and wet and heavy. Cramps come stronger, in waves, and more clots follow like slippery lemons. I run a bath and call down to my husband. In a half hour, we are meant to host a workshop for a dozen parents and children. I tell him he must figure out a way to cancel it.

The cramps last a half a minute, or maybe longer, one after another, four or five minutes apart. Like contractions. I have a vague memory to lower my voice and vocalize through them. I get halfway through an *om* before a sob takes its place.

The bathwater turns pink and then red. I drain the tub to start over.

As the tub fills, I look down at my body on hands and knees. Blood is streaked across my legs. A pile of clots, maybe a gestational sac, lie on a washcloth by the tub's edge. I put my head down in child's pose, so as not to faint. All I can smell is blood.

I call for my husband. He appears breathless, holding our daughter who has just awoken in tears from her nap. As I look up at them, stars ring the edges of my vision. I tell him to call the midwife, to ask about signs of hemorrhage. I can hear my daughter's voice as they fly down the stairs, *Papa, Papa! Is Mama ill?*

I squat as I drain the tub again. Another cramp begins, with that strange sensation of things falling out from deep inside. I reach down and deliver the placenta into my hand.

My husband sits on the edge of the bath with a cool washcloth and a shot glass of tincture to stem the bleeding. It burns like whisky, and I chase it with honey. He holds my arm steady as I climb out of the tub and walks me to bed, then dashes back down the stairs.

I lie down and close my eyes. I can hear him dodging my daughter's endless stream of questions. I am too tired to cry.

I spend late afternoon knitting. A tiny lace pattern runs around the hat's brim and three ribs corkscrew up to the crown. When I am finished, I cut the yarn, weave in the ends, and go downstairs to join my family.

After my daughter is asleep, my husband and I go out into our tiny garden. I am not sure what kind of ceremony we should have, but it feels wrong to throw everything away. I ring a Tibetan singing bowl and burn some sage while my husband unwraps each piece and lowers it into a hole in the dirt. After he fills in the hole, he sets down the shovel and clears his throat. I turn him to me by the shoulder and hold him for a long time.

Days later, my friend calls to announce the arrival of her baby. She and her partner are ebullient, riding a postpartum high. Our daughter is transfixed by the sleeping newborn—tiny and ancient and squished. I hand my girlfriend the hat wrapped in thin tissue. Later at home I will cry, but in that moment, I am happy for them and nothing else.

The Storm

Jenifer Richmond

Sitting on my porch tonight, I see lightning bugs. I wonder what joy my son would have chasing them. I look up to the sky and see a storm is coming. A flash of lightning shines in my eyes, and the thunder rumbles through my ears. A tear falls as I whisper, "I miss you, Noah." I bury my head in my hands, looking down at the sidewalk. A slow rain begins to fall. Each drop darkens the sidewalk, as if to represent the years and milestones of my son's life that I have and will miss. The rain becomes heavier and faster as I become more upset at the increasing raindrops on the sidewalk. The thunder grows louder as my cries grow louder, silencing the daily pain I struggle to hide because it makes everyone else more comfortable that I do so. My mind becomes infused with every detail of my pregnancy, my labor, the delivery of my son, the funeral, the aftermath...and here I sit... on my porch...still facing the aftermath. The storm.

Then I look at the bending trees and the shaking leaves. My son is reminding me that I am strong. That I may bend, but I do not break. It is because of this strength from my son that I was able to become pregnant again, and inside my home now lies Noah's little sister. I fought to get her here. I fight to keep her here. She is my rainbow after the storm. I know that I have my rainbow—beautiful and perfect, full of life and color—but here I am, still facing the storm.

How does one live that way—incomplete? Half of my heart went to heaven with my son and half remains here with my daughter. How can I ever give either of them my whole heart when each has a half so far away from the other. This is what consumes my mind—the things a mother should never have to consider. That's what makes me a different mother, full of insights and appreciation. The insights I wish I did not have to learn the way that I have.

I decide I should wrap up my grieving for the night. I walk back inside, wet with the raindrops of my son's life. No one will know the grief and tears I have left lying on the floor tonight; by morning it will be dry. That's what is expected of me: to move on, to not be so depressed, and to be thankful for my life. I sit in my home, "protected" from the storm that carries on despite the shelter—the shelter that is still standing but damaged regardless.

I watch my daughter sleep and thank God that she is so healthy, that she is even here with me. After Noah died my world was over, but when she arrived, there was a little hope, a reason to live. My dear son, I have some work to finish in this life, but do not give up on me. I will meet you at home when my time is through. And my final thought rests in this before I go to bed: Three minus one does equal zero. But what does four minus one equal?

Tear Drop Toes
Amy Dahlenburg

"Not Again"

Kelly Kittel

*A*ndy kissed me awake early. I drew in my breath, realizing my contractions were getting more uncomfortable.

"I hope these are working," I said. "That nurse better check my dilation today, or you'll have to."

"Gladly," he said, grinning.

Easing out of bed, I followed him to the kitchen. After months of bed rest, waiting and worrying, I was ready to have this baby.

"Have a great day," I said, kissing Hannah and Christiana. "Maybe today we'll have a baby." For the first time in ages, I watched them skip off to school. The sun reflected off their blond hair and the dew in the grass, the spring air sparkling with new growth and possibility.

Andy and I headed back down the hall—I to shower, he to dress Micah—and soon I heard them arguing. "Pleeeeze, you only have to wear them for an hour."

Micah skipped in, dressed in the corduroy pants he hated. "See, Mom? They swish when I move. Are you coming to my music?"

"I wouldn't miss it." I laughed. I'd missed so many of my kids' milestones over the past months, and today was his final performance of the year. My appointment with the nurse was at 10 and his program at 9; I'd stay for half and go directly from there.

Andy drove us right up to the front door of my neighbor's house, and Micah and I eased our way down the basement stairs to where Joanne was busy setting up. "I hope my water doesn't break on your couch," I joked.

"Oh, it's an old couch," she said.

My friend bustled over and sat next to me, excitedly asking, "So, do you think today's the day?"

"I sure hope so, fingers crossed," I said, rubbing my belly. I'd already arranged for Micah to go home with her to play after the program.

The recital began with the kids singing a few songs before Joanne said, "Now grab a partner for the circle dance."

"Come on, Mom!" Micah said, pulling my hand to help me up. All the parents were joining their kids, so I waddled over a few steps to take our place in the circle. The song began, and we all shuffled around like a large, undulating amoeba in a small petri dish. Whenever the music paused, we followed the instructions, clapping our hands or standing on one foot. I moved only my upper body, happy to simply stand there holding Micah's hand while the others touched their noses to the carpet.

Andy arrived soon after and caught my eye, gesturing from the stairs. I rose and was taking the handful of steps to meet him, when I felt a gush between my legs and thought, *Oh my God, my water* has *broken!* Scooting into a bedroom at the bottom of the stairs, I whispered, "Quick, get me a towel!" Andy tossed me a hand towel from the adjoining bathroom, and I stuffed it between my legs. Leaning forward, I pulled the front edge of the towel away, tentatively, expecting to see the telltale wetness of my baby's bathwater.

The white towel was bright red with blood.

Andy and I exchanged wide-eyed looks of panic. I managed to get off the bed and up the stairs without creating an incident, our crisis unfolding to the sweet voices of five-year-olds singing "Slow Poke Fred." Nobody missed a note as we made it out the door and into Andy's red Blazer, speeding off to the hospital while Andy phoned the doctor on his cell phone.

Inside, I was screaming, but "Hurry" was all I managed to say as I clenched my legs together, trying to seal my leaking cells, my fingers pressing firmly against my baby's life, now ebbing into a towel.

We arrived in about ten minutes—an eternity—and parked at the entrance. I was just starting to tell the admissions gal what was happening when I spotted our favorite nurse. "The Kittels are here," she sang with glee.

"Terri, I'm bleeding," I said, wiping the smile right off her face. She rushed me into the nearest room, handed me a Johnnie, and pushed me into the bathroom to change

I hope I haven't ruined Joanne's towel, I thought, pulling it from between my legs and tossing it in the sink. *What am I doing in here? Hurry, hurry, please God, hurry, hurry*, I chanted to myself, pulling the gown closed behind my back but not bothering to tie it.

"Get on the bed," Terri instructed. She climbed right up, kneeling over me and palpating my stomach while peppering me with so many questions. "How long have you been bleeding like this? How long has your tummy been hard like this? When was the last time you felt your baby move?"

"I don't know," I repeated. "I don't know. I don't know."

I didn't even know my tummy was hard. All I knew was that I was bleeding. A lot.

I couldn't think. I couldn't answer her questions. My mind spun away from my body in panic.

"How long has your tummy been hard like this? How long has it been hard?" she demanded over and over.

I kept saying, "I don't know I don't know I don't know." It was all happening so fast and yet so slow.

"When was the last time you felt your baby move?"

Finally my brain recognized a word.

"Baby?"

"When was the last time you felt the baby move?" Terri repeated, saying the magic word again: *baby*.

My mind snapped to attention, flashing to the night before, me reclining in my Lazy Girl chair, the three kids settling down, ready for bed. The baby was doing its nightly gymnastics inside of me, flipping around, throwing out a knee or elbow. We all felt my belly, laughing and playing with the pointy protrusions. Hannah said, "Mom, I think this is a heel!"

Christiana and Micah danced around until they each grew tired, leaning over to kiss both me and the baby's bumps. "Good night, baby. Good night, moon."

"When was the last time you felt your baby move?" Terri's voice interrupted my reverie.

My adrenaline-filled brain finally managed to stop the video filling its screen, directing my mouth to answer, "Last night?"

While I was busy with my flashback, an ultrasound technician had arrived by my side and hooked up her machine. She had a student shadowing her, who stood at the foot of my bed next to Andy. As her mentor set to work, she turned to Andy, smiling, and crooned, "Sooo, is this your first baby?"

Maybe I should have answered, explaining that no, in fact this was our fifth baby; we buried our fourth nine months ago.

But neither of us said a word.

The tech squirted her bluish gel and I felt the coldness spreading in concentric circles around my distended belly while she searched and searched with her ultrasound wand. I prayed it was a magic wand. She paused to turn the screen away from me, then continued examining my baby in its watery world, pushing harder to carve her pattern like an ice skater drawing compulsory circles around the frozen surface of my skin, but selfishly keeping her figure eights all to herself. I held my breath, waiting for her to exhale a sigh of relief. Waiting for her to say something. Her silence was deafening. I examined her face, her eyes, her hands, like it was my job, not hers, waiting for her to smile, begging her silently—keep looking, keep skating, don't stop. I beseeched God to get in here. Paging God to my room, *now*.

And I repeated over and over to myself, *This cannot be happening to me, this cannot be happening, this can not be…*

Silence filled the room.

No tiny foot kicked her magic wand away.

Nothing moved beneath the stretched skin and clenched fist of my belly, once so lovely to touch, now as hard as ice, an icy oligotrophic lake—nothing living in it.

I lay there, waiting. Waiting for the inevitable pronouncement. Slamming my ears shut and blocking them to keep my baby in the present tense.

Don't you say anything, don't you dare say a word, I warned everyone wordlessly while I waited impatiently for someone to do something. Whisk me off to surgery, cut me open, save my baby, take my life if you must, but *just do something!*

Instead, everyone seemed to move even slower, like we suddenly had all the time in the world. Slowly, slowly, they unplugged and wheeled their machines out of the room, asking no more questions, and leaving me lying there with my protruding belly exposed, a dead end covered in cold gel.

While I was holding Micah's hand, shuffling around in a circle, changing into my Johnnie, or trying to find answers for too many questions, my baby was dying. My baby had drowned.

Dr. H entered the room and dared to break the silence. Abruption, she'd explain later. For now, she kept it simple. "There's no heartbeat. There's nothing we can do."

I wanted to plug my ears like a child and scream to keep from hearing her terrible words. They had given up. But I hadn't. I was stubborn. I was desperate. I was Irish. But I didn't know how to save this baby. I didn't know what to do. My mind reeled: *No way, no way, no way, this can* not *be happening.*

"I'm so sorry," the doctor said.

I closed my eyes and thought, *Not again.*

Taken

Maria B. Olujic, PhD

Some names have been changed to protect the privacy of individuals.

*I*t's Wednesday. I am waiting alone in the Petrova Teaching Hospital in Zagreb, Croatia, while my husband is leisurely having a Turkish coffee across the street. The hallway with the flaking orangish fiberglass chairs serves as the waiting room. All the chairs are bolted to the wall and filled with ladies who are "inpatients," as well as people like me who are "outpatients." The inpatients are wearing hospital gowns of varying colors and shapes, with deep pockets that bulge with boxes of cigarettes and lighters. Some of them are chain-smoking, and all of us are waiting patiently for our turn with the ultrasound.

I notice a woman coming out of the ultrasound room wearing a flower robe and a radiant smile. "It's a boy!" she exclaims. "I guess she'll keep it," whispers a woman sitting next to me. Her statement reminds me of a colleague's work in demography and the "one child policy" in China. I ponder how technology has enabled women in the Third World to have selective abortions because they are carrying a daughter—ending a life is a lot easier when the desired gender is male. Even now, the summer of 1988—on the eve of the Yugoslav war—an ultrasound is used as a tool for selective abortion of unwanted female babies.

Finally, it's my turn. I am lying on the hospital table, and above my head large windows are covered with *cerada*, army green tarpaulin. The room is semi dark except for the monitor that is blinking a bluish-green light. There are several men and women in the room, all in white lab coats and white clogs. I later learned they were interns. Dr. Ferić slides his chair closer and applies cold gel to my lower abdomen and swipes the wand back and forth. He asks one of the interns to help him apply more gel. The pressure on my abdomen is hard as he swipes the wand sideways, up, and down. "Is the professor back?" he asks casually. This is an honorific reference to a physician, Professor Kuzmić, a leading gynecologist at the teaching hospital.

After fifteen minutes Professor Kuzmić walks in—the one who verified my pregnancy five months earlier. He looks at the monitor; at the same time Dr. Ferić shoots out a single word in English: "Without."

I look up at Dr. Ferić, trying to make sense of what he tried to say as Professor Kuzmić said emphatically, "It's okay, you can tell her. She understands because she speaks English."

"Without what?" I croak.

Dr. Kuzmić looks at me and asks, "Where is your husband?"

"In the coffee shop across the street," I reply.

"Let's go get him. I need both of you."

As we exit the old Petrova Hospital all the sounds are muffled and acrid diesel fumes engulf my nostrils. The sunlight feels opaque, as if there's an eclipse of the sun.

My husband is reading the *Slobodna Dalmacija* newspaper and sipping his coffee. When he sees us, he stands up in deference to Dr. Kuzmić, whose wiry figure towers slightly over my husband's six-foot-four frame as he asks, "Can you come with us?"

"Sure," my husband responds as he pulls out dinar notes to pay for the coffee. We go up two flights of stairs to a set of doors on the top floor of Petrova Hospital. "These must be doctor's quarters," I mutter to myself. I feel privileged that Kuzmić brought us here.

"The baby is without a neural tube on the very base of its skull, a small but critical anomaly. We will verify with other tests, such as alpha-fetoprotein to make sure."

"What does this mean?" I choke on the words.

"We are not sure yet, and we need to wait—"

I interrupt him. "But if the diagnosis is right, what then?"

"Then you will have to terminate the pregnancy. But no need to think of that right now," Kuzmić concludes.

It's Thursday now. The blood is drawn. "There is nothing for you to do since Monday is a national holiday, *Dan Borca* (Day of the Hero). We are closed to outpatients," Kuzmić reminded us. "So, it's best if you take a few days off and just relax until next Tuesday, when we will draw more blood to compare the alpha-fetoprotein levels. Do you have a place to go?" He knows that our village is in the Dalmatian hinterland three hundred miles from Zagreb.

"Yes, we planned to visit friends in Bosnia," I whisper.

As soon as we leave Dr. Kuzmić, my husband demands that we get a second opinion. The diagnosis is quickly confirmed.

"Let's go and talk to another physician; our child's life is on the line," he keeps saying. After two days we have four additional opinions.

It's Friday night in Brčko, Bosnia. With our hosts we are watching the annual Split Music Festival and the only televised event on the single Yugoslav channel. The winner is a young performer, an unknown Matko Jelavić, for his song, "Majko Stara," (Old Mother), which will become an iconic melody across Yugoslavia—reminiscent of Bosnian *sevdah* pathos blended with Dalmatian lament:

Old mother, listen to your son's song
Mother,
Who decided to take away my dearest?
No tears left to cry out my sorrow
Night is quiet, the sea is breathing peacefully

The weekend is spent in a blur of colors and emotions. Shots of *šljivovica*, a plum brandy, are taken before every meal "to open the appetite." Instead of opening my appetite, the brandy sears my innards, and I can barely taste it. The family we stay with gives us a tour of the villages near the River Sava. I feel my visit was an omen—in a short time the smell of smoldering fire and bullets will be echoing throughout the valley. Everything seems to happen too quickly. With each step the ground feels liquid. In me and all around me I can see the destruction about to erupt. My own tears of anguish will soon bathe my country with tears of war, and "ethnic cleansing" will become the norm.

It's Tuesday morning, and Dr. Kuzmić meets us at the door to Petrova Hospital. "The alpha-fetoprotein test verified the diagnosis. You will need to terminate the pregnancy, but we could still wait and do another ultrasound and one more blood test," he says.

"No need," I say. "Before the weekend I went to four more locations within Zagreb—a clinic, a private physician, and two other hospitals. They all confirmed the same diagnosis."

Kuzmić looks at me with a gaping mouth and finally utters, "That's quite incredible. We can induce an abortion this afternoon, but you will have to be admitted to the hospital for a few days."

Once I am admitted, my husband is told to stay at the front door—or the coffee shop across the street. No family is admitted into the ward.

I am in a room with three other woman, all three pregnant and well into their last trimester. They are "bed resting" in the hospital "to protect their pregnancy" during their last weeks. They look at me with pity. I look at them and at their swollen bellies with wariness. I roll on my side and curl up. I am given a concoction of medicine and Nurse Barbara tells me that, "Professor Kuzmić will stop by after his afternoon exams and rounds."

After a couple of hours the room begins to spin, and I feel separated from my body. I do not want to accept the fact that I am a person in this body. The spinning continues and after hours of asking for help, the Professor walks in, and I try to explain that something is wrong. He says, "Don't worry, that's the feeling of hallucinating when one takes narcotics."

The lights become fuzzy and blurry. I am wheeled into the adjoining room, an exam room of sorts. I see the Professor lift the lid from a steaming pot and grab worn-out rubber gloves that have been disinfected in hot water. My eyes close as his hands slip on the heavy latex.

Several hours later I wake up to hear the Professor's words to my husband. "It's too bad—it was a boy."

When Nurse Barbara returns I ask her if I can see the baby. She says, in a manner suggesting she has uttered these words a thousand times, "It's best that you don't see it. It's down there in the basement room with all the formaldehyde." I freeze and words lodge in my throat. The nurse looks down at me as if to decipher what the problem is. In an anguished voice I say, "But he's my son." I close my eyes, and everything becomes dull.

The Final Thread

Heather Lynne Davis

1. Going Under

Yesterday, during the ultrasound,
the doctor called it
fetal demise.

Today, these are
the last words I hear
before going under.

I know so many women who have
staggered through this loss.

I used to think how awful
to carry a fetus
dead
inside you
for hours, days, or even
weeks. How gruesome, how
wrong that must feel.

But now
I don't want to
let you go,

give you over
to the operating room, its machines,
this whiteness,
these lights, cold
containers, stainless
steel.

You are mine.
You are me.
We are

safe together.

When the D and C is over,
there'll be no trace,
nothing on heaven or earth
to show.

I want only to rise up
off this gurney and walk away,
take you with me
before the terrible
theft begins.

2. The Stain

Bright bright red in long rounded rivulets
divides the white of my thighs, surprises me because
there is no pain. I am standing
after the D and C, all miscarried
tissue gone. This is
the first rising, the first moment
upright in a flimsy gown, hidden
by pale blue curtains. A drop

falls, makes a crimson fractal
on the beige suede of my sandal.
I wipe my legs with the wet
paper towels they give me. I
stare at the blood on my shoe—
one drop on one shoe—
her blood, his blood, our blood,
the last blood.
I don't wipe it. I want to walk
with this touching my skin,
the final
thread between us.

I put my clothes back on.
I walk.

Rae of Hope

Tiffany Pitts

In memory of our sweet girl, Elliston Rae.

October 26, 2012. In one moment I inhaled the breath of a first-time mom, voided of any real sense of pain or loss, and exhaled the breath of a mother whose heart, dreams, and life has been ripped apart. In that moment I lost my daughter. In that moment I said good-bye to the self I had always known.

I had a normal pregnancy—just enough sickness to make me aware that we were still pregnant and successfully moving along through the first trimester. This was not my favorite part, although it calmed my anxiety over our miscarriage five months prior. At our thirteen-week ultrasound, we watched in amazement as this shockingly human-looking little baby jumped and turned and jumped some more. It was really happening! At our twenty-week ultrasound we confirmed our thoughts from the moment we found out we were pregnant—we were having a girl! A perfect, healthy, active little girl.

During my pregnancy, two people I knew had stillbirths. I had never heard of this before. Out of fear and out of ignorance, I did not reach out to them. At the time, I felt that any words I could muster up would be so insignificant. I would come to find out the only thing that comforted my husband and me was knowing that we were thought of. Knowing that someone shed a tear for us, for our situation, and for our perfect daughter who should not have died. And most of all, knowing that people were not afraid to say her name.

When I was thirty weeks, we surprised our family who had traveled into town for my shower by having an ultrasound done at our home. When the technician walked in the door my first words were, "Hi! Please check the cord. I just need to know that the cord is not around her neck." He was a bit taken aback. Probably not the greeting he was expecting. It took about forty-five minutes for our little girl to even look in our direction, but once she did, I was thinking more about her plump lips and nose than about asking more questions about the cord. I figured if there was a problem, he would let me or someone else know. Any fear I had carried up to that point was now gone.

At thirty-eight weeks, I went in for my weekly appointment. I told the doctor that I hadn't been feeling my baby girl move. She quickly checked me with the Doppler—without hesitation, loud and clear, there was the heartbeat: 151. Nice and strong as ever. We even had an ultrasound to determine just how big this not-so-little one would be. Nobody seemed worried about anything, so why should I worry?

But within twenty-four hours of leaving that appointment, things went terribly wrong, and I had no idea. The little person who was growing inside me, whose life was my responsibility, was taking her last breaths, and I was oblivious. I would like to say that the events of the next morning were a total blur, but that is not the case. I remember every detail. I remember walking into the hospital, in labor, thinking I would be holding my little girl in a few hours. That part was accurate. I just did not envision that I would be holding her, but she would not be alive.

As I write this almost a year later, I can still picture the faces of every nurse in my tiny room in triage. I remember the look they all passed around the room when they couldn't find our baby's heartbeat. I remember the exact moment of seeing our baby on ultrasound as her heart sat still. I suddenly forgot about the contractions, and what felt like morphine ran through my veins; my body, my mind, and my emotions went numb. Little did I know I would spend months in this numb state.

After eleven hours of enduring an epidural that never seemed to last very long, conversations I never imagined having, and decisions I don't wish on anyone, and pushing out a baby who will never experience any of the dreams we had for our new family, Elliston Rae Pitts was born at 10:06 p.m. As soon as she came out, I heard nothing but shock in the doctor's voice as she began counting the number of times she had to unwind the cord from around her neck. Seven times. Something she said she had never seen in her entire career and never even heard of. Along with the seven loops around her neck was a tight knot. Although I would give anything for none of this to have happened, I am glad we at least know what the problem was. After the cord was removed, we were handed the most beautiful baby girl–six pounds, nine ounces of pure perfection. Long toes, which did not come from me or my husband. Long fingernails already in need of a baby manicure. Lots of dark hair. My nose. My husband's ears. Lips so beautiful, they were made to be kissed.

As devastating as the day's events were, nothing was as painful as handing our baby over to a nurse and walking away. The baby I had carried for nine months. The baby my husband had dreamed of taking on daddy/daughter dates. The baby who opened our hearts up to a whole new level of love in a way only a child can. I put her in the arms of a stranger, and we left. I am still completely frozen in despair when I think about that moment. We walked through the same hospital doors that for nine months we had imagined walking through with our baby. Now, however, we were empty-handed.

I see pictures of myself from years, months, even days before we lost her, and feel as though I am looking at a different person. I see an innocence in my eyes that I will never have again. I think I am one of the few who does not find comfort in the phrase "Everything happens for a reason." I refuse to believe that this happened on purpose. Rather, my husband and I have committed to giving her life purpose. We will be better parents to our future children because of our sweet Elliston. We will enjoy life to the fullest because we know we are not guaranteed tomorrow. And we will not fear what lies ahead, because we have one spunky, beautiful girl waiting for us on the other side.

It's a crazy dance. I had a baby, who was more beautiful than I'd ever imagined. Even in her death, she brought us such joy. Balancing that with the hurt and the grief is complicated. It is a combination of feelings I never knew existed. However, somehow they can go hand in hand.

The Fire This Time

Adina Giannelli

You get to do intellectual work all day long, he says. His voice is jealous. *I am never alone in my thoughts.*

Well, you have your work and your other children, I say, *and I have graduate school and a computer.*

And I only have this time, I think to myself, *because Talya is not here.*

But I don't ever say these words aloud. I can't bring myself to say these words aloud.

Still, somehow, through the noise of his other children and my weeping and his rage, in spite of our sadness and our anger and ourselves, he hears me.

I know you'd give anything to have her here, he says. *We all would.*

We talk about her, sometimes, but these times are rare. More often, we say nothing at all. Silence is the hallmark of her absence, the truest feature of our presence. And the silence is impossible—cavernous, captivating, shocking.

I cannot retrieve our daughter, cannot will her tiny body back to life. Instead, I try to capture her father's feelings. I want him to talk to me about his grief, but he cannot. His refusal reverberates; it is an echo that affects my own mourning. Its effect is silence. And everybody knows: silence begets silence, itself a sort of death.

We cope in different ways, to the extent that we cope at all. I cry and rage and read and convince my advisor that I should write my thesis on parental response to infant death. He works and makes music and focuses on his other children.

It's not as hard for me, he says, *I have other children.*

It's worse for you, he says, *at least I have other children.*

I don't know what I'd do, he says, *if I didn't have other children.*

Fuck you, I think.

He doesn't like to talk about it. He is English, he is older, he has to hold it together, he says—for the sake of his other children.

I understand, I remark, my voice thick with irritation. *She did not matter to you as much as the girls do.*

Don't be snide, he says, but he does not deny it.

So I weep, and he snaps. I talk about Talya, all the time, to anyone who will listen and to many who won't. He keeps her to himself. I beg him to talk about his grief. *It's personal*, he says, *I don't want to share it with anyone, not even you.* I go to her burial site regularly; he will not return.

We don't know how to manage our grief; the best we can do is endure its jagged contours and pray that we won't do too much damage to each other and everyone else around us in the process.

I write, and write, and write, while he commits himself to the yard, where he builds a gorgeous garden shed out of pine. He affixes a wooden cutout of a broken heart to the shed's facade. The heart is painted red, and in the sunlight, it looks as if it's bleeding.

That was all about Talya, he explains, but I already know.

I am beside myself with sadness, crying in the car and in the bathroom and in my Sunday-morning yoga class. He does not cry—his grief manifests itself in other ways—in frustration, in anger, and in his ongoing work. Furious, he escapes further into physical labor, targeting the abandoned cabin at the edge of the property. With a smattering of tools and two strong hands, he tears down this hundred-year-old shack, ripping it down bit by bit, one board at a time.

And I realize: that was all about Talya, too.

I am not yet aware that I am pregnant with our second child, who will be a healthy, robust, spirited, and energetic boy that lives. I am not yet aware that he is involving himself with other women, *to cope*, he later explains, *because you are so sad all the time*. I am not yet aware that in time, I will fall deeply and headlong in love with another man—kind, generous, connected. But I am beginning to understand that our relationship is not going to survive this trauma; we will not be able to power on, to put the pieces back together in the aftermath of our terrible loss.

Really? I ask him, incredulous and indignant, when he tries to justify his affair. *Our daughter just died. I did not realize that this was supposed to be a happy time for us.*

But late at night, while I throw down words on my laptop, in the kitchen, aware that our relationship is disintegrating, he migrates from the backyard, where he gathers cabin wood, to the living room, where he tends the fire, and back again.

He chops the cabin's pieces into firewood, and burns them in the woodstove, night after long winter night, leaving a thick, stagnant smell that never goes away. Its efficiency appeals to him; that is its catharsis. He is breaking his grief into manageable bits, and making it disappear.

But for me, the cabin is not his grief, but our relationship in the face of our daughter's death. Where we once lit cordwood, what's between us is engulfed in flames.

And cabin wood is not like cordwood; it never lasts for long. The embers glow, radiating a low burn long after the flame goes out, but it is not real fire—it gives no heat. The fire needs constant refueling, or you have to start all over again. And we try to keep up. I used to be so good at lighting fires and keeping them alight. My hand was always steady, and I was right in time. I lost my skill the winter after Talya died, the winter of the cabin wood. For in that final season, almost every time I'm near the stove, I burn my hand. And when I lift the latch to add another slab of wood, I can see: it is too late. But for the embers, there is nothing left.

Early Second Trimester

Tiffany Johnson

You're past the twelve-week point of a typical miscarriage, yet not to the twenty-week "stillbirth" mark. Somewhere in between. No name for what you've experienced so they call you a miscarriage, but that word doesn't even begin to describe your loss. That word doesn't give credit to your baby's life. You're too early to have been able to feel your baby kick much. You missed that. Your OB will not consider this a stillbirth or include it as a "para" on your chart. It's your second delivery, but your chart will still say only one. If you didn't make it to twenty, it doesn't count. It didn't happen. The photographers will not come to you, even if you ask; your baby is too young and doesn't qualify. It would not be appropriate for you to have a funeral. People will tell you "at least you weren't very far along." Most will not want to see pictures of your baby because of her underdeveloped skin. You will keep them to yourself. Loving and missing your baby alone.

But your baby is fully formed and human, just a tinier version of all other babies who are recognized as stillborn. You go through labor and delivery and hold your baby. You name her and take pictures with your cell phone. You grieve like any other mom would grieve. You hurt the same and mourn the same. Brynn Erin Johnson lived for sixteen weeks before being strangled by her cord. She was a baby. Planned for, wanted, and loved. She was real, she was mine, and she is gone. She counts. My loss counts. Yours does too.

When Grace is Gone

Kerry Ann Morgan

*H*er name was Ava Grace, and she wasn't meant to be.

The name had yet to embellish embroidered pillows or baby books—it could have been Mia or Julia or even Jack—but from the moment I felt her blooming within me, I imagined her every detail. Her strawberry-blond pigtails bounced as she giggled at tickly belly kisses; a smattering of inevitable freckles danced across her nose; dimpled hands grasped a pink blanket, her fingers working the silky fabric as she drifted off to sleep. She was radiant…and she was mine.

My beloved Cabbage Patch Kids, vintage Barbies, and antique Betsy Wetsy doll decorated her nursery. Below her ruffled dress, Band-Aids plastered her constantly scraped knees, for after she spent hours lost in magical storybook worlds, she tore through our garden searching for fairies hidden amid the sunflower stalks and rose blooms.

She was real—the tangible, thriving child born of my dreams— then she was gone.

Three times I let her slip away. My body failed her. My love wasn't strong enough to bind her to me, to keep her alive. Somehow I just couldn't make her *be*. Though technically it was never my fault, and I did everything in my weak powers to hold on to her, my guilt is a scar that will never fade.

When you have one healthy, amazing child, no one understands that fortune may not fall upon you again. An uncomfortable shrug and downcast eyes became my only response to the constant barrage of questions about when we were going to provide our son with a sibling. Losses were brushed aside as savage words bit to the bitter core. *You already have one kid—there's no reason you can't have more. It's just not in God's plan right now. There must have been something wrong with it. You don't need another mouth to feed, do you? It's for the best. God will give you another baby when you are ready. It happened early, so it's not a big deal. It's not like it was a "real" baby you had held or anything.*

The wait consumed me each month. Days ticked by in a blur as I obsessed about recreating her, dreaming I was worthy of breathing life into her tiny cells. Fertility drugs sent me teetering to the edge. Prayers went unanswered. What little faith I once held was washed away in a tide of blood.

While I lamented the child denied to me, I neglected the son that lived. Twice I'd hugged him and lied about my nasty tummy aches the doctors had healed, but he'd seemed to know, as if he'd seen a light, a life, flicker out in me. He'd remained my slight shadow ever since, protective yet wary.

Constant failure beat me down until I could no longer withstand the jabs of frustration, the gut-punches of heartbreak and grief. I finally broke. A dull husk shivering on the bathroom floor was all that remained. I surrendered while my shattered spirit still had a chance to piece itself back together.

Life goes on, forever fluid as a river, at times flooding my heart with joy, yet occasionally receding, leaving me brittle and barren. There will always be a lingering part of my soul adrift. A glimpse of a shy smile on a young girl in a crowd, graceful laughter carried on the breeze—that could have been her.

In time, I chose to declare peace with the past so I could embrace my family's future. I chose to find grace in the bounty of beautiful moments life granted me instead of bemoaning what had been denied. Though our threesome may not be all I'd once longed for, it is now complete, and it is enough.

Her name was Ava Grace, and her soul was not meant for this world.

Dear Little Mizuko Bean
Lauren Vasil

Dear Little Mizuko Bean,

Twice as much time has passed since you stopped growing as you ever lived. I'm learning to live with the void you left.

I had a feeling I was going to get pregnant in January. Then, three days after you were conceived, I was sitting at my computer drinking my afternoon cup of tea and smelled Old Spice aftershave—the kind my grandfather used to wear. And I heard his voice say quietly in my ear, *"It's a boy."* Was it his ghost or my body giving me a message? No matter, you somehow shyly announced yourself.

Ten days later, I enjoyed a margarita with dinner. I told S., your dad, that if my temperature was still high the next morning, I was going to take a pregnancy test. I ordered the best tequila and savored my margarita, figuring it might be the last time I enjoyed a cocktail for a while.

Twelve hours later, you boldly announced yourself with two pink lines. I had long-imagined this moment, and had pictured whooping and happy tears. Instead, my knees knocked and my hands trembled. *I'm pregnant.* Did I dare say the words aloud? *I'm pregnant.* S. took a deep breath and said, *"I knew it."* He sounded more stressed than happy. I felt more stressed than happy. When those two pink lines appeared, our lives changed forever. I put the test in my desk drawer but kept taking it out again to hold it, look at it, marvel, and let the proof sink in that I was pregnant.

Pregnant. *What kind of mother would I be?* We sat down to our favorite lunch, a simple meal of bread, cheese, fruit, and homemade habanero-peach jam. I barely tasted it. *Pregnant.* I tested the word out, feeling my lips, breath, throat, tongue, and teeth form the word. *Puh-RE-GUH-nunt.* It seemed foreign. Did it really describe *me*? I looked at the test in my hand. Yes it did. The next morning, another test revealed a slightly darker second pink line. A third consecutive morning, a third set of double lines. The tests lay side by side in my drawer. I looked at them affectionately and placed my hand over my flat belly. There was life in there. I could feel it.

The changes in my body were almost immediate. Tired all the time. Hungry all the time. Thirsty all the time. I couldn't make it through the night without getting up at least once to pee. My boobs became sore to the touch and swelled a full cup size. I timidly entered a maternity store to pick out a new bra. I was pink with pleasure when I was asked how far along I was. *"Five weeks and two days,"* I said, and grinned shyly. *I was overcome with happiness. To celebrate,* I thought about buying myself a top or a tunic to accommodate my extreme bloating and hide the hair band I was using to fasten my jeans. I was tempted, but didn't want to invite bad luck. As I waited at the checkout counter to pay for my new bra, a pull-on foxy little black lace number, I admired the blonde ahead of me who was about five months pregnant. *Now I, too, am part of this club.*

I don't recall feeling happier in my life than when I was pregnant with you, Bean. I made lifestyle choices that would be considered sacrifices by some, but for me it was a delight to forgo coffee, deli meats, soft cheese, and alcohol. I never paid more attention to what I put in my body or on it. I checked myself out in the mirror: my thighs were rounder, my belly fuller, and my breasts heavier. I gained ten pounds, and wondered if my usually fast metabolism would be permanently slower, if I would lose my figure—but I didn't mind too much. You were coming.

You were coming. We began to share the news of you. When I think back to our friends' and families' delighted reactions, there is a tug at my heartstrings.

You were coming, and S. began to get really into the idea. He started touching my belly and referring to you as "the baby." He was so protective of me, anxious to minimize any stress, because "it's not *good for the baby.*" I caught a glimpse of the terrific dad I hope he'll someday be, and I miss it so much. I miss you so much.

You were coming. Every day, I was aware of minor cramps that felt like stretching, pulling, and tugging. With my hand over my swelling belly, I began talking to you first thing in the morning, last thing at night, and in quiet moments in between: *"Grow, little bean. Grow strong, grow beautiful. Grow."* I pictured myself in silhouette: a woman in profile, with bent neck, lovingly cradling her belly, which radiated light.

And then your light went out.

After weeks of a flurry of activity, it slowed down, and came to a grinding halt. My belly felt dark and lifeless. I googled my absence of symptoms, to no avail. I posted on Reddit. I called the nurse at the clinic where I wouldn't have my first ultrasound for another three weeks. Everyone agreed that a *lack* of symptoms was nothing to be concerned about. I put it down to first trimester nerves and reminded myself that now came a lifetime of worry. I still had some signs of pregnancy, so I wasn't too concerned that I didn't have morning sickness—after all, my mother didn't until about week eight or nine, she said when I casually asked. But your light had gone out. Deep down, I knew it. I was reluctant to say *I'm pregnant*. When I did, I felt sheepish. I didn't *feel* pregnant. I felt like a fraud.

The day of the first ultrasound came. I noticed my boobs were no longer sore. I was dreading the appointment. I joked with the receptionist about finding out one way or another. Part of me couldn't believe that I would fall headlong into an unfortunate statistic. After all, what were the chances? Besides, I did everything right. I ate well and took care of myself. I thought positive thoughts. I radiated happiness, felt stress-free, loved the world and everyone in it. I instinctively knew you were there from the moment you burrowed into me. I loved you. YOU ARE COMING…aren't you?

After cheery (and, as it turned out, ill-timed) congratulations from the nurse practitioner, the ultrasound began. It was like in a movie where a character picks up the receiver and tries to listen for any sign of life at the other end of the phone. *"Hello?"* they say over the crackle. *"Hello? Anybody there? Hello? Hello?"* There is no answer, only static. *"Pick up!"* I begged. When I found out you had stopped growing on the day I began to worry something was wrong, my heart stood still and I felt the blood drain from my face. The most powerful call of my life has been put on hold.

These days, I see the things I will never share with you. Two weeks ago, I was riding in a forest. It was so green. I thought of you—that you would never see color and be so moved by nature. My horse reared up, and I thought of you—that you would never know fear or discomfort. We ambled along a muddy path on a hill past a doe standing nervously and protectively over her hour-old fawn. Something of her wide-eyed and alert watchfulness, assessing if our slow parade of horses was a threat, reminded me of myself. In some small way, I envied her new motherhood.

Instead of looking forward to meeting you sometime in October, I am trying to move forward with the greatest loss of my life. I have never known such visceral grief. I am wrestling with complex pain that ripples into difficult feelings that affect every moment. I don't know what lessons I can learn from losing you, but I'm determined to not let your loss be in vain.

You were conceived six months ago today, but you are not here. Since losing you I have felt that getting pregnant again would be the final piece in the puzzle to mend my broken heart. I wonder if I am pregnant again: my boobs are tender, and there has been a strange pulsing below my navel. Are you quietly announcing yourself again or is it the most magical thinking? I study my face in the mirror and my intense gaze is returned. I wonder if I look changed, if others notice a perceptible difference in me. Are those the eyes of a woman who miscarried? Do they reflect a small hope returning? Or is life dancing quietly behind them?

Loving Grace
Star and Judi Corvinelli

The End

Dafna Michaelson Jenet

I changed. In the moment I noticed that my baby's heart was not beating on the ultrasound screen. When the words that now play over and over again in my head in slow motion—"I'm so sorry, that's the heart, and there is no heartbeat"—reached my ears, I changed. A part of me died in that moment too.

I lay there in shock. I was confused. I didn't know the script, but I knew that I didn't know my lines. What was going to happen next? What was I supposed to do? I had a dead baby inside of me. I asked my husband, "What do we do?" And while trying to comfort himself and me, he also tried to keep me calm. "We'll ask the doctor when she comes in."

We waited for what seemed an eternity. In hindsight we understand we were close enough to the office closing for lunch and the staff wanted to give us as much time as we needed and dignity to leave without having to pass a waiting room full of healthy happy pregnant women. When she came in and I asked what comes next, she told me about the clinic they send women to who are in my situation. She gave me the name of the doctor and his number written on a prescription pad. She hugged me and asked to see me two weeks after the procedure.

I don't know what I expected. It had only been two hours since we'd heard the news. But I called the number. I sobbed to the woman who answered the phone. She suggested I call back later. That put me off a bit, but really, I was incoherent. I pulled myself together and said, "No, I need to get this scheduled now." I explained that my baby had died and I needed a D and C. She scheduled me for the next morning.

My head was spinning. I did not know how to behave. I did not know how to feel. I knew I felt awful. I knew I felt robbed. I knew I was still in shock. I also knew that I wanted to bury my baby. I did not know how to do anything. I reached out to my rabbi, and he gave me the name of someone to contact. He was a close friend, which made it a little easier. I could not speak on the phone—I was not ready to hear the voice of another; in truth, I am still not ready—so I sent him a message on Facebook. It was already late at night.

The next morning we went to the clinic. I began bleeding on the way. By the time we got there, I was in shock.

Now, I beg you to not politicize the sentiments I am about to share with you. This is not intended to be political or to reflect my beliefs about any form of medical practice.

We entered the clinic, where there were two young women behind a glass partition. I told them who I was, and they asked for $545. It would not be put on my insurance. I questioned them further. "It's a termination, so that is not covered by insurance." I was confused, and angry—this was no termination, had they not heard me? "My baby died." I repeated firmly. I could see that my husband was confused and did not know how to protect me or how to help—and let's not forget, his baby died too. The woman in the back of the room stood up and came to the window. "If you want to use your insurance, you have to go to the emergency room. I'm not sure if they will help you, though." I was confused, and hurting, and bleeding. Why would she send me away? Why would I go to the emergency room and sit there just to be sent home? Why were they being so crass? I knew I did not want to leave. I also did not want to stay. I also did not want my dead baby inside of me for one more minute. I wanted my live baby back.

As we sat and waited, all I could think about was that I had not arranged a burial and I did not know what to do about that. When they called me back and I asked to have my husband come with me,

I could tell that I had made an unusual request. This confused me further, but by this point, after signing all the paperwork, it finally hit me. This was an abortion clinic. Yes, they also perform D and C for fetal demise, but ours was the rare case.

My husband came back, and they began to prep me. The room was spartan. The equipment seemed old. I started to have nightmares about rusty needles. I could see that everything was wrapped and clean, as it should have been, but I still felt awful.

They pulled out a small ultrasound machine. They were looking at the baby. They kept the screen turned away from me. I really wanted to see my Peanut one more time, but I was too afraid to ask. This becomes a theme for me…When they asked Michael to leave me so they could start the procedure, I asked, "What will you do with the baby?" A nurse responded quickly, "It will all be incinerated."

My mind went blank and then I got scared. Incinerated? I did not want my baby incinerated. I wanted my baby buried. Well, I did not want that either; I just wanted my baby to be alive and healthy. Once more I failed myself and Peanut as I said nothing.

As I was waking from the procedure, I asked the nurse, "Was the baby formed?" She said no, but I still think she was lying. I asked a second nurse—I think it was a second nurse; I was still very foggy— "Was the baby formed?" She too said no.

I did not have any strength. They helped me to the recovery chairs. A room of five recliners. Five recliners? I could not imagine having to recover with five other women around me. Fortunately there were none. I asked for my husband, and when he arrived all I could say was "no more Peanut." Even then I could not ask him to help me find the baby and get him buried.

I still panic thinking of my poor baby in an incinerator, and knowing I put him there because I did not have the strength to ask for a burial. I had so few tasks here on earth for Peanut, and I could not complete this most basic and most important one. I could not give him a respectful end. I sent him to the incinerator.

I have nightmares. They happen while I am awake or asleep. They happen when I am alone. I wish I had known what to do. How to handle myself. What to say to get help and to get the dignified end I wanted for a too-short life. But who wants to be prepared for that? We make birth plans when we are pregnant, not funeral plans. I will be giving this to my obstetrician, a truly wonderful woman, in the hopes that something can be done to make the process one that provides dignity to the mom, respect to the dad, and closure for the spirit of a baby they'll never get to meet. I want to say rest in peace to my little Peanut, but I fear I did not provide him with such an end.

Spring Baby

Monica Wesolowska

Spring is the hardest. April 27 to June 4. Every year, I spend those days in vague dread over an end we have already lived through. Even as the thirty-eight days of Silvan's life shrink proportionally against the growing of my subsequent children—soon Miles and Ivan are one and three, then two and four—I spend those six weeks each year waiting for the end. In the pregnant bellies of passing women, I catch glimpses of him. Holding others' newborns, I smell him. In every stranger's six-week-old, I lose Silvan all over again.

On one of those spring days—a lovely, balmy one—I'm sitting on a park bench, chatting with the other parents, when I notice Miles lying splayed on the sand, unblinking, staring straight up. Perhaps he is dead. A dead child is not something I have to imagine. My heart beats wildly. Perhaps, I tell myself, trying to stay calm, he's merely playing dead to get my attention, to see how I will love him if he dies as his brother did. Suddenly, I am alone, no other parents near, though they sit beside me on the bench. "Miles," I say with quiet urgency. "Stop it."

To my great relief, he's alive. To my greater relief, he listens. He gets up and returns to activities that bother me less but probably bother the other parents more—throwing rocks, balancing large plastic toys on the tops of the monkey bars below which Ivan and the other younger children play. Like any parent, I worry about my children dying. Like most parents, I try to live as though they won't.

As the work of having young children eases slightly, as dinner becomes somewhat civilized again, David and I begin to look for rituals to bind us as a family. We start by lighting candles every Friday night. This is not about a god so much as it is about pausing to be grateful. How grateful we are for our children. How hard it is to pass that gratitude on. Usually we're tired on Friday nights, and the children wiggle and giggle until we yell at them to stop, but surely they can find something to be grateful for. We make suggestions. David suggests they feel grateful for the meal I've cooked. I suggest they feel grateful for having food at all. This gives them pause, as it should. For they know about death. They have seen dead flies and snails; they know that their older brother is gone.

Their questions start early, startling me.

"What if Silvan were in this box?" Miles asks one day as he's opening a present.

"Why would he be in a box?" I ask.

"Wouldn't you like that?" he asks.

A few years later, Ivan pipes up from the backseat of the car. "What if Silvan comes back to life? Would you like that?"

"People don't come back to life," I tell him.

"Maybe," he says.

"Maybe," I concede because it's true; I don't know what's possible.

In dance class, I'm stunned one evening by a vision of Silvan and me and centuries of dead, pressed up against each other in the dark, at the edge of an underground stream. Since losing Silvan, I don't know if I believe in souls that way anymore, but I am in awe of all that a mind can contain, more than we will ever know.

If I could, I would hold Silvan again.

But for now, I have only his ashes in a vase in the living room—after scattering a few on the trail where once I imagined his conception, I couldn't let the rest go. And in a drawer, his pale-blue terry-cloth pajamas. And I have his bench in the backyard. Every year on his birthday, we sit on it as a family. It's a child-sized wooden bench with a plaque attached to the back engraved with his dates and a quote from his song, the one we used to sing to him. "You'll never know dear," the bench says, "how much we love you..."

Over time, the bench becomes hidden.

To find it now, you have to cross to a back corner of the yard, walk up three little stairs of stone, and duck beneath the drooping flowers of an angel trumpet. That was our idea, a place to find if you make the effort. A place to sit and love him.

Often it is other people's children who find it first. They lead their unsuspecting parents there. When the adults reemerge from under the plants, I wait to see if they will say something.

Some do, some don't.

And then one day, I find I can forgive those who don't ask. Not everyone has to know.

Sometimes even I forget, if only for an hour.

One April, a friend tells me, "I had my Silvan dream again last night. I always dream about him this time of year. Is it okay I told you that?"

Yes, of course, I say.

Another April, I run into Silvan's neonatologist, the one who gave us the news about Silvan's brain damage, the one who told us we could let Silvan die, if we thought this was the best way to love him. He lives in our neighborhood. "Wasn't it Silvan's birthday yesterday?" he asks.

Yes, I say, yes.

Every birthday, David's sister makes a donation to children's hospice in his memory; and David's stepmother calls to thank us for being brave enough to have more children. At my brother's house,

I see Silvan's picture. At my obstetrician's office, too. There he is, golden among a swirl of babies.

If there is a miracle to this story beyond Miles and Ivan, it is that Silvan is remembered. Not by everyone, but by enough. He is my boy, so specifically mine; but in death he can belong to anyone who wants him.

Excerpt adapted from *Holding Silvan: A Brief Life (Portland: Hawthorne Books, 2013).*

Firstborn

Barbara Crooker

The sun came up, as it always does,
the next morning, its pale gold yolk
bleeding into the white room.
I remember how cold I was,
and how young, so thin,
my wedding ring rattled
on my finger. How the tea
the nurse brought
broke in waves on the rim
of the cup, spilled over
in the saucer; how nothing
could contain my tears.
Three days later, I left
in a wheelchair,
with nothing in my arms.
The center of this gold ring
is a zero. The horizon,
where the sun broke through,
is no longer a straight line,
but a circle. It all comes back
to you.

First published in *More* (C&R Press, 2010).

Space Within My Heart

Karin Morea

I'm a perfectionist, a planner, an organizer. I am patient. I patiently waited through five years of marriage—planning, organizing, making sure everything was perfect for the arrival of our first baby. Our son, Bennett, was born two days before his due date on September 10, 2012 after a seemingly healthy pregnancy and labor. He slid into the world at 8:18 p.m., and the doctor held his perfect, beautiful body up for me to see. It was the most anticipated moment of my life, and I knew in an instance, it would forever be the most painful. Having the best and worst moment of your life share the same space within your heart is indescribable, and my mind wasn't prepared.

As I look toward my son, the only thing I focus on are his eyes, his closed eyes. He isn't moving; he isn't breathing. The reality of this moment is that nurses and doctors are running in and out of the room trying to resuscitate my son, my doctor is delivering the placenta, and my husband is crying, but in my memory, this moment is silent. I'm not moving, not screaming or crying, and I'm fairly certain I'm not breathing. I don't remember much of the following moments, hours, and days, but I know at some point my husband asks me to blink, and I do.

The NICU doctor who has taken my son out of my room returns to tell me he doesn't know why, but my son is not likely to live much longer, and I need to come see him. I don't hear him. I already know this—I knew it the moment I saw his closed eyes. I speak for the first time since his birth. I find the doctor's face and say, "I killed my son."

He shakes his head. He's crying. He tries to tell me that's not what he is saying, but he has to leave the room, as he can't control his emotions.

I am taken to see my son. I'm wheeled up next to him. He's covered in wires and connected to machines, and I ask the nurse how long he will live. When Bennett hears my voice he wakes up and searches for me with his eyes, unable to move his body, trying to find the only voice he knows. I stand, look into his dark-blue eyes, and tell him how sorry I am.

I'm taken back to my room to face the worst night of my life. My husband holds me as I cry, surrounded by the sound of healthy babies being born, endless crying that goes on throughout the night. I rattle off a list of demands to my husband that make no sense— we're moving, I'm never going back to work, I don't want to see any of our friends and family again. He doesn't bother trying to reason with me; he lets me believe that if I can leave everything I've ever known, I can leave my baby behind as well.

The next day we hold our son and listen to test results confirm that although there is no known reason at this time, our son can't and won't ever breathe on his own. We now face the decision of when to remove life support. We wait until our mothers arrive from out of town to spend a few minutes with our son, then we prepare to say good-bye. Thirty hours after entering this world, at 2 a.m. the morning of September 12, he is placed in my arms for the last time. When the breathing tube is removed he wakes up, looking into my eyes, asking me why he can't breathe. I don't have an answer. I try to comfort him and make a memory of this moment—I know it isn't going to last long and within seconds, his eyes close. His heart beats longer than expected and then he's gone and taken from us, forever.

We arrived at the hospital only two days earlier with our son; now we are leaving without him. So little time has passed in the world yet our lives have been changed forever. We drive home in the middle of the night, the car seat empty. It has been in the car for weeks but now feels so much more present.

I stay in a state of shock for weeks, my body slowly letting me come to terms with the death of my baby. Because Bennett's body looked so perfect, I have panic attacks that I killed him—he was healthy and I just hadn't given him enough time. I stare at pictures of us I don't remember taking, trying to piece time together. I make my husband tell me over and over again what he remembers. My husband asks the NICU doctor to walk me through all the tests again when he realizes he is getting nowhere with me.

My strongest emotion is guilt. I can't overcome it. I must have done something wrong. He was in my body. He was my responsibility. I keep a running list—I exercised too hard, I swam in the lake, I traveled too much. I am aware of the absurdity of these thoughts. I would never allow another woman to think she had caused the death of her baby, but I can't control them.

I start to measure a successful day by if I'm able to get out of bed, take a shower, cook a meal. I try to pull the car into the garage, but I don't know the gas from the brake so I just cry and leave it there. I stare at the microwave not knowing how long to cook the food before giving up and walking away. I make it through the doors of the grocery store and turn to leave. My anxiety makes it hard to leave the house, as everything is overwhelming—the cars, the noises, the bright lights. I want to wear a sign that says "my baby died" so everyone knows what I am feeling. I question if I will ever again be a functioning member of society.

Being a first-time mother, I also have no idea that the love for your child, whether he lives or dies, continues to get stronger over time. I long for my son with an intensity I have never felt before. My arms physically ache to hold him, a sensation that makes me feel crazy. My love for him grows every day and with that comes more pain. The reality of everything we had lost becomes more and more real to me. I am grieving for so many things at the same time it's overwhelming. I grieve my loss, Bennett's loss, my husband's loss, and possibly the loss of future children. I spend weeks doing nothing but grieving, letting my emotions come and go like waves, experiencing and surviving each one.

Then one day without thinking about it, I turn on the TV. I not only shower but I dry my hair. I buy a little pumpkin and place it next to Bennett's urn. I go back to work. I feel myself starting to return to a world I no longer recognize but must live in.

A moment doesn't go by when I don't think of our son, of our loss, but I learn to live with this sadness. It helps us to talk about Bennett, so we go back to the same conversations we had before he was born, wondering what our son would be like. Despite our grief we are grateful for the moments we had with him, that we know he looked like my husband and that he was able to see us, hear us, and feel our touch.

Two months after Bennett's death, the autopsy report shows that he died from a genetic disease of which my husband and I are both carriers. It is the leading genetic cause of death in infants. There is no cure. It is estimated that one in forty people are carriers. A disease we had never heard of is now all we know.

Brayden William Porter

Jaimie Porter

"*I* knew it." I grinned at Tom after we found out we were having a boy at my twenty-week ultrasound. Upon leaving my obstetrician's office with the news, I joyfully began planning for my son's arrival. One month before his due date, we were ready. His nursery was decorated, his clothes were washed and put away, and his tiny diapers were piled high on the changing table. We just needed our baby.

On January 30, our moms and my sister-in-law huddled around Tom and me at my thirty-six-week ultrasound appointment. Overwhelming excitement filled the room as the image of our baby appeared—his hands, his feet, his profile. I thought I was going to burst. With our baby's picture in our hands, Tom and I then moved into another room to talk to Dr. Sullivan. Simply routine.

His face told us otherwise. "There is a problem with the baby," he stated matter-of-factly as he sat down on a stool. "Your son has fluid around his brain." In our baby's case, the condition, hydrocephalus, was most likely "not conducive to life." I'll never forget those words. Tom and I stared at each other in utter disbelief. As we sobbed, the doctor asked if we wanted our family to come in.

"There's a problem with the baby," I managed to say as they came through the door.

Dazed and numb, we left the office out a side door. Once home, we had to make the tearful phone calls to the rest of our family. With each retelling, I thought, "This can't be true. This can't be happening to us." For hours I scoured the Internet to find out whatever I could about hydrocephalus. Devastated, thoughts of long-term care and unending complications haunted me as I tried to sleep.

The next day I had a Level 2 ultrasound, and the news just got worse. Our baby definitely had fluid around his brain in addition to other abnormalities. Even more afraid for our son, we were then sent to Cincinnati Children's Hospital Fetal Care Center for an MRI and several other tests. Exhausted, we went home and waited for the results. And waited. And waited. A full week later, the longest week of our lives, we sat in a conference room surrounded by doctors and our family. The neurologist spoke first. His words were terrifying. Our baby did not have hydrocephalus; in fact, he had very little brain tissue. If he lived past birth, he would have no brain activity. He would be deaf and blind and would eat and breathe through a tube. This treasured baby, whose heart was beating below mine, was not going to survive. How would I survive? I found myself wishing and praying for the original diagnosis of hydrocephalus. Even though he would endure hardships, we would still have our beloved baby to hold. A selfish thought.

We had so many questions, some of which were answered when we met our genetic counselor. She explained that our baby's case had been shown to doctors all over Cincinnati. Although each was familiar with our son's problems, none had seen them all occur in one baby. The doctors were doubtful that the cause was genetic, which somewhat eased our concerns about a future pregnancy, but they could not rule it out. Together we decided we did not want an autopsy performed, since the results may not be conclusive.

During this time I didn't want to leave the house. Everywhere I went, well-meaning people would see me, very pregnant, and would start asking questions. Is this your first child? When are you due? Are you having a boy or a girl? I was not ready to tell our story; I just wanted to hide at home.

Two weeks before my due date, instead of being in heaven, I was in pure hell. Instead of choosing the clothes my child would wear for his trip home from the hospital, I was choosing the clothes he would wear for his funeral. We had decided on cremation for our son but not until after a viewing and memorial service. Our baby deserved to be celebrated.

We went to the hospital at 6 p.m. on February 25, one day before my due date. We weren't sure if our son would be alive when he was born, and if he were, how long he would be with us. Fortunately, we had a compassionate nurse, who held my hand and shared the loss of her own child. As painful as the situation was, it was comforting to have someone by our side who knew exactly what we were going through. I will never forget her.

My labor progressed normally, and with friends and family waiting for him, our son, Brayden William, was born on February 26, 2008, at 5:57 p.m. Through tears and smiles, we all held him close, felt his heart beat, felt his breath on our skin. People filled the room; this was our chance to share our beautiful baby boy with those we loved. At 3:20 a.m., February 27, Brayden William gained his angel wings as his grandmother held him. My mother's voice softly woke me as she gently placed him in my arms. I thought my life had ended, too, as those we loved held him and said good-bye, but I was thankful for the nine and a half hours we had had with him.

We would never be ready, but at some point we knew we were going to have to let Brayden go. When that moment arrived, I had been promised that I would be putting my son into the arms of one of our nurses rather than a stranger from the funeral home. However, there was a horrible miscommunication. I will never forget the moment when a man dressed in a dark suit walked into my hospital room and introduced himself as funeral home staff. I froze. I simply could not give Brayden to this stranger, knowing I would never hold him again. As I bawled my eyes out, I reluctantly placed him in my dad's arms. He then turned and tearfully did for us what we were not capable of doing ourselves.

I was released from the hospital that morning. The same nurse who had held my hand made sure that I had not been moved from labor and delivery, so I was not wheeled past all the new mothers with their healthy babies. Because of her, I also took with me Brayden's footprints and a lock of his hair. I walked into the house without my child, past his closed door, and into my bedroom. Mercifully, I fell asleep.

The days preceding the funeral were a blur, as was the funeral itself. I do remember being touched by the streams of people who came. I was exhausted, but I was so grateful for their support I hugged everyone in line. I was especially touched when my obstetrician, Dr. Sullivan, walked through the door. He had been there for the beginning of our journey with Brayden and he was there now, at the end. From him and others I took strength that I no longer had. During the service, Tom and I sat gazing at our son, who was wrapped in blanket and laid out in a bassinette, and my eyes filled with tears as "Amazing Grace" softly played. I will see my son every time I hear that hymn.

Afterward, surrounded by our family and friends, I just sat there thinking, "How can we just walk away and leave our baby boy behind? What are we supposed to do now?" It was then that everyone left the room, and Tom and I were alone with our son for the last time. Before we rejoined our friends and family, Tom held my hand and said quietly, "We have been through the worst together. Whatever comes in the future, we will handle it together."

After the funeral, life went on...for everyone else. I just stared at the walls for weeks. When Brayden's death certificate arrived before his birth certificate, I crumbled. However, Tom's words when we were alone with Brayden at the funeral home sustained me on my darkest days, days when I had thoughts of ending my own life. When I forced myself to get out of the house, telling our story to anyone who asked helped us both to heal, and his story touched everyone who heard it. Brayden changed not only our lives, but also the lives of others.

Life did go on. When Brayden died, we closed the door to his room, thinking we would never be able to open it again. But that door, along with our hearts, soon opened to welcome our daughter, Emma, and were never closed again.

My Daughter

Brandon Bodnar

In memory of Ada MaryJo Bodnar, born still on June 30, 2013.

The doctor places you gently in my cradled arms.
I close my eyes and dream of another world, another life.

I take you home and lay you in your crib.
I wrap the blanket around your tiny frame.
I stare at my smile reflecting in your eyes.
You smile back and laugh with innocence.

Your first steps, first words, first thoughts.
You tell me all about your first day of school.
You tell me all about your first childhood crush.
I take it all in, relearning my world through you.

You leave home for college, bound to fix this world.
You call home, joyfully professing to have found love.
You dance gracefully, as I clumsily step on your gown.
You place my grandchild gently in my cradled arms.

I open my eyes, and you are still there.
I hand you to the doctor, and dry my tears.
I held you but for a moment of eternity.
My Daughter, good-bye.

Our Bloody Secrets

Susan Rukeyser

I remember how it was. Every month, the blood. Usually met with indifference, occasionally relief. For women, just the way it is. We don't talk about it much, but blood unites us.

I remember how it was, when I was pregnant. I was older this time, my son already eight and eager for a sibling. (With him, I bloomed with happy pregnancy. I delivered without drugs. I felt invincible. I thought, *I should do this for other women. Be a surrogate for those who want babies, but month after month see nothing but blood.*)

I remember how it was, when blood came when it shouldn't. In week ten, the embryo becomes a fetus. It looks like a comma: big head, a curve of body. Just over an inch long, the size of a kumquat. If it's wished-for, it's a baby.

First, just a hint. Then undeniable pink. Loathsome red. I staggered to the bathroom, all of me pouring out.

I lowered myself to the tile, afraid of how much would come. I affixed one pad to another. I scrubbed at a drop on my sock, making it worse.

"By the time you see blood, it's too late," a nurse later told me.

My son, the child who lived, grew from kumquat to avocado to butternut squash. Then he slipped from me, not a day too soon, ready for the world.

One morning before kindergarten, we buried his tadpole in a grassy hill behind our house. His baby frog, dead too soon. It dissolved into dirt, reduced to fluid and thin tissue that clung to the surface. Some life isn't meant to last.

We called the doctor's office; the nurse said to come in. She emphasized: "This happens more often than people realize." Women are united by their secrets, too.

"You may need a D and C," she said. "There's a risk of infection, serious bleeding."

I winced at "serious."

"You'll need a shot, if you're Rh negative, and the baby was—"

"Was?" I asked, but she pretended not to hear.

In the doctor's waiting room, I was surrounded by bellies swollen with success. Beige walls pressed in, reflecting too much light. I was bent with surging waves of pain like labor, or almost. My husband asked the receptionist, again, if I could wait somewhere else. He was told, again: No. Mothers-to-be glanced sideways at my sweatpants, my puffy eyes, and unbrushed hair. They knew. I was humiliated, but sorry, too, for the bad omen I was. *Don't look*, I whispered into patterned carpet.

"Deceased for days, probably," announced the doctor. My body, bare and empty, shivered beneath a paper gown. He said I should've brought the expelled material. Sometimes it offers an explanation. They run tests. I didn't have anything to give him, but if I did I wouldn't tell.

Back home, I avoided the bathroom. My grief lived in the grout between tiles, in the toilet. I should have thrust my fingers into blood, in case there was something to retrieve. I should have tried to find something to bury in dirt, like the tadpole reduced to fluid and thin tissue.

For days life drained from me. I collapsed to soggy rubble. "What kind of a mother?" I whispered, too many times. My eight-year-old didn't know. He went to school. My husband went to work. They went out among the living. I was glad to be spared my son's questions. I had no answers, only guilt.

Choice is power. I've always believed this. Free women choose to accept or deny lovers, to welcome children or delay them—or refuse them. As I lay in bed, still in sweatpants and layers of pads, I wondered if losing this tiny fetal comma—to me, my baby—would weaken this conviction. My thoughts tumbled: Is it punishment? I'd never believed in a vengeful God, but I fretted because of all those years I'd considered a fetus a collection of viable cells, not a baby. Perhaps that's why?

I wanted this blame, but I couldn't convince myself. I didn't believe it any more than I believed a ten-week-old fetus was really a baby, for any reason besides our love for it. For him, or her.

Miscarriage didn't turn me against choice. I was relieved when I realized this. The blood didn't wash all of me away. Although it did humble me. I was never invincible. What was lost wasn't a comma, or a kumquat, or a fetus. Loved already, it was our child.

Now I know a woman's power results from choice but also voice: speaking aloud our bloody secrets.

Afterward, when the monthly blood arrived on schedule, I was not indifferent. Not relieved. How long would all blood remind me of that blood? How long would my shame keep me silent? Too long.

A woman's body may betray her, lose its hold on a wanted child. Likewise, it may implant an egg fertilized by someone she doesn't love, someone uninterested in parenthood. Someone bad. The betrayal goes both ways.

Some life isn't meant to last. Every month, another bloody reminder.

One Could Not Stay

Natalie A. Sullivan

We don't know exactly when she died. We said good night to her on the Monday. On the Wednesday, the doctor delivered the terrible news. She was born just after midnight on that Friday. The pregnancy had overjoyed us, and then stripped us of life as we knew it for the next eight and a half months.

The sickness was severe—hyperemesis gravidarum, they called it. It was followed by endless calls to the doctor's office, insomnia, dehydration, IVs, emergency room visits, hospital stays, medication, extreme weight loss, and the psychiatrist who ultimately saved my life. In between the tears and the terror, there were moments we still hold onto: sweet good-night kisses, pictures of our hands laid gently on my pregnant belly, a baby shower with family and friends. We took silly pictures in front of the cake. We oohed and aahed over each little outfit. There was so much pink. At home, we set up her crib, a lovely wooden oval bed. I ironed a shiny decal onto a crisp white onesie. It said "I ♥ Daddy," and I put it on a stuffed rabbit and lay it in the crib to surprise him. She loved to twirl and spin in my stomach at night as I lay on my back. She loved to hear her daddy's voice and feel his touch. When she was born, she had his eyes. After so many months of waiting for her, she was everything we could have ever wanted. Burying her was the hardest thing we've ever done.

Our daughter's birth, albeit still, brought more joy than sadness, more pride than pain, and overwhelming beauty and love over anything else. We often talk about her now—our baby, our daughter, our firstborn. She's an angel on a charm bracelet, a locket on a chain, a heart on a pair of cufflinks. She's a wind chime on the terrace, a flower in the baby garden, and a pinwheel in the wind. After she died, there were tears. There was pain. There was counseling. There was hopelessness and fear. There was anger and blame. There were words that could only be written and pain that could not be contained. There was restlessness and uselessness. There were pointless distractions. And then, there was him.

We found out about our son only weeks before he was born. There was no time spent together before his birth. There was no swollen belly, no sickness or pain. There was paperwork, and there were meetings. At the one we will always remember, his pregnant mother looked at us and said, "He's yours," with such certainty that we allowed ourselves to hope. Still, we promised ourselves we wouldn't get attached until everything was certain. We wouldn't prepare. We wouldn't set up a nursery. We wouldn't even see him until the signature was secured. Then, when we knew he was coming, we dropped everything and rushed to be with him. Over the hours and the miles of highway, we tried to manage our expectations, but when we had the chance to see him, we couldn't stop ourselves. He came through the door of the nursery swaddled in a blanket into the hallway where we were standing, and he smiled. He smiled, and that was it. We were his, and he was ours. At that moment, our joy, our pride, and our love were as strong as they had been only once before.

Since bringing our son home, our days have been filled with his footsteps and his laughter. Our nights have been filled with his little cries. Our months have been full of celebrations, and our plans are now focused on one thing: what is best for him. Every night we say a prayer with our son. In it, we thank God for his sister whom he will never meet and for his birth mother whom he will probably never see again.

As our son grows, I can't help but think about the age our daughter would have been. I think about how the two of them would have played together and how much she would have loved her baby brother. I think about how different, yet alike, they would have been. Then, without fail, I am gripped by a thought that never ceases to amaze me: if she were here, he probably would not be. Under different circumstances, it is unlikely that they both would have been ours. I can't say that our daughter's death "happened for a reason," and, at the same time, I can't imagine a life without our son.

I am so grateful for the time we spent with our daughter. I will always wish we had more. She made my stomach rise and fall, but her little chest could no longer do the same. He never moved inside me, but now he keeps us on our toes. I carried her for months, but could only hold her for a few moments. I hold him each day and feel like I'm holding my heart in my hands. Through some divine miracle, he finished what she started. We made her, but she was taken away. He was born to another mother, but was always meant to be ours. We have two children, but one could not stay. He's what I lived for. She's the reason I'm not afraid to die.

Touching Heaven
Lee Cavalli-Turner

Losing Luna

Shannon Vest

The white heron sat calmly listening to me as I unraveled right there on the beach into a steady stream of tears. I apologized for not being able to save its life. I had just thrown a glass bottle into the ocean; it was filled with sparkly beads, herbs, and a letter to the daughter that I had lost. I told the heron my story because I had not told anyone else. All of my friends were too busy to listen or to bother with my current predicament. The father, who was normally insanely intuitive, had drifted back into his own little world, which did not currently include me.

In LA, people get caught up in their own lives. It was easy to feel alone. The whole experience had been so strange. I knew that I was pregnant the morning after it happened. I woke up with a swimmy feeling in my belly, and my fluffy Turkish Angora cat curled up in a purring ball on top of it. He draped himself across my belly every single night, purring happily until February 14, the night I came home from a friend's house covered in blood from the waist down. It was a twisting pain that had made me get up from the couch that I had been lounging on watching a movie. I went to the bathroom and found my skirt already saturated with dark blood. The cramps were horrendous. It felt like death was writhing out of me. I informed my friend that I had to leave because my period had started. I asked for an old towel so that my car seats wouldn't get stained. She seemed a little concerned about my behavior, but let me go. I laid the towel on the seat and drove home telling myself that my period had finally started after three months. As I crossed Suicide Bridge in Pasadena, I fantasized about driving my car over the side. The barriers were too high, though.

I got home and immediately peeled off my ruined clothes. I showered, realizing that the bleeding had stopped and all that was left was a sick feeling in my stomach. I curled up on the bed and began to cry, knowing that I had not taken care of myself—this was my fault. I should have been stronger. I should have told him. I had tried, but the conversation had always turned back to him. I was also in a bizarre state of denial, which was unlike me.

Over the previous three months, my hormones had taken me on the roller-coaster ride of my life. I would feel waves of euphoria and then crash into the pits of despair. I got nauseous, but never threw up. I had vertigo. My breasts itched and grew. I had heartburn every night when I lay down. I wore empire-waist dresses to cover my small, rounded belly. I had this amazing glow that seemed to emanate from within. I wandered through my days distracting myself from the truth. I felt amazing except for the fact that I was utterly alone. I desperately needed to be held. I felt like a child myself.

One friend accused me of being pregnant because of my glow and recent cleavage. I told her that I was getting fat. My mother watched me suspiciously as I waved away nausea before having Christmas dinner. I asked her nonchalantly if she'd had morning sickness with me. She said no, her pregnancy was blissful and easy as she watched me carefully. My mother was never one to pry, but I wanted her to so badly. I needed someone to take my hand and guide me through this. I was an only child. I was used to doing things alone, but someone needed to break my stubborn silence and force me out of denial. I have always been the person that people come to with secrets. I needed someone to be me, to keep asking, to sit with me until I admitted to what they suspected. No one did.

It was the holidays, so it was easy to drink excessively, which was also out of character for me. I went to bed each night feeling the life in my belly grow. I called her Luna. I spoke to her each night, begging her to only be born if she had both of us. I was too scared to raise her on my own. I thought I would be disowned if I told my father that I would be a single mom. The fear was intense, but so was my love for the life inside me. I wished for a miracle, because I really wanted this child. I pictured her dark hair and big blue eyes. I felt her spirit with me, speaking to me, and comforting me. She was pure love.

Two weeks after the miscarriage, I finally called him and told him what had happened. His first reaction was terrible, but he quickly apologized and became the caring friend that I had needed all along. It was too late, though. I blamed myself. He held me in his arms and told me that he had dreamt of our daughter, Luna. He described her exactly as I pictured her and said her name with the sweet intuitiveness that I had known for years. He assured me that everything would be all right. He was there for me.

The tide was coming in quickly, and the white heron would soon be carried out to sea. The seaweed that I had carefully unwound from around its body lay a safe distance away. I had hoped that the sweet young bird was simply caught up in the umbilical cord of the sea and would fly away when freed. Instead, the bird gathered its broken body carefully into a nesting position. The long graceful neck looked a little too twisted. The bird's breathing calmed and the vivid orange eyes stared at me peacefully. The lack of fear was astounding. The heron had allowed me to unravel it and sit close enough for its sharp beak to pierce me. It seemed to understand every word, and as I looked into those eyes, a feeling of absolute love came over me. The symbolism of meeting this graceful dying creature was powerful. I wanted so badly to save it, but fate had decided to take the white heron. As I stood up to leave, the wind picked up, tickling my ears with what sounded like a child's giggle. I knew that meeting this creature was no accident. I knew that the spirit of the white heron would guide Luna safely above the crashing waves. One day I would be ready, but the universe had made it painfully clear that now was not the time.

Luna's father and I had a terrible fight two weeks later and stopped speaking for years. I had a car accident weeks after the fight that left me with a crooked spine and a concussion. I had contractions that night and figured that I would have miscarried no matter what. I sat in my wrecked car at the intersection of Wilshire and La Brea in my beautiful blue Easter dress. Wasn't Easter about birth? I wanted to die. The Smiths sang "There is a Light That Never Goes Out" on the radio. Perfect. A man knocked on my window telling me to get out of the dangerous intersection or I would get hit again. I was crying hysterically and shouted that I didn't care. If that car hadn't hit me, it would have barreled into a dozen pedestrians crossing the street. Technically, I saved a few lives that night, but a part of my spirit left me—it shot right out of me, leaving emptiness. A girl can only take so much. Holidays became painful reminders of loss.

I left LA in 2009, but the pain has been slower to leave me. As soon as my back allowed me to dance and run again, the emotions came rushing in, and I had a breakdown. I couldn't believe that it was still so fresh four years later. I read recently that new studies have shown that mothers forever hold DNA in their bodies from every child they carry beyond a month. It makes so much sense. Think about that powerful fact for a moment. Is it any wonder that women often have a hard time letting go of the past? A man can walk away, but a woman carries the past inside her body until she turns to dust. If more people knew that, would it make a difference in how we respond to one another?

Whenever I walk along the river near my current home, a blue heron likes to grace me with his presence. He flies alongside me often, then lands to watch me pensively. It comforts me. It assures me that I am never really alone.

Miscarriage

Patricia Dreyfus

My husband rubs his graying temples,
rests his thumb and little finger
on his eyelids, speaks softly into the phone,
consoles our daughter.
Are you okay?
Any pain?

Years ago, standing in my blood,
alone at our doorstep,
I held our child, perfectly formed,
torn from my body too soon.
I called her name, wept.

He turned away.
Still, he won't speak
of this child.
If only he would
whisper to me,
Are you okay?
Any pain?

Luca D'oro: Our Golden Boy

Carla Grossini-Concha

When I am with Gina, it feels like home.

I met her in the summer of 2007. My outlook changed completely, because for the very first time, I felt like I had met my match.

A whirlwind romance began, and before we were dating even a month, we moved in together. We laughed as we took pictures of ourselves in front of the U-Haul, and we said that one day, we would show these photos to our children.

We loved, we laughed, and we lived. We wanted everything life had to offer. We couldn't wait for our future together to begin, because the love we felt was so big.

We married. We traveled. We experienced. We planned.

I remember clearly the clipboards with Gina's drawings, ideas of what we thought we wanted to do in the future, but hadn't decided on yet, and choices of "yes" or "no" on them.

Europe…yes.

AIDS/LifeCycle…yes.

Baby…yes.

We decided we were finally ready to settle down and start our family. Inspired by dear friends and neighbors who were showing us how it could be done, and by seeing these sweet babies grow into little people, we wanted badly for one of our very own.

We went through the process of finding the perfect donor, and were thrilled to have found one that Gina felt a connection to. So we began trying.

We experienced the ups and downs of the insemination process—the weeks of preparation for the magic of ovulation, the testing, the ultrasounds, and then the waiting game, holding our breath for two weeks in the hopes that it would happen. Starting all over again the next month, and the next, until one morning at 3 a.m., I couldn't believe what I was seeing. Two lines. We were pregnant.

We were going to be mothers.

For thirty-nine weeks we loved him, we talked to him, and we planned for how life would be with him. Life was beautiful, and waiting for him to join us brought us so much excitement and joy. There are so many happy pictures of the belly and us. We sent out our first holiday picture with Luca and the dogs. We anticipated the arrival of this little man entering our lives. We wanted him so very much.

"Think about it, there must be a higher love
Down in the heart or hidden in the stars above…"

We had thirty-nine weeks and two days with Luca. He was born, and he never woke up.

We welcomed him into our world; then we hugged and kissed him good-bye into the starry sky.

All those plans we had, dreams of his first smile. His first laugh. His first steps. The first time he called Gina mommy. These dreams were going to remain just that. They were never going to come true with him.

My Luca was never going to wrap his baby arms around me and give me a hug.

Life went on for everyone else around us. But our lives stopped. Those first few months were a blur of tears and a constant feeling of being pulled completely apart, being split wide open at the heart.

"Things look so bad everywhere,

In this whole world, what is fair?"

How was this fair? Why us? Why him? There was no indication of his sickness, why did he have to leave?

These questions, the frustration of trying to make sense of that which is absolutely senseless, filled our minutes for days and weeks.

And the darkness became so evident and ever present. Losing him was like having the entire ground fall out from underneath us. How do you have faith in anything ever again, when your baby dies? How do you trick your mind into having hope?

But eventually, and little by little, I was reminded of the love that made Luca even come to be in the first place.

A love that felt like home, a love that was my family—my life with Gina.

This family, my family, that will forever hold Luca as our firstborn, our eldest son.

We try every day; we take steps forward. We live for Luca, honoring him. And we hold on to hope that one day, Luca will help us welcome his sibling into our lives, and into this world.

September 10 marks six months. I think of him every minute of my day. I get up in the morning and I pass by the altar we've created for him, and I talk to him. I tell him how much I miss him, and how much I love him. I cry. I sob. The tears flow, cleaning me out for that moment. And then a calm comes over me. Luca comes over me.

His presence is bigger than we ever could have expected. Even though he's left our world, he's present in everything we do, in everything Gina and I experience.

"Let me feel that love come over me

Let me feel how strong it could be."

I do wish our story were different. I wish that I could write about Luca at five and a half months old and share his beauty, his laughter, and everything he loves.

But I cannot deny, nor will I ever take for granted, this higher love he has brought us.

Quoted lyrics are from "Higher Love" by Steve Winwood.
Our favorite version is sung by James Vincent McMorrow.

If

Susan Ito

*T*he nurse from the women's clinic said yes. "Congratulations!" News that she delivered daily, altering lives with one syllable. Yes. No. I immediately bought a book on pregnancy, and ran my finger along the due-date chart, counting months. Early January. New year, new life.

Months later, my husband and I were on a beach holiday. I swelled in the humidity like a sponge, my breasts enormous, my face squishy with fluid. "*Look* at me," I said, frowning in the mirror.

"You look wonderful," he said. That wasn't what I meant. I hadn't been complaining about feeling fat or unattractive, although I *was* fat, in a strange, swollen way.

"You're pregnant, sweetheart," he said. "That's how you're *supposed* to look."

When I got home, I saw that I had gained thirteen pounds that week. I pulled out the pregnancy book. In red print, it said, *Call the doctor if you gain more than three pounds in one week. If your face or hands or feet are swollen. If. If. If.* I checked them all off. I called my obstetrician friend, Lisa. I whispered, "I think something is wrong."

Lisa's voice was calm. "Swelling is common," she said, "but can John check your blood pressure?"

We stopped by his gastroenterology office near the Greek restaurant where we had reservations. We planned to eat, then browse a bookstore: our usual date. I eased onto the exam table and held out my arm, impatient for spanakopita.

I heard the Velcro tearing open the cuff, felt its smooth blue band. I dangled my feet and smiled at John, the stethoscope around his neck. I loved this small way he took care of me. I felt the pounding of my heart echoing up and down my fingers, through my elbow.

I will never forget his face, the change in color from pink to ash, as if he had died standing at my side. "Lie down," he said quietly. "Lie on your left side. *Now.*"

The numbers were all wrong. He shook his head. "What's Lisa's phone number?"

His voice was grim—numbers, questions, a terrible urgency. He ordered me to pee into a cup. "We've got to check your urine for protein."

He dipped a paper strips into the cup of gold, cloudy liquid, and the color changed from white to powdery blue to indigo. My protein level was off the chart. "No," he whispered. "No, goddammit, *no.*"

"What? What *is it*?" I asked. I couldn't believe that things could be as bad as what his face was telling me.

"Your kidneys aren't working," he said. He pulled me across the street to the hospital. He rushed me to the nurses' station, shouting numbers. I thought, *don't be a bully*, but they scattered like quail, one of them on the phone, another pushing me, stumbling, onto a bed. They pulled at my clothes, my shoes; another blood pressure cuff; the shades were drawn. They moved so swiftly, with such seriousness.

Suddenly, I had a new doctor. Lisa, obstetrician of the normal, was off my case, and I was assigned a high-risk neonatologist. He was bald, with thick glasses, wooden clogs, and a soft voice.

A squirt of blue gel on my belly for the fetal monitor, the galloping sound of hoof beats, the baby riding a wild pony inside me. What a relief to hear that heartbeat, although I didn't need the monitor; I could feel the baby punching my liver.

There was a name for it. Preeclampsia.

Well, preeclampsia was better than eclampsia, and as long as it was *pre-*, they could stop it, right? And what was eclampsia? Explosive blood pressure, a flood of protein poisoning the blood, kidney failure, stroke, seizures, blindness, death. But I didn't have those things. I had *pre-*eclampsia, which felt like less of an emergency.

They slipped a needle into my wrist, attached to a squishy bag of magnesium sulfate to prevent seizures. *You may feel a little hot.* As the drug oozed into my bloodstream, I felt a flash, like my tongue was baking. My scalp prickled, and I threw up onto the sheets. I felt as if I was being microwaved.

I was wheeled down to radiology. I stared lovingly at grainy images of the baby onscreen—waving, treading water. A real child, not a pony or a fish. The X-ray tech asked, "Do you want to know the sex?" I sat up. "Yes!"

She pointed. A flash between the legs, like a finger. A boy. I nearly leapt off the gurney. "John! Did you see? A boy! It's Samuel!" Sahm-*well*, the Spanish pronunciation, named after the beloved host father we'd lived with in Nicaragua.

He turned away from the screen; he didn't want to look, or celebrate having a son. He knew so much more than I did.

The neonatologist recited numbers slowly.

"Baby needs at least two more weeks for viability. He's way too small. But you…" He shook his head. "*You* probably can't survive two weeks without having a stroke, seizures, worse." He meant I could die.

"What are the chances…that we could *both* make it?"

"Less than ten percent, maybe less than five." The space between his fingers shrunk into nothing.

I was toxemic, poisoned by pregnancy. The only cure was to not be pregnant anymore.

I looked at John hopefully. "I can wait. It will be all right."

"Honey. Your blood pressure is through the roof. Your kidneys are shutting down. You are *on the verge of having a stroke.*"

I smiled. Having a stroke at twenty-nine would not be a big deal. I was a physical therapist; I knew about rehab. I could rehabilitate myself! I could walk with a cane. *Lots* of people do it. I imagined leaning on the baby's stroller handles, supporting myself the way elderly people use a walker.

We struggled through the night. "I'm not going to lose this baby," I said.

"I'm not going to lose *you*," he said. "Think: a baby born this small could have problems. *Severe* problems."

I had worked in a cerebral palsy clinic; I knew children who could not walk or speak or meet their mother's eyes. But we could cope with those things, couldn't we?

After the longest night of my life, I relented.

I lay with my hands on my belly all night, feeling Samuelito's limbs turning this way and that. There was nothing inside me that could even think of saying good-bye.

Another day of magnesium sulfate, the blood pressure cuff, the fetal monitor. No change in status for either of us.

I signed papers of consent, my hand moving numbly across the paper, my mind screaming, I do *not* consent, I do *not*, I do *not*.

The doctor entered with a tray, a syringe, and a nurse with mournful eyes.

"It's just going to be a beesting," he said.

And it was: a small tingle, quick pricking bubbles beneath my navel; and then a tube like a tiny glass straw that went in and out with a barely audible *pop*. It was so fast. I thought, *I love you, I love you, you must be hearing this, please hear me.* And then a Band-Aid, with its plastic smell of childhood, was spread onto my belly.

"All done," he said. All done.

My child was inside, swallowing the fizzy drink; it bubbled against his tiny tongue like deadly soda pop.

It had been injected into my womb to stop his heart. To lay him down to eternal sleep, so he wouldn't feel what would happen next, the terrible, terrible thing that would happen. *Evacuation* is what it is called in medical journals.

I wondered if he would be startled by the taste—if it was bitter, or strange, or just different from the saltwater he was used to. I prayed that it wouldn't be noxious, that it wouldn't hurt. That it would be fast.

John sat next to the bed and held my hand as I pressed the other against my belly. I looked over his shoulder into the dark slice of night between the heavy curtains. Samuel, Samuelito, jumped against my hand once. He leaped through the space into the darkness and then was gone.

All gone.

After losing Samuel, I was frightened by my body's betrayal. We began pursuing adoption; it seemed safer than the gauntlet of pregnancy. However, our two daughters insisted on showing up in our family, in spite of our attempts at contraception, and I am infinitely grateful that they did.

I do not forget that son—my small cowboy—or the way he galloped through me. Part of me that believes I failed a test of motherhood—the law that says your child comes before you, even if it means death. But I look at my girls, the life that fills our family, and I know none of this would be here if I had chosen differently. Maybe not even myself.

Our Family Love Story

Carissa Kapcar

Valentine's Day is a tricky holiday for my husband and me. In 2006, Valentine's Day stopped being Valentine's Day and started being simply "the day." As my husband hurried off to work, he gave me three cards, one from him, one from our two-year-old son, and one from the baby who had been growing inside of my stomach for 38.5 weeks and who we were excited to meet just eight days later.

As I opened the card from the baby, a feeling of dread came over me. I had been worried about a lack of fetal movement since the evening before, and I felt that pang of panic that all pregnant women experience right before the reassurance sets in. I read the card from "Baby" and thought, *I don't even know if this baby is alive anymore.* About ninety minutes and some phone calls later, I found myself next to an ultrasound machine in my ob-gyn's office, cold jelly rubbed on my stomach, hearing an anguished phrase from my doctor that is forever etched in my mind: "I'm so sorry, Carissa. There's no heartbeat."

The remainder of that February 14 was filled with consultations from medical professionals and perinatal loss specialists, phone calls to our parents and siblings four hours away, and e-mails to friends. Having a priest come and sit in your living room is not usually a part of Valentine's Day celebrations. We spent the day making decisions and deliberations that no parent should have to make. It's never natural for a parent to plan their child's funeral arrangements…but it's especially unnatural when it's done at the same time they are planning their child's labor and delivery.

I don't even remember if my husband and I originally had plans for that Valentine's evening. Since then, I've never thought to wonder that or try to recall that memory. It's doubtful, given that it was the middle of winter in Chicago, we had a toddler at home, few babysitters, and I was at the end of my pregnancy. But if we had made plans, I am certain the reality of our evening was far from what we would have done on that lover's eve: we spent that evening in a hospital, where laminaria, which were described to me as "seaweed sticks," were inserted into me to induce labor for a deceased child.

Doesn't sound very romantic, does it? No. It wasn't. But while this is a story about heartbreak, it's also a very true love story. A true love story between my husband and myself. And a true love story between us and our children.

Together, we faced one of those terrible and beautiful life moments. For better or for worse, we did it. My husband/life partner/co-parent held my hand during the laminaria insertions and patted my back when I awoke a few hours later, back in our home, to contractions. Together, we tossed and turned overnight until at 4 a.m.; together, we kissed our toddler and left for a cold, gray drive to the hospital. Together, we parked the car in the garage and quietly put one foot in front of the other and walked to the check-in area. Together, we tried to ignore the happy faces of expectant parents in the elevators or the balloons that bopped up and down tied to floral arrangements that said "It's a Boy!" Together, we looked the other way, choked back tears, and steadily made our way forward.

Together, we delivered our baby. For many heartbreaking hours, I labored and breathed. He paced and analyzed my contractions on the eerily silent monitor. There was no baby's heartbeat to listen for. And when it came time to push, there was an ironic wave of adrenaline that swept over us both. While we knew the outcome was going to be tragic, we still were eager to see the beautiful child that we, together, had created. And so I pushed, and he locked eyes with me and together we heard our beloved nurse inform us in a whispered voice, "It's a girl." Together, we processed the silence, which was immediately filled not with a newborn baby's wail, but with her mother's wail.

We spent the next twelve hours together with our daughter, admiring her, bathing her, taking in every single thing about her beautiful, perfect body…knowing that our time with her was fleeting. Together, we gave her the name we had always hoped to give a girl. Together, we beamed with pride while her grandparents held her and admired her features. When it was time to leave, our son arrived to briefly see his sister, and together we left with no wheelchair, flowers, or fanfare. We looked back at our daughter, and our little son turned around and said, "Bye, Baby." Hand in hand, we stepped out of the hospital and back into a life that would be forever changed.

In the seven years since our daughter's birth and death, our family has grown and happiness has returned to not just most of our days, but to all of our days. Together, my husband and I grieved—and continue to grieve. Side by side, we went to support groups and counseling and doctor appointments. Together, we met with specialists around the country who told us there was no explanation for this event that happened in an instant. Together, we prayed and cried and screamed—sometimes at God, sometimes at Life, sometimes at each other. When one of us would wake to the other silently sobbing in the middle of the night, we never said a word, but just quietly reached over and grasped our hands together. Together, we continued to be lively and fun and busy with our toddler. We left him with grandparents and took a trip together and drank way too much wine together.

Together, we made the painstaking and brave decision to go through more pregnancies. Together, we have welcomed two more daughters and wept with joy and relief upon hearing their borning cries. Today we are a chaotic, busy, grateful, and happy family, and together we have created four beautiful children, each of them a miracle. But only three of them are living.

We've made our daughter a part of our story. As a family, we reference her often. Early on, we decided that we didn't want this day to be associated with sadness or despair, so we decided that every year on February 14 we'd earmark it as a special day for our family to celebrate each other. We take a vacation or spend time at a special place and call it her "Birthday Trip." We laugh and play and think about each other—and we think about her.

So on February 14, we don't celebrate Valentine's Day, we celebrate something else: a gift from our daughter, our love story. It's a story that begins with us being wiser, more confident, and more protective of our emotions and one another. A story that shows us the resiliency of our marriage and allows us to love more deeply. In this story we have perspective. We are better, more compassionate listeners and friends in this story. As a family we will always LIVE, have adventures and fun. We will find a way, not find an excuse. And in this story, we have a depth of gratitude that was impossible before. We know just how low the lows can be, so we cherish and savor and defend these highs. I'm so proud of our family love story.

First published on *The Huffington Post* on February 13, 2013. It has also appeared on iVillage Australia and on Carissa's blog, www.carissak.com.

Rockabye

Carol Folsom

At sixteen I cringed
at black-and-white photos in *Life* magazine
girls sprawled in alleys
dead on hotel rugs
in puddles of their own last blood,
desperate girls like me.
Coat hangers, knitting needles, poison:
they all worked
and plenty of folks would do it
for easy cash from
desperate girls like me.

Then came Rowe
it's legal now
the gavel pounds:
desperation dismissed
a closed file.
But oh the bag of rocks around my neck
the neon-bright regrets
in my heart's sad eye.
I rock you still and always
my unknown unborn
in aching, empty arms,
sentenced for life to wonder
who you would have been.
Oh, I'd have loved you so.

Three Minus One Baby Loss Mums
Amy Dahlenburg

Anneka's Story

Cherrie Gustafson Moore

On a beautiful July morning, late in my pregnancy, I woke, startled and disoriented, from a sound sleep. My heart was racing, and I felt sure something was terribly wrong. I pushed my belly, prodded and poked, desperate to feel my baby girl move. My heart hammered, and I felt dizzy as she remained still. Finally, after a few more moments, I pushed deep into my belly and felt pure relief as my sweet girl pushed back. I breathed deep, my heart settling into a normal rhythm, and sank back into my pillow thinking all was well. I didn't know then, in the breaking dawn of that brand-new day, that it would be the last time I would feel my daughter move.

A few hours later, while at the clinic for my regular appointment, I began to tense as nurse after nurse came into the exam room searching for my daughter's heartbeat. They were cheerful, blaming a faulty stethoscope, or her breech position. Finally one nurse heard a rapid *kachoo, kachoo, kachoo*, which bounced loud off the walls, and I was reassured when she said, "Ah, there she is. C'mon, little sweetie, stop hiding." We laughed together, imagining her eluding the nurses. Moments later the doctor on call came in. He was all business—unsmiling as he checked and rechecked. Lines of concentration mapped his face as he asked for another stethoscope and finally, the portable ultrasound machine. The room was silent as he rolled the wand over my distended belly and we listened for the steady rhythm of my daughter's heart. Somehow, even in those moments I didn't consider the worst. My head was turned toward the ultrasound monitor, and I grinned when my daughter's image filled the screen. "Oh, look," I said. "She's not breech anymore; her head is down," and I actually laughed in that moment, feeling the joy of her impending arrival, any day, any hour.

It was only as I began to focus closer on the image that a horrible realization began. I saw, and I said, as a wave of dread and fear came upon me, "Where's her heartbeat?" In that moment, that surreal, terrifying moment, it was as though the world stopped spinning. Silence pulsed in my ears, and all life narrowed to a pinpoint of held breath as the doctor said abruptly and matter-of-factly, "There is no heartbeat…Damnation!" He threw down the ultrasound wand and strode from the room. In that instant, as I struggled to grasp the meaning of such impossible words, I felt thrown from the earth—my feet, my heart, my entire life were unanchored, free-falling into my worst nightmare, hurtling into a place of darkness and calamity.

The following morning my beautiful daughter, Anneka Marie Moore, was born. When she slid from my body, a holy hush filled the room, and we marveled at her beauty, her dark curls, her delicate piano player fingers. She was stunning, beautiful and precious even in death. We held her, my husband and I and some of our children, and sang "You Are My Sunshine" while raining kisses and tears on her velvet cheeks, stroking her skin, inhaling the new baby scent of her—trying to memorize her and impart a lifetime of love into just one day. Our joy was deep, sharing space with the grief that was already digging channels into our lives and the life of our family. In that beautiful heartbreaking day—the day of hello and good-bye—God was present, a breath in the room, and having and loving Anneka was to me sacred, like touching the edge of Heaven.

Saying good-bye to my daughter was the hardest thing I've ever done. I held her into the night, quietly whispering mama love to her, singing lullabies, resting her cheek on mine—trying to absorb her into me, to cement the look and feel and smell of her to my heart and mind for all time to come. I sobbed when it was time to release her. I unwrapped her from her blanket and kissed each little finger—fingers that would never shake a rattle, touch my face, tie a shoe, wear a wedding ring, or stroke the face of her own babies. I kissed each precious toe, thinking of the miles she would not travel—the first steps and climbing and racing through this life that would not happen. "Good-bye little fingers. Good-bye little toes," I whispered as I cradled her to my heart, and spoke a prayer and last good-bye into her tiny ears.

It went against every instinct I had, to let her go. As I released her, held out my precious girl and relinquished her tiny body, I knew I would never be the same—the landscape of my entire life had changed. In that small hospital room on that terrible night, I couldn't hear the voices of the people around me over the wail of my own heart as I sat, stunned and silent, my empty arms already aching at the impossibility of a lifetime without my daughter. Good-bye, sweet girl of my heart…good-bye…

Since that bittersweet day, I've learned the loss of a child is staggering and carries a pain beyond measure. There is no "getting over it" but rather learning to live with it. In the first months I wasn't sure I would survive the tidal waves of longing, the empty cradle, empty arms, breast milk leaking in maddening rivulets down my belly. I spent days at the cemetery bringing little gifts of wind chimes and flowers and praying angels, and on the first cold day of autumn I tucked her quilt over the little patch of land that had become her resting place. Some days I raged at God, calling him a thief, a robber, and then in the night wept as I tried to imagine my girl in Heaven, held and loved, but not by me. I felt quarantined in my grief—not shut out but shut in, in a place that no one wanted to enter. There was no map of that place and I felt twinges of bitterness as I wondered whether I had become completely invisible, and how it was possible that the world went on while my daughter, heart of my heart, lay in a grave.

On better days, and there were some, I recognized shafts of light even in my mourning. I took some comfort in moments of love and goodness from a precious few who offered kindness, who spoke her name, who looked in my eyes and offered to listen. These gifts were my treasures, seeds of strength that grew as I resolved to not let the loss of my daughter diminish me but rather allow it to enlarge and deepen and enrich me. Music healed, as did shared tears, talk, prayers, touch, and laughter. I clung to the good, even while crashing my way through those deep dark woods, and I took to heart the words and hope from those who had survived such pain. As weeks turned to months turned to years, the path became less tangled, my stride strengthened, and I was able to look around and glimpse beauty and hope and promise. The grief triggers quieted, and I began the blessed part of healing when reminders of Anneka became more precious than painful, and singing "You Are My Sunshine," or looking close at my granddaughter, who shares her Auntie Anneka's dark curls and sweet face, brought deep joy and privilege rather than pain.

Recently, my family went to the beach and released sky lanterns to celebrate Anneka's fourteenth birthday. My heart was full as lantern after lantern lifted high and was carried in the breeze heavenward, each lantern symbolic of a year without her, glowing and growing smaller and smaller in the night sky until finally they disappeared, one by one. I stood on the beach, and with tears in my eyes, I looked up, straining toward Heaven, still longing to hold my girl, to touch her, to braid her hair or listen to her teen-girl giggles. As the last lantern flickered and disappeared, all was still except for a soft breeze.

I can't help but contemplate how much Anneka's life and death have impacted me. She has shaped me in beautiful ways—this precious one who lived only beneath my own beating heart. Surrounded by my other children, I feel wrapped in peace, as though I am part of some sacred dance heavy with mystery and unknowns. I will never understand the whys of my daughter's death in this lifetime and I will long for her until my dying day, yet this peace, this deep down gratitude for having known and loved Anneka, is enough. Once again, it seems I am touching the edge of Heaven.

Acknowledgments

*T*his book is, in its own way, a miracle.

For those of us who have lost children to stillbirth, miscarriage, or neonatal death, we are all too familiar with things falling apart, futures not happening, and beginnings that quickly become endings.

The same is true with books, films, and almost every creative endeavor I can think of, which is why the very existence of these pieces that come from our hearts and make it into the world are cause for celebration.

This book would not exist without the incredible talent and enthusiasm of the *Return to Zero* community, of which nearly one hundred members are represented in these pages. Every tear, broken heart, and drop of blood is evidenced in your stories—thank you for baring your souls and reliving your experiences so that the world can better understand this unique and devastating loss. Every story is important, and these extraordinary pieces were culled from nearly one thousand submissions, all of which are testaments to the love and loss we have experienced as a community. I wish we could have included every single one in this book.

This book would not exist without the dedication of my co-editor, Brooke Warner, and publisher She Writes Press. Their commitment to bringing this compilation together and taking it out into the world is remarkable and should not be taken lightly. She Writes Press is a brave and beautiful publisher, and Brooke is a joy and an inspiration to work with on a daily basis.

This book would not exist without the film *Return to Zero*, which in itself would not have come into being without the bold "Magnificent Seven" investors who put up the equity necessary to make a quality film—one with world-class actors—about a subject matter that is so very difficult to tackle that it could not have been made inside today's studio system. From the bottom of my heart, thank you. And to the *Return to Zero* community who, through our Kickstarter campaign and donations directly through our website, helped us to cover the costs to complete the film: Without each and every one of you, the film—and therefore this book—would not have come into the world.

I would like to thank four people without whom I could not have done any of this. To my wife, Kiley, who is my strength, and who I love and admire more than anyone on earth; to my daughter, Roxie, who lights the way for me with her spirit and love every day; to my son Cannon, whose energy both grounds and elevates all of us; and finally to my son Norbert, who would have been eight years old the year of this book's publication—I would give every experience, every frame of the movie, every page of this book, everything away if I could just hold you in my arms for one more hour. You never breathed a breath of earth's air into your lungs, never took a sip of its water on your own lips, but you will be forever loved and remembered as our firstborn, Roxie and Cannon's older brother, and someone who, through his presence on this earth, has helped to change, heal, and break the silence forever. I'm so very proud of you, son, and I love you.

—Sean Hanish

*F*irst and foremost I want to thank Sean Hanish for his commitment to his own story and passion, and for his enthusiasm and energy in partnering on this project. I also want to thank each and every person who submitted their work to be included in this book. The hardest part about working on it was making the selections. Thank you to Caitlyn Levin and Krissa Lagos, my team at She Writes Press, for everything they did to make this project a reality. To our proofreader, Carissa Bluestone, and our designers, Dede Cummings and Kiran Spees. This project has been a work of love, and She Writes Press is honored to be playing a role in birthing it into the world.

—Brooke Warner

About the Contributors

Courtenay Baker is a single mom of four: Milo (8), Violet (6) and twins Juliet and Willa (3). She miscarried her first and fourth pregnancies; the twins were conceived using fertility treatments. Courtenay has a degree in Secondary Speech and Theatre Education from the University of Northern Iowa. She manages a full-time job, a part-time job teaching tap dance lessons, the activities of her children, and she sometimes gets to blog at Soup: Midwestern Mama Cooking up Life in the Heartland. http://www.iasoupmam.com

Jessica Schlabach Baldanzi teaches writing and American Literature at Goshen College and blogs about comics and graphic novels at goshencommons.org. She also is a regular student at Spacious Heart Yoga, where all the instructors are awesome.

Heather Bell's work has been published in *Rattle*, *Grasslimb*, *Barnwood*, *Poets/Artists*, *Red Fez*, *Ampersand* and many other publications. She was nominated for the 2009, 2010 and 2011 Pushcart Prize from Rattle, won the New Letters 2009 Poetry Prize, and most recently was a finalist for the 2013 Consequence Prize in Poetry. Heather has also published four books. Any more details can be found here: http://hrbell.wordpress.com/

Jane Blanchard resides in Georgia. Her poetry has appeared in many venues in the United States, in Ireland, and in the United Kingdom.

Susan Blanco is a wife, mother, and elementary school literacy specialist. She is also a volunteer group facilitator of the Peninsula chapter of HAND, Helping After Neonatal Death. This is her first professionally published piece.

Brandon Bodnar lives with his wife, Anastasia, in Alexandria, VA. He served an enlistment as an Arabic Linguist in the U.S. Air Force, studied Computer Science at Iowa State University, and recently graduated from Cornell Law School.

Jessica Bomarito is a writer and editor living in Michigan with her husband Dwayne, and children Logan and Savannah. Her daughter's Tessa and Sabine were stillborn at 36 weeks following a complete abruption. They will always have a piece of her heart.

Ian Byrd is husband to Alyssa and father of three beautiful children Liam (9), Henry (3) and Sydney Grace. Our story began on November 30, 2007 when we learned that Sydney had passed at 31 weeks due to a fully concealed placental abruption, probably in the middle of the night. Upon upgrading to a new fixer upper home in 2012, our first task was to beautify the barren backyard landscape with a cottonwood tree and place Sydney's ashes back to the earth. It was a beautiful healing moment for us and the aptly named "Sydney Tree" is thriving and reaching for the heavens.

Since the stillbirth of her son in May of 2013, following a miscarriage a year and a half before, Kate Camp has been outspoken on matters of grief and pregnancy loss. She lives in Louisiana with her husband, daughter, and pets. Kate is a veterinarian by trade and writes for pure enjoyment.

Amy Cartwright is 32 years old and lives with her husband John and two children Georgia (3) and Alfie (1) in Cheshire, England. After 2 early miscarriages her first daughter Lucy was stillborn at 37 weeks after Amy went to the hospital with reduced movements and was told that there was no heartbeat. Amy was induced immediately and Lucy was born silently at 00.58am on 24th September 2009, weighing 6lb 13oz.

When **Lee Cavalli-Turner's** son Albie died at 34 weeks and 5 days, his mum was left with not only a broken heart but also a gift she had never known existed. In the time that followed Albie's death, due to IUGR, the smaller, everyday things in life appeared even more beautiful. Now, Lee rarely goes anywhere without her camera as capturing beautiful images is her way of showing Albie the world he never took a breath in.

Alexis Marie Chute is an award-winning Canadian artist, photographer, and writer. She writes a blog called *Wanted, Chosen, Planned* about life after the loss of a child and has penned two books for bereaved parents. Alexis Marie uses her art to find healing and this work may be viewed on her website, www.AlexisMarieChute.com, or in one of her many international exhibitions.

Stacy Clark is a freelance writer and the mother of two daughters, by birth and adoption. She has an MFA from Goddard College and her writings on adoptive parenting have appeared in numerous publications, including *Adoptive Families, Adoption Today*, and *The Pitkin Review*. Ever grateful to her daughter's birthparents in China, she lives with her family in Florida.

Colleen Lutz Clemens lives in Bucks County, PA, with her husband, daughter, and dogs. She teaches literature at Kutztown University. She is co-editor and contributor to *Philadelphia Reflections, Western Washington Reflections*, and *Western Pennsylvania Reflections* and has been published in several magazines, books, and journals. When she isn't wrangling those in her charge, she is reading, writing, and knitting.

Born and raised in the Garden State, **Lainie Blum Cogan** is an alumna of Barnard College. She is a teacher, consultant, and aspiring writer.

Wendy Staley Colbert's personal essays have been featured in *Salon*, *The Feminist Wire*, *Whole Life Times*, *ParentMap*, *This Great Society*, *Writing in Public*, *Feel More Better* and *Writing Is My Drink* and in the anthologies *We Came to Say*, and *We Came Back to Say*. Her essay "Shopping for Breasts" will be featured in Kerry Cohen's anthology, The Dressing Room, forthcoming from Seal Press in 2014. For more information, see wendystaleycolbert.com.

Judi and **Star Corvinelli** reside in Brooklyn New York and have been happily married since 2006. The couple has always wanted to be parents and began their journey in 2011. Finally, their wish came true and Star became pregnant with their daughter Grace. In July of 2012, during a routine checkup, they found out that their daughter's heart had stopped beating and she was born still at 24 weeks. Star, as a counselor expresses her self through words. Judi, an artist and musician created many pieces throughout the last year to express how she feels about the loss. The piece "Loving Grace" is one of the couple's favorite and was created by Judi about a month after the loss of their daughter.

Franchesca Cox is a creative soul, dream-chaser, wife, and mom. Since her loss, she is in a passionate pursuit to not only live life but squeeze every last drop out of it. She writes a blog, *Small Bird Studios*, and has authored a book, *Celebrating Pregnancy Again*, for bereaved moms who find themselves expecting again.

Barbara Crooker's work has appeared in journals such as: *Nimrod*, *The Green Mountains Review*, *The Valparaiso Poetry Review*, *South Carolina Review*, *Tar River Review*, and anthologies, such as *The Bedford Introduction to Literature*. Her books are *Radiance*, winner of the Word Press First Book Award (2005) and finalist for the 2006 Paterson Poetry Prize; *Line Dance* (Word Press, 2008), winner of the 2009 Paterson Award for Literary Excellence; *More* (C&R Press, 2010); and *Gold* (Poeima Poetry Series, Cascade Books, 2013). Her first child, a daughter, was stillborn in 1971.

Amy Dahlenburg is a 31 year old married mum of 7 children, only two are here on earth with her though. She has endured 4 miscarriages and one stillbirth. Her stillborn son's name is Noah. Amy's life turned upside down when he died, and to cope she took up photography as therapy. It's now her life's passion and she hopes to bless others with this gift that has blessed her and provided much healing. Amy's two earthly children, Charlotte and Josiah, give her a little bit of healing everyday and a lot of comfort as she continues to grieve her other children that were too precious for this earth.

Erica Danega is a mom of three, Damon and Reese here on earth and their big brother Seth, an angel. She lives in Central New York with her loving husband Brent and their children. She's a life long dreamer who loves to create new and beautiful things. Erica blogs about her experience with the seasons of loss and her quest to be inspired by the beauty of the simple moments of life. Follow her journey at www.mysonflower.com.

Heather Lynne Davis received her M.A. in Creative Writing from Syracuse University and has published poems in journals such as *Cream City Review, Gargoyle, Poet Lore*, and many others. Her book *The Lost Tribe of Us* received the Main Street Rag Poetry Book Award. She works in the international public health field as a communications manager and lives in Virginia with her husband, the poet Jose Padua, and their two children.

Janet Lynn Davis, a former technical writer/editor and communications specialist, lives with her husband in a rustic area north of

Houston, Texas. Her poetry, both free verse and tanka, has appeared in numerous online and print venues over the past several years. Currently, she is serving as the vice president of the Tanka Society of America; she also maintains a poetry blog called *twigs&stones*.

Paul De Leon and his wife live in San Antonio, Texas with their three living children. One week away from delivering their fourth, their daughter's heart suddenly stopped beating. They delivered a stillborn baby on March 5th, 2011 and have since decided to take the story of thier loss and help as many others as they possibly can.

Marina DelVecchio is a writer and college professor in writing, literature, and Women's Studies. Writing mainly about feminism and violence against women, her work has been published by the *Huffington Post, Her Circle Ezine, BlogHer*, and anthologized in CenGage Learning's *Media and Violence against Women*. She is currently pursuing her MFA in Creative Writing at Queens University of Charlotte and writing about her childhood experiences with homelessness, orphanages, and her mother's prostitution in a memoir titled *Hanging Loosely from the Darkness*.

Patricia Dreyfus studied writing at University of California Long Beach, University of California, Irvine, Iowa Summer Writing Festival, A Room of Her Own Retreat, and in San Miguel Allende. She belongs to The Writing Well, The Greater Los Angeles Writers Society, Academy off American Poets and PEN. She has been published in the *LA Times, Travelers' Tales*, and *The Best Travel Writing*. She was a finalist for the Anderbo Poetry Prize and has won numerous other poetry awards.

Brooke Taylor Duckworth is a wife, mom, and professor of literature in St. Louis, Missouri. She started her blog "By the Brooke" before starting a family, and after the death of her first child, Eliza, it became an unexpected lifeline for processing her grief and connecting with other bereaved parents, many of whom are now dear friends. These days she's busy keeping up with her high-energy husband, David, and daughter, Caroline, while teaching, writing, embarking on various DIY projects, and carrying Eliza in her heart. Brooke blogs at http://bythebrooke.blogspot.com.

Chiyuma Elliott is an Assistant Professor of English and African American Studies at the University of Mississippi. A former Stegner and Cave Canem Fellow, her poems have appeared in the *African American Review*, *Callaloo*, *The Collagist*, the *Langston Hughes Review*, *MARGIE*, the *Notre Dame Review*, the *PN Review*, and *Torch*.

Latorial Faison is an American military spouse, mother, poet, educator, and author whose poetry and prose have been published in *Southern Women's Review*, *Kalyani*, *Chickenbones*, *Stars and Stripes*, and elsewhere. She is a graduate of U.V.A. and Virginia Tech and currently works as an English professor. www.latorialfaison.com

Shannan Fleet is a mother, artist, and home educator. She carried her second child, Mary Bernadette, from 19 weeks to stillbirth without knowing when Trisomy 18 would end their time together. Shannan is honored to have her first venture into the literary world accepted into this collection. She lives in San Francisco with her husband and children.

Carol Folsom is a retired attorney in Jacksonville, Florida, who writes poetry, fiction, and essays and is about to complete her first novel. Her work has appeared in three anthologies and a variety of online publications.

A writer and teacher, **Adina Giannelli** lives in western Massachusetts with her young son. Her essays have appeared in publications including *Book Lovers* (Seal Press), *Babble,* and *Salon.*

Aoife Goldie is a daughter of two, sister to five and a wife to the most beautiful soul she's ever met. She is a proud mother of three: two boys and a little girl due imminently. Sadly, she'll never see them all in the same room together.

Meagan Golec lives in Portland, Oregon with her husband, living son, and two cats. She loves to learn, makes a mean cheesecake, and has a newfound sense of purpose as a self-proclaimed "grief ambassador." She misses Anderson every day.

Carla Grossini-Concha is a New Yorker, born and raised, transplanted to the West Coast over 10 years ago and embracing her inner hippy ever since. She is a dog-lover, yogi, and most importantly, fierce warrior mama to Luca D'oro, her first-born son. Her hope is to share Luca's story with the world and help people in grief allow the love behind the pain, to enhance their lives and transform them.

Keleigh Hadley is the author of the YA series, Preacher's Kids and Christian fiction novels; Revenge, Inc. and Favor Ain't Fair. She lives in the San Fernando Valley with her family.

Jennifer Hannum is a photographer excited about capturing all of life's moments. Her first inspiration came after she married her supportive husband Josh and documenting the growth of their 5 amazing children became her focus. She studied at Owens State Community College and is employed at Wurzell Studio and Gallery in Perrysburg, Ohio. Jen is thankful to God for the gift He has given her and Now I Lay Me Down to Sleep has given her the welcome opportunity to share her passion with the community.

Laura B. Hayden is the author of STAYING ALIVE:A LOVE STORY, a memoir described by Readers Views as "a beautiful reminder of what really matters." This moving, humorous, and inspiring view into the grieving process received an Honorable Mention at the 2013 New York Book Festival and a 2012 Readers Views Award naming it one of its three top memoirs of the year. It has also been recommended by the American Institute of Health Care Professionals. Excerpts and more info at http://laurabhayden.com/

Elizabeth Heineman's memoir of her stillbirth is *Ghostbelly* (Feminist Press, 2014). She teaches at the University of Iowa.

Corrine Heyeck is a public relations professional, wife, and mother of four. Following a healthy pregnancy, her second child, Brenna, was stillborn at full-term for causes unknown. In addition to her daughter, Corrine has three sons, including rainbow twins.

Loni Huston-Eizenga and her husband Matthew lost their firstborn daughter, Aisley, during childbirth on August 5th, 2012. She has since committed herself to helping other bereaved parents both by sharing her raw emotions and experiences through her writing and in her involvement with Colorado non-profit organizations that provide resources and support to those devastated by pregnancy and infant loss.

Susan Ito co-edited the literary anthology *A Ghost At Heart's Edge: Stories & Poems of Adoption* (North Atlantic Books). Her work has appeared widely, including in *The Bellevue Literary Review, the Kartika Review*, and *Making More Waves*. She is a creative nonfiction editor at *Literary Mama*. She writes and teaches at the San Francisco Writers' Grotto, and can be found at http://susanito.com.

Gabe Johns is the father of four children, three boys and a girl. By day, he works in the financial sector of city government and by night, is a superhero dad and husband. He and his family currently live in Kingman, Arizona. His third child, Kian, was stillborn from a cord accident in July 2012.

Writing fiction since 2011, **Julie Christine Johnson**'s work has appeared in *Stories for Sendai, Granny Smith Magazine, River Poets Journal, Cirque*, and *Flash of Fiction*. She was short-listed for the

2011 Santa Fe Writers Project and the 2013 New Millennium Writing Fiction Awards Programs. She recently left a career as a wine buyer to work on her first novel. A native of the Pacific Northwest, Julie Christine makes her home with her husband on the tip of a peninsula where the Salish Sea meets the Puget Sound.

Tiffany Johnson is a NICU RN in the Kansas City area. A busy mom to three living children, two of which were "rainbow" twins following her loss. She enjoys marching band, swimming, and holidays.

Carissa Kapcar is a happy, grateful, sometimes funny and often times tired mother of four (three living) shuttling a mini-van around the suburbs and clinging to just enough irreverence to stay sane. In addition to her blog, CarissaK.com, her work has been featured on The Huffington Post, iVillage Australia and LeanIn.org.

Jessica Killeen is a writer, researcher, sociology professor, and mother of two living children, Molly and Duncan. Her second daughter Maggie Marin was stillborn in September 2010. Born and raised in Australia, she now lives in Missouri with her husband and children.

Ashley Kimberley is the mother of four precious children. Her second baby was stillborn in 2009, and his death has changed her life in infinite ways. She still loves fiercely, creates art, and is in love with her husband. She works and lives with her family in Bellingham, WA.

Shoshanna Kirk is a writer and editor who lives in San Francisco. She is currently at work on a memoir, *French Bred: How I Had a Baby in France and Lived to Tell the Tale.*

Kelly Kittel is a fish biologist by trade but a writer at heart. She is married with five living children, her best work beyond compare. She lives with her husband and two youngest children in Rhode Island but her favorite writing space is in her yurt on the coast of Oregon. She has been published in magazines and other anthologies. "Not Again" is an excerpt from her first book, *Breathe*. (She Writes Press 2014).

Gabriela Ibarra Kotara, 23, lives in San Antonio, TX with her husband Rob. They are hoping for another child.

Susan Miller Lawler lives in Tacoma, Washington with her precious, wee family. She reminds herself daily to throw out the rulebook and just make it up as she goes along; it always seems to work out better that way.

Rachel Libby lives in Sacramento, California with her husband Daniel and their son Samuel. A preschool teacher by trade, Rachel is now grateful to be spending her days caring for Sam and writing the story of his brother Oliver.

Deborah Linker is a retired speech-language pathologist and author of *Living on the Edge*, a collection of poetry She also maintains the website *Rocky Road Adventures* at www.deborahclinker.com. Deborah divides her time between South Florida and Aix en Provence, France. Her motto is "May All Your Roads Lead to an Adventure."

Barbara Mulvey Little is a freelance writer-editor, communications professional, spiritual director, and wisdom-seeker but her favorite roles are wife, mother, grandmother, sister, daughter, and friend. She lives in the Pacific Northwest with her husband.

Robyna May lives in Brisbane, Australia with her husband and two living sons, Isaac and Elijah. In July 2012, Robyna's world shattered when she lost her middle son, Xavier, to SIDS. Since that time, healing has come in many forms—writing, creating, talking, and welcoming baby Elijah into her family.

Dafna Michaelson Jenet and her husband Michael Jenet are the parents of "Peanut." The Jenet's live in Colorado with their three children and run a non-profit called The Journey Institute which focuses on creating opportunity through building community. They have begun The Peanut Project in memory of their son with the mission of helping women and their families get the support they need in the first 24 hours to 2 weeks following the devastating loss of their unborn child.

Christina Melendrez is the only child of Ed and Betty Melendrez. She grew up in the United States Army and spent the first 16 years of her life traveling from base to base with her parents. She was born in Kentucky, and moved to Holland, Missouri, and Germany, before settling in Southern California. She attended UCLA, where she majored in History, with a minor in Political Science, and now works for a large investigations company outside of Los Angeles. Christina will soon be moving to Iowa to start a new chapter in her life. Her writing is dedicated to Maddison Marie, born November 10, 2011.

Mike Monday is an attorney who lives in Omaha, Nebraska with his wife, Ann, and his two children, Ben and Sadie. He and Sean Hanish, the writer and director of *Return To Zero*, have been friends since their first day of first grade in 1974, when their cubbyholes were fortuitously adjacent to each other.

Cherrie Gustafson Moore lives near the shores of Lake Superior, where she is nearing completion of her BS degree in Family Wellness at the University of Wisconsin-Superior. Her writing has appeared multiple times in *Dust and Fire: Anthology of Women's Writing* and *Livingstone News*. She is passionate about advocating for people suffering loss or living in crisis. She is mom to six beautiful children, one whom she held for just a day.

Karin Morea lives in Seattle, WA with her husband Nathan and their 3 dogs. She works as a wellness program manager and volunteers as the Vice President of Parent Support of Puget Sound, a support group for parents of stillbirth, infant loss, or miscarriage.

Kerry Ann Morgan is a lover of words and wit. She lives with her family in Florida, where she devotes her time to writing, reading too many books, and dreaming about her next adventure. Visit her website at KerryAnnMorgan.com.

JS Nahani is a writer, coach, and expressive artist living in Vancouver, BC. She loves to find music in the mundane, swim in the sea, and dance with her two young children at teatime.

Stephanie Nalley has a wonderful husband, Blake, and three children under 2--one in heaven and two living. Together, they live to bring glory & honor to God in their loss. Family means everything to her.

Maria B. Olujic has a Ph.D. in Anthropology from U.C. Berkeley. She works in education and lives with her husband and two sons in the Bay Area.

Anne Phyfe Palmer is a yoga teacher, studio owner, and blogger (www.8limbsyoga.com/blog). She lives with her husband and two daughters in Seattle, Washington. Anne Phyfe is at work on a memoir about ambition, yoga, and how loss brought the two into alignment.

A longtime magazine editor and contributor, **Jennifer Massoni Pardini**'s work has appeared in various publications, most recently *The New York Times*, *San Francisco Chronicle*, and *Literary Mama*. She earned her M.F.A. in English and Creative Writing from Mills College and blogs at www.jennifermassoni.com. She also collects hearts in her son's honor with The Chain-Link Heart Project (chain-linkheartproject.blogspot.com).

Rebecca Patrick-Howard is an author and lives in the mountains of eastern Kentucky with her husband and two living children. She lost her youngest son, Toby, in 2010 to SIDS.

Faith Paulsen's poetry and prose have appeared in journals and collections including philly.com, *Apiary, Wild River Review, Blast Furnace, Sprout, When Women Waken, Canoodaloodaling, Literary Mama*, three "Cup of Comfort" collections and three "Chicken Soup for the Soul" books, and "In Gilded Frame, a collection of ekphrastic writing. She lives in Norristown, PA.

Colby and Tiffany Pitts are located in Phoenix, Arizona. They have been married for 6 years, and are currently expecting rainbow baby boy due in June, 2014.

Jaimie Porter is a fulltime mother, wife, and police officer. She and her husband, Tom, have been happily married since 2007.

Bobby Richmond lives in West Virginia with his wife and our 18-month-old daughter. He works as a paramedic. Their first child, Noah, was stillborn in 2011. They founded an organization in his honor to provide awareness and support for other parents.

Jenifer Richmond resides in West Virginia with her husband, daughter, and memory of her son. She is an emergency room nurse and paramedic primarily, but also an advocate for pregnancy loss awareness and education. She established an organization in honor of her son called Now Our Angel's in Heaven (N.O.A.H) and works daily to give lost babies a voice.

Born in Minneapolis, Minnesota, Jeannie E. Roberts is the author of *Nature of it All*, a collection of poetry (Finishing Line Press). She is also the author and illustrator of *Let's Make Faces!*, a children's book. Her poems have appeared in several publications, including *Verse*

Wisconsin. Jeannie lives in Chippewa Falls, Wisconsin. For more, visit www.jrcreative.biz.

Lisa Roth-Gulvin, a retired fashion designer, has been actively writing for eight years. Her work has been published in *Literary Mama* and *PATHS* Literary Journal. She is currently working on a novel and lives in New Jersey with her husband and eight-year-old daughter.

Susan Rukeyser usually writes fiction and sometimes tells the truth. Her work appears in *Monkeybicycle, SmokeLong Quarterly, Necessary Fiction,* and *Hippocampus Magazine,* among other publications. This piece originally appeared in *The Mom Egg.* www.susanrukeyser.com **Bar Scott** is a singer-songwriter and recording artist. *The Present Giver* is her first book. She lives in Colorado now, with her new husband, Brent Bruser.

J.lynn Sheridan writes in the Chain O' Lakes of northern Illinois in a very ordinary house, but she'd rather live in an old hardware store for the aroma, ambiance, and possibilities. She has recently been published in *Beyond the Dark Room* and *Storm Cycle* 2012, *Of Sun and Sand, Mouse Tales Press, Four and Twenty Literary Journal, The Plum Plum, Jellyfish Whispers,* MouseTales Press, and *Enhance.* She is currently working on her first novel. Find her at writingonthesun. wordpress.com and @J.lynnSheridan.

Besides being a high school English teacher and college English Adjunct Professor, **Katie Sluiter** has also appeared as an elite blogger for *US BabyHuddle,* a featured writer on Borderless News and Views, and in syndication on BlogHer. She also currently works as a freelance journalist for iAquire. Her writing has appeared in the 2012 poetry anthology by Every Day Poets and the May 2013 issue of *Baby Talk Magazine.* Katie lives with her husband and two sons in West Michigan and blogs about their life at sluiternation.com.

Abbie Smith is the mother of Isaiah, born still July 24, 2008. Passionate about stillbirth awareness, she is a co-founder of Stillborn Still Loved, a Seattle Children's Hospital guild benefiting the work of the Global Alliance to Prevent Prematurity and Stillbirth. Smith recently earned her master's degree in International Community Development from Northwest University with a thesis project focused on creating stillbirth awareness through shared narratives.

Kelly Smith lives in Ohio where she is wife to her college sweetheart James and the homeschooling mother to their four children. Her great love is the written word. She also has a passion for gardening, running and supporting those suffering through infant loss. Visit Kelly at www.whaleletters.com. Her piece is dedicated to her two angel babies, Elijah Mark and Jeremiah David.

Natalie Sullivan is the grateful mother of two beautiful children. She is a lawyer by training and a writer by heart. Natalie lives in New York City with her husband and their beloved son.

Sarah Elizabeth Troop writes and recreates historical and cultural recipes for her blog, *Nourishing Death*, which examines the relationship between food and death in rituals, culture, religion, and society. She is a member of The Order of the Good Death and serves as the Social Media Editor for Death Salon.

Lauren Vasil began writing her blog OnFecundThought.com as a way to make sense of the bewildering grief she experienced over her miscarriage. She believes it is important to break the silence surrounding pregnancy loss and is honored that her story has been included in this anthology. The London-born graphic designer lives in San Diego with her husband and dog.

Jessica Null Vealitzek is the author of *The Rooms Are Filled*. She lives near Chicago with her husband and two children. She can be found online at www.jessicavealitzek.com.

Shannon Vest spent over a decade in the film industry. She loves to travel and often takes off for months at a time to explore new places. She currently lives in Chattanooga, Tennessee and writes full time.

Jessica Watson is the mom to five, four in her arms and one in her heart. Her daughter Hadley passed away on her third day of life due to complications of prematurity. Jessica has since left the corporate world behind and vowed to soak up every minute with her husband and four surviving children. She blogs with her heart on her sleeve at FourPlusAnAngel.com and writes for sites such as *Still Standing Magazine*, *The Huffington Post* and *Mamalode*.

Monica Wesolowska is the author of *Holding Silvan: A Brief Life*. With an introduction by Erica Jong, *Holding Silvan* was named a "Best Book" of 2013 by *Library Journal*. She teaches fiction and nonfiction writing at UC Berkeley Extension. Read more at www. monicawesolowska.com

Mercedes M. Yardley is a dark fantasist who wears stilettos and red lipstick. She is the author of the short story collection *Beautiful Sorrows*, the novella *Apocalyptic Montessa and Nuclear Lulu: A Tale of Atomic Love* and her debut novel *Nameless*. Her website is www. mercedesyardley.com.

After the death of her second daughter, **Angie M. Yingst** began writing about grief, art, religion, and parenting at her blog *still life with circles*, chosen in 2010, as one of the top Fifty Must-Read Mom Blogs by *Parenting Magazine* and *Blogher*. Angie's essay, "Mothering Grief", appears in a collection of essays about stillbirth called *They Were Still Born* (Rowman and Littlefield 2010). She has a poetry chapbook called *of this, we will not speak*. Her poetry will be included in the upcoming collection called *To Linger On Hot Coals* (Spring, 2014). Angie holds a B.A. in Religion from Temple University in Philadelphia, PA.

Kristin Camitta Zimet is the Editor of *The Sow's Ear Poetry Review* and the author of a collection of poems, *Take in My Arms the Dark*. Her poetry is in countless journals including *Poet Lore, Salt Hill,* and *Lullwater Review*. She volunteers with patients in the hospital and in hospice.

About the Editors

© Michael Benatar

Sean Hanish is the writer, director and producer of the first feature film ever made on the subject of stillbirth, "Return to Zero", starring Minnie Driver, Paul Adelstein and Alfred Molina.

An award-winning filmmaker and commercial director, Sean works in a variety of mediums. While his passion is storytelling, he has created, directed and produced commercial campaigns for top international celebrities and brands such as Cindy Crawford, Oscar De La Renta, Liz Claiborne, the NFL and Disney.

His first play "Acts of Contrition" played to sold-out runs in both New York and Los Angeles and his short films "Sales Tribe Grashecki" and "Real Men" won film festivals in the US and internationally.

Sean Hanish is a member of both the Writers Guild of America and the Directors Guild of America, and lives in Pasadena, California with his wife, two children and two cats that he is allergic to but loves too much to give away.

*B*rooke Warner is founder of Warner Coaching Inc., publisher of She Writes Press, and author of *What's Your Book? A Step-by-Step Guide to Get You from Inspiration to Published Author* and *How to Sell Your Memoir: 12 Steps to a Perfect Book Proposal.* Brooke's expertise is in traditional and new publishing, and she is an equal advocate for publishing with a traditional house and self-publishing. Her book was a finalist for the Foreword Reviews Book of the Year Award for 2012 and her website was selected by the Association of Independent Authors as a winner of "Best Websites for Independent Authors." She lives and works in Berkeley, California.

SELECTED TITLES FROM SHE WRITES PRESS

She Writes Press is an independent publishing company
founded to serve women writers everywhere.
Visit us at www.shewritespress.com.

Four Funerals and a Wedding: Resilience in a Time of Grief by Jill Smolowe
$16.95, 978-1-938314-72-8
When journalist Jill Smolowe lost four family members in less than two years, she turned to modern bereavement research for answers—and made some surprising discoveries.

Breathe: A Memoir of Motherhood, Death, and Family Conflict by Kelly Kittel
$16.95, 978-1-938314-78-0
A mother's heartbreaking account of losing two sons in the span of nine months—and learning, despite all the obstacles in her way, to find joy in life again.

Warrior Mother: A Memoir of Fierce Love, Unbearable Loss, and Rituals that Heal by Sheila K. Collins, PhD
$16.95, 978-1-938314-46-9
The story of the lengths one mother goes to when two of her three adult children are diagnosed with potentially terminal diseases.

Splitting the Difference: A Heart-Shaped Memoir by Tré Miller-Rodríguez
$19.95, 978-1-938314-20-9
When 34-year-old Tré Miller-Rodríguez's husband dies suddenly from a heart attack, her grief sends her on an unexpected journey that culminates in a reunion with the biological daughter she gave up at 18.

Americashire: A Field Guide to a Marriage by Jennifer Richardson
$15.95, 978-1-938314-30-8
A couple's decision about whether or not to have a child plays out against the backdrop of their new home in the English countryside.

Loveyoubye: Hanging On, Letting Go, And Then There's The Dog by Rossandra White
$16.95, 978-1-938314-50-6
A soul-searching memoir detailing the painful, but ultimately liberating, disintegration of a twenty-five-year marriage.

CPSIA information can be obtained
at www.ICGtesting.com
Printed in the USA
FSOW02n0511060416
18830FS